The West Indies and the Arctic in the age of sail: the voyages of *Abram* (1806–62)

Rob David and Michael Winstanley
with Margaret Bainbridge

Centre for North-West Regional Studies
Lancaster University
2013
Series Editor: Sam Riches

The West Indies and the Arctic in the age of sail: the voyages of *Abram* (1806–62)

This volume is the 60th in the series of Occasional Papers published by the
Centre for North-West Regional Studies at the University of Lancaster

Designed, typeset, printed and bound by 4word Ltd, Bristol

British Library Cataloguing in-Publication Data
A CIP catalogue entry for this book is available from the British Library

ISBN 978-1-86220-302-0

Contents

Preface

The rescuing of *Abram* from obscurity can be credited to Dr Margaret Bainbridge, who retired to Lancaster in the 1990s after a varied and distinguished academic and teaching career in Istanbul and at the London School of African and Oriental Studies. In retirement she set about exploring her family history and while researching in Cockenzie she discovered that an ancestor, Alexander Horn, had died at sea on board the whaling ship *Abram* sailing from the nearby port of Kirkcaldy. She traced the ship back to its earlier career at Hull and from there back to Lancaster where it had been launched barely a mile away from where she was living. Intrigued by this, over the next decade Margaret amassed copious notes relating to the ship and came to the opinion that the story should be more widely known. She felt that her own advancing years and declining health would prevent her achieving this and sought assistance. The problem was finding people who were able to encompass both the West Indies and the Arctic. She approached Dr Michael Winstanley, an historian then at Lancaster University who had researched Lancaster history; he in turn invited Dr Rob David, another academic local historian but with a life-long interest in the Arctic, who was then Honorary Research Fellow in the History Department, to join him. Margaret generously made her notes freely available to us and resourced our further archival research. Although she did not wish to be listed as an author, without her initial research and support *Abram's* story would never have been told.

While Margaret was researching *Abram* she was given assistance by many people, many of them unknown to us. We would like to express our gratitude to them as well as to those who are now continuing to assist her in whatever way.

Acknowledgements

We are grateful to Melinda Elder and George Howson for sharing their expert knowledge of Lancaster's maritime history; Sue David for proof reading and literary research; Len Smith and Ann Savours for explanation of nautical terms; Arthur Credland of Hull Maritime Museum; Bernard Stonehouse of the Maritime Historical Research Centre, University of Hull and Emma Sakamoto Ferranti for drawing the maps. We are also indebted to the following institutions for preserving and making available the documents and illustrations without which this research would not have been possible: Anstruther Museum; The British Library; Dundee Central Library; Dundee University Archives; Fife County Archive Centre; Hull Trinity House; Hull History Centre; Kirkcaldy Central Library; Kirkcaldy Museum and Art Gallery; Lancashire Archives; Lancaster Central Library; Lancaster Maritime Museum; Lincolnshire Archives; London Metropolitan Archives; Manitoba Provincial Archives; The National Archives; National Maritime Museum; National Portrait Gallery; Orkney Library and Archive; Scott Polar Research Institute, University of Cambridge; Shetland Archives; Whitby Literary and Philosophical Society; and Whitehaven Beacon Museum. Any errors of fact or interpretation are, of course, our own.

Introduction
Abram and her worlds

In 1953 Lancaster's amateur dramatic, choral and musical societies combined forces to celebrate the Coronation of Queen Elizabeth II with a grand theatrical historical pageant which illustrated episodes in the history of the town. Episode Five, 'The Port of Lancaster', dramatised the town's trading connections with the West Indies. Among the characters it allegedly portrayed was 'Captain William Trasure (Master of the "*Abram*")'.[1] A copy of an oil painting of *Abram* by James Wheldon is now displayed in Lancaster Maritime Museum but it depicts her in a very difference guise, as an Arctic whaler. This book explores these very different aspects of her career, a career which is more remarkable that any semi-fictional dramatic portrayal could have imagined.

Ships are integral components of Britain's historic global trading and cultural reach, and *Abram*'s story is among the most vivid and illustrative of their histories. Three aspects of her career single her out from her contemporaries. First is her longevity; she survived at sea for over 56 years. Secondly, she sailed in two of the most dangerous regions of the world. As one of the many merchant vessels plying between the Caribbean and Britain she escaped unscathed from the extended wars with European powers and the United States as well as the hazards which tropical climates posed for wooden sailing ships and their crews alike. Her connections with the tiny British and Danish Virgin Islands, and the fact that she was named after one of the planters on these islands, were also unusual at the time. For the majority of her life, however, she was part of the Northern Whale Fishery traversing the dangerous polar seas. Although other ships were employed in both trades,[2] her 44 years in the Northern Whale Fishery were not only a remarkable record, given the dangers of navigation in the ice-bound seas of the Arctic, but one which connected her to many of the significant events in the whaling history of that time, including the search for Sir John Franklin whose entire expedition went missing searching for the North West Passage in the late 1840s. Finally, viewed from a twenty-first-century perspective, she was engaged in what are now probably considered to be the two most emotionally-charged and heavily criticised aspects of British expansion at the time: the enslavement and subjection of native peoples and the mass destruction of the largest mammals in the cause of economic gain.

This book aims to do more than describe *Abram*'s voyages although these are clearly the threads which knit her story together. The intention rather is to use her career to explore these key aspects of Britain's trade with other parts of the world which have now all but disappeared. This is not to suggest that Britain's West Indian possessions and her involvement in whaling in both the northern and southern hemispheres have not been extensively studied before; far from it. But in both cases such studies have largely overlooked the ships and the individuals involved with them, and how their histories shaped and reflected those trades. Conversely, studies of individual ships have tended to focus on just one aspect of their careers. For possibly the first time the full history of a ship sailing in such contrasting regions is told here.

Historians of the West Indies in the late eighteenth and early nineteenth centuries have approached the region's history in very different ways. The best known and possibly the most widely read are studies of the African slave trade; its growth, financing, potential profitability, exploitation and the campaigns to abolish it. The functioning of the slave plantation system and the lives of those involved in it have also attracted much attention, along with the potential impact the system had on British economy and society. Recent debates have focused particularly on issues related to emancipation; on the families of slave owners, slaves and their descendants; on the possibility that West Indian profits fuelled the acceleration of British industrial growth; on the potential existence of a 'trans-Atlantic mercantile community'; and on military conflicts and rebellion in the region. The ships themselves, those who built, owned and manned them, their changing destinations and the composition of their cargoes, have remained relatively unexplored. The intention here is to show how one ship's history can provide insights into many of these aspects.

In contrast, whaling historiography has been dominated by the study of individual whaling ports and the seasonal voyages of their whaling ships and the documenting of the return cargoes, their processing and subsequent uses. Consequently neither the earlier nor often later histories of individual ships, nor the connections between individual whalers and contemporary Arctic exploration, have been explored in detail. The few overviews of the whaling trade and the industry's contribution to the British economy which have been written have enabled *Abram*'s history to be set within the wider context of the Northern Whale Fishery.

To a large extent these contrasting historiographies reflect the inevitable fact that historians are constrained by the source material available to them. Whilst the cargoes of whaling ships were extensively but often inaccurately recorded and published, the more diverse outward and inward cargoes of West Indian vessels often have to be pieced together from stray surviving manifests or shipping reports in local newspapers. Conversely, the identities and activities of West Indian merchants and planters have been easier to document than those of the owners of whaling vessels. Although crew lists survive for both trades they provide only basic information about individuals while detailed ships' log books and journals are rare. While there are no surviving log books for *Abram*'s West Indian voyages, some of her whaling expeditions are exceptionally well-documented, most notably through the eyes of her surgeon, Thomas Phillips, in 1839. There is also good evidence of her involvement in the search for the explorer John Franklin ten years later.

The contrasting approaches adopted in this study reflect these different historiographies and the sources on which they rely. It has not proved possible to adopt a strictly comparative approach throughout, although similarities and differences are discussed in the conclusion. Part I primarily sheds light on the commercial world *Abram* served as a West Indian trader rather than her exploits on the seas, since there are fewer sources relating directly to the ship than those documenting the networks of individuals connected with her voyages. Part II, however, draws more directly on manuscript sources primarily concerned with her individual voyages – log books, journals, crew lists and press reports. The insights which they offer are necessarily and understandably different but they are equally valid. Perhaps the most remarkable aspect of her long history is not that we cannot fully document it throughout, but that, over 200 years since she was launched, it has been possible to discover so much about her and those whose livelihoods depended upon her.

Notes

1. *Beneath Hadrian's Tower: a historical pageant* (programme, 28–30 May 1953), copy in Lancaster City Museum. As the programme notes acknowledged, however, 'historical accuracy has at times been freely adapted to theatrical need' and the pageant was not to be viewed as 'a document of precedent'.

2. Whaling ships from east coast ports were usually conversions from Baltic traders, but the Lancaster-built *Harmony* and the Whitehaven-built *Alfred* also transferred to whaling at Hull from the West India trade around the same time as *Abram*. Many ships built for the Caribbean trade were later utilised in trade with other parts of the world.

Locations in Britain and Ireland with which *Abram* had connections.

Part I
Lancaster and the West Indies, 1806–18

Michael Winstanley

CHAPTER ONE

'The new ship *Abram*'

John Brockbank's shipyard on the River Lune at Lancaster, established as early as 1738, was a well-regarded business. By the end of the century over 100 ships of progressively larger tonnages, many of them for the West Indian trade, had been launched from his yard on Cable Street.[1] (Figure 1.1) In the late 1790s, like many shipbuilders around the country, his order book had been full with commissions from merchants. In 1799 alone, seven new Lancaster-built ships of over 200 tons had been registered in the port along with vessels recently launched in Ulverston, Liverpool, North Shields, Hull, Holderness, Thorne (Yorkshire), Whitby and Elgin.[2] Since the depression of 1801–2, war, coupled with a collapse in prices, had sapped

1.1. Lancaster from Cable Street 1798, by Julius Caesar Ibbetson: Lancaster Maritime Museum, LANLM.1930.2. (Reproduced by courtesy of Lancaster Maritime Museum, part of Lancashire Museums.)

Lancaster merchants' confidence. In 1804 Brockbank had sold only two vessels over 200 tons to them, and in 1805 only three ships (on four voyages) entered the Lune from the West Indies.

On 27 July 1805 the 50-gun *Minerva*, at 551 tons the largest vessel ever built in Lancaster but sold to merchants elsewhere, had been launched from his yard, but he had no further orders on his books. The following month, therefore, his daybook (Figure 1.2) records his progress on a 'Specn' or speculation ship: 100 ft.10 in. long, 26 ft. 9 in. broad, and weighing 318 tons.[3]

On 21 December 1805 Brockbank sold her for £4100 to two local men who had purchased another ship, *Neptune,* from him a year earlier, Thomas Burrow and Thomas Mason, together with Abram Chalwell [*sic*] Hill, after whom she was named, listed as non-subscribing partner.[4] Payment was to be made in two instalments: £2,050 in cash or bank notes on 6 July 1806 and the remainder, with three months' interest added, by 6 January 1807. In the sale contract Brockbank agreed to finish the hull and recaulk if necessary, to complete all joinery work, scuppers, hawseholes and mortices, carve a 'neat Head, Taffrail and Quarter pieces', find and 'make a complete set of masts, yards and other poles' and to coat them with resin, prime and paint all paint work and find a 'pinnace or well boat suitable for the vessel'.[5] The purchasers were to supply several items which were also to be fitted by the builder: pumps for the pump well, iron for the masts, rigging, caps, guns and gun ports, sleeves and deadeyes, iron stanchions and guards, hatchbars, copper and brasswork, inside glasswork and any mahogany for fittings. As on earlier Brockbank ships, this metal work was sourced from another established local business, almost certainly Abraham Seward, 'plumber glazier, brazier, brass and bell founder' with whom Burrow and Mason had an account.[6]

Just 16 days later, on Monday 6 January 1806, she was launched.[7] Seward's accounts show that he continued to fit her out with four large brass canisters, a brass compass, and various unidentified sundries. The entry in Lancaster's shipping register (Figure 1.3) seven days later described her of 295 tons, 'a square-sterned ship with a flush deck', with three masts and a man's 'figure' on the prow.[8]

Over the next 12 years under a variety of masters, *Abram* was to make 21 voyages to the West Indies, all of them to Tortola and often also to the

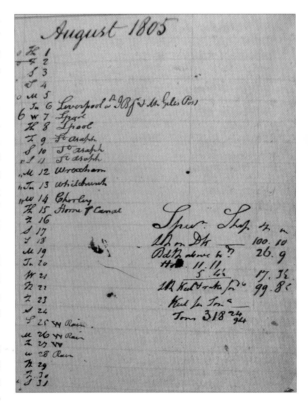

1.2. *Abram* as 'Specn ship' in Brockbank's daybook, August 1805: Lancs. Archives, DDX 2743 MS 241. (Reproduced with permission of Lancashire Archives.)

1.3. *Abram* in Lancaster Shipping Register, 1806: Lancs. Archives SS5/1. (Reproduced with permission of Lancashire Archives.)

neighbouring Danish islands of St Thomas and St Croix, before being sold at Liverpool in 1818 (Appendix 1). Although it would probably have been considered inconceivable at the time of her maiden voyage, she was to be one of the last ships regularly to ply between Lancaster and the Caribbean and the men who owned her were to become the last of the town's West Indian traders.

This brief account of *Abram's* origins raises several questions. Why was she being built in and sailing from Lancaster, a port which, by all accounts, had suffered considerably during the financial crash of 1801–02 and had been all but eclipsed by its larger neighbour Liverpool? Who were her owners and why were they investing in a new ship at that time? Why did she sail to the British Virgin Islands, often portrayed as one of the most economically marginal of the Caribbean colonies and, even more intriguingly, to the Danish possessions of St Croix and St Thomas? What were her outward and inward cargoes and who were they carried for? What sort of men sailed in her and what can we glean of their experiences? What light does the ship's history over the next 13 years shed on the prosperity or otherwise of the West Indies in general, and Lancaster and the Virgin Islands in particular? What might be the significance of her sale in 1818?

How did those who had owned and sailed in her fare in the years which followed her sale, as *Abram* herself embarked on a remarkably different trajectory which was to take her away from the familiar landmarks of her early years and into the dangerous waters of the Arctic. The first half of this book seeks to answer these questions.

References

[1]   Origins and history of the shipyard taken from Nigel Dalziel, 'Trade and Transition, 1690–1815' in Andrew White (ed.), *A History of Lancaster,* 2nd. edition, Edinburgh University Press, 2001, pp. 96–7; Eija Kennerly, *The Brockbanks of Lancaster: the Story of an 18th century Shipbuilding Firm,* Lancaster City Museum monograph, 1981.

[2]   Lancashire Archives (Lancs. Archives), SS5/1, Lancaster Shipping Registers.

[3]   Lancs. Archives, DDX 2743 MS 241, John Brockbank's daybook , 1794–1805.

[4]   Abram is regularly lengthened to Abraham in many official documents but he always signed 'Abram' so this will be used throughout unless Abraham is part of a direct quotation. Chalwill is largely used in official documents although Chalwell is occasionally substituted. Abram Hill usually abbreviated this to an initial C in his signature.

[5]   Scuppers and hawseholes were holes in the side of the ship through which water could drain and through which hawsers were passed; the taffrail was the railing around the stern; the quarter or fashion piece was used for fashioning the stern; deadeyes were pieces of wood with holes for directing and controlling rigging.

[6]   Lancs. Archives, DDX 2743, MS 8127 John Brockbank's instructions for building ships; DDX 2743 MS 3726 Abraham Seward Account Book, 1805–13; *Holden's Triennial Directory 1809, 1810, 1811,* London, 1811, p. 245.

[7]   *Lancaster Gazette,* 11 Jan. 1806; Lancs. Archives, DDX 2743 MS 242 John Brockbank's daybook, 1806–13.

[8]   Tonnage in shipping registers was calculated differently from that recorded by shipbuilders. Lancs. Archives, SS5/1, Lancaster Shipping Registers.

CHAPTER TWO

Lancaster and the West Indian trade

In the eighteenth century Lancaster had been transformed from a provincial market, administrative and judicial centre into a prosperous transatlantic entrepot.[1] Much remains as witness to its prosperity at that time. In the 1750s new Port Commissioners laid out the building plots on St George's Quay for the warehouses and a Palladian style Customs House.[2] Elegant Georgian mansions lined newly created streets and squares.[3] A town hall, now a museum, was erected on Market Square in 1783, while the 'New Bridge', also in the fashionable Palladian style, and John Rennie's monumental canal viaduct over the River Lune provided impressive approaches to the town from the north and east. In 1787, when both trade and ships had expanded further in size, the Port Commission financed the construction of an outport at Glasson Dock on the mouth of the Lune. A Merchants' Coffee House functioned as a centre for exchange of information and goods, while local banks established by leading merchant families, Thomas Worswick Sons and Co. and Dilworth and Hargreaves, provided financial services which underpinned business operations.[4] The

2.1. The Custom House and St George's Quay (detail) by Gideon Yates, 1790s: Lancaster Maritime Museum, LANLM.1986.117. (Reproduced courtesy of Lancaster Maritime Museum, part of Lancashire Museums.)

wealth which generated Lancaster's 'Golden Age' was almost exclusively derived from just one source: the West Indian trade.

'The most valued possessions in the overseas Imperial world'[5]

By the late eighteenth century over 85 per cent of exports from the British West Indies were consigned to the home country and by 1807 the trade employed, directly or indirectly, half of the nation's long distance shipping with duties levied on it contributing a staggering 12 per cent of total government revenue.[6] The Caribbean was the source of exotic produce which underpinned the dramatic changes in British economy and society influencing fashions for furniture, textiles, clothing and diet.

What constituted the British West Indies had changed dramatically over the previous two centuries. The islands of St Kitts or St Christopher (1624), Barbados (1627), Nevis (1628), Antigua (1632), Montserrat (1632) and the major acquisition of Jamaica in 1655 were the main components of the first phase of acquisitions. The position remained virtually unchanged for the next century before Grenada, Dominica, St Vincent and Tobago were all ceded to Britain after the Seven Years War with France in 1763. Although all of them were temporarily lost during the American War of Independence (1776–83), they were subsequently regained. During the French wars of 1793–1815 Britain seized St Lucia from the French and the Dutch colonies of Essequibo, Berbice and Demerara on the South American mainland in 1796. All were restored in the Treaty of Amiens in 1802 but retaken the year after and retained when the war ended. The British also took and retained the Spanish colony of Trinidad in 1797. In addition the British temporarily occupied French Martinique (Martinico), Swedish St Bartholomew, Dutch Surinam and Curacao and the Danish Virgin Islands of St Thomas, St John and St Croix, all of which were then opened to its merchants.

Sugar dominates popular images of the region and not without reason. By the second half of the century most of the longstanding British Caribbean possessions had taken on the characteristics of fully developed, highly capitalised, plantation colonies with Jamaica dominating production in volume terms. Production expanded dramatically over the course of the century fuelled by rising domestic consumption and a thriving re-export trade to Europe and Ireland. As the price and production of sugar rose from the 1750s it became Britain's most valuable single import. Trade with the West Indies rose fourfold over the 50 years and accounted for around 60 per cent by value of all transatlantic cargoes by 1815, although a significant proportion of the increase during the wars can be attributed to the acquisition of new colonies rather than rising production in established colonies.[7] Many of the longstanding colonial plantation economies were serviced and funded by merchants from London and Bristol and domestic

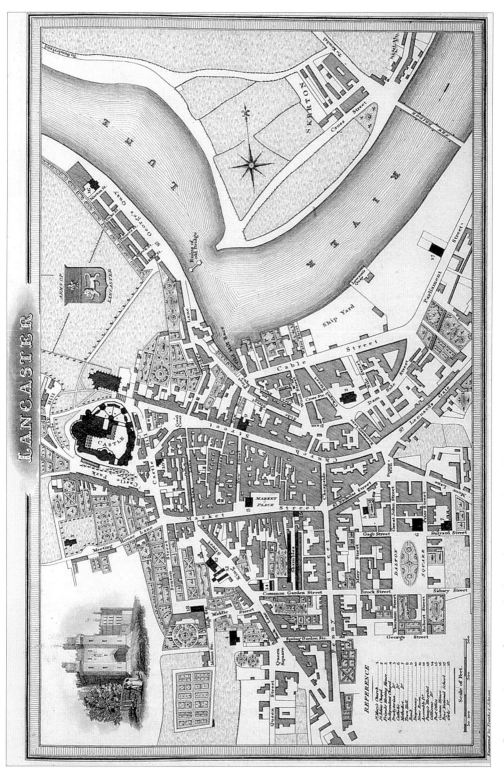

2.2. Lancaster in 1824 showing St George's Quay and Brockbank's shipyard, from Edward Baines, *History, Directory and Gazetteer of the County Palatine of Lancaster*, vol. 1, Liverpool, 1825.

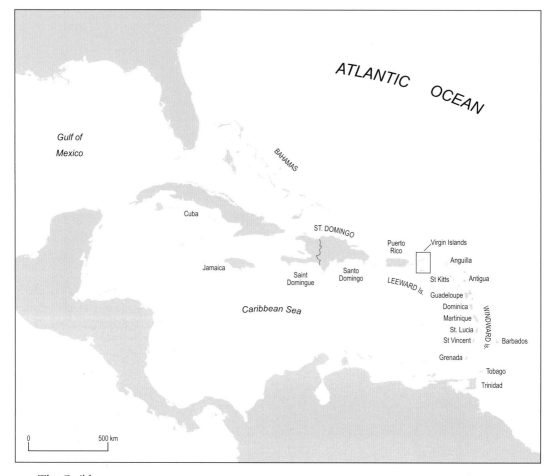

2.3. The Caribbean.

and re-export markets were also heavily dependent on the metropolis. Not surprisingly, with just one exception, all the colonial agents who lobbied parliament on behalf of the planters had their main residence in London, as indeed did many of the planters who increasingly enjoyed the luxuries of the capital while delegating the chore of managing their plantations to factors, agents and attorneys. Therefore, although sugar featured prominently in cargoes unloaded at North West ports, it probably did not have the overwhelming significance for many of the merchants as it did in London.

Cotton has been overshadowed by sugar in modern perceptions of the West Indies and by production on the American mainland which later came to dominate supplies for the burgeoning Lancashire textile industry in the nineteenth century. But the United States' dominance was not established until after 1800. Cotton cultivation was particularly attractive to smaller planters since it was less labour- and capital-intensive than sugar and could be grown successfully on poorer soils. Output expanded in the last quarter of the century in response to the rising demand generated by the introduction of water-powered spinning mills from the 1770s, particularly in Lancashire, and further encouraged from 1786 by a variety of government initiatives and by the introduction and rapid diffusion of Joseph Eve's self-feeding roller gin which used water, wind, or animal power to process the long-staple cotton which was grown on the islands.[8] During the late 1780s the Caribbean supplied over 70 per cent of the British market, as opposed to less than one per cent for the United States, and even as late as 1815 it accounted for approximately 30 per cent of British imports, then greatly increased in volume to some 16–17 million lbs. per annum.[9] Prices fluctuated considerably, however, since they were dependent on the variable profitability of the British domestic industry. Cotton exports mushroomed in the mid-1780s before stagnating with the onset of the French war, picked up again from the mid-1790s but crashed in 1799. The increasing volume of trade in the 1800s was helped in no short measure by British colonial acquisitions during the war, particularly the Dutch colonies of South America. Not surprisingly, much of this cotton was shipped to Britain on ships from the North West of England, including Lancaster and Liverpool.

'The emporium for all the world'

Ships from the West Indies, however, brought back more than sugar and cotton grown in British colonies. Merchants traded with other powers' colonies and the United States through a number of 'free ports', where goods could be imported and exported free of duty. The government assisted this by negotiating access to other countries' products, such as the valuable logwood plantations of Spanish Honduras. By the 1780s there were several of these free ports scattered throughout the region, including Jamaica, but possibly the most important was the Dutch Leeward island of St Eustatia (or Eustatius) which Edmund Burke described in a debate in the House of Commons in 1781 as 'an emporium for all the world'. Not surprisingly, shipping records for its close British neighbour, St Kitts, confirm that it was a regular port of call for British merchants, including those from Lancaster, and that they either traded themselves, or employed ships owned by local men or British agents there, to transport cargoes between free ports and other islands and the American mainland. In early 1784, for example, *Commerce,* a Lancaster ship captained by William Trasure, who was later to captain *Abram* on her maiden voyage, called at St Kitts from Lancaster and then made round trips to Boston and Philadelphia with tropical produce returning with lumber, staves, coins and fish, some of which he took to St Eustatia. From St Eustatia he returned to St Kitts with yet more provisions before loading with sugar, cotton and fustic and returning to Lancaster in April 1785. Not all vessels spent so long transhipping cargoes in the region, relying on smaller locally-owned sloops which regularly plied between the islands; some of these sloops were owned by British merchants' agents residing temporarily on the islands, and others by freelance local merchants.[10] When St Eustatia fell to the French in 1795, British and other European merchants switched their base to Charlotte Amalie on the Danish island of St Thomas, which had been established as a free port in the 1760s. Return cargoes into Liverpool and Lancaster were consequently very varied. As well as sugar and cotton, they consisted of indigo, fustic, logwood, mahogany, tamarind, Nicaragua wood, lignum vitae, rum, coffee, cow and ox hides, staves, satinwood or yellow sanders, tortoise shell, succades, arrowroot and coker [sic] nuts.[11] (See glossary for further details.) Ships which called at Madeira on the outward voyage often brought wine. Those who engaged in the triangular slave trade with the Africa coast carried ivory and gold.

London and Bristol men dominated initial trade with the British colonies and consequently the acquisition of plantations, but west coast ports such as Liverpool, Whitehaven, Glasgow and Lancaster rapidly developed as suppliers of labour, provisions, raw materials and goods, and as recipients of a wide range of produce. As Colonel Gascoyne, MP for Liverpool, noted in 1799, 'The London merchants were mostly agents for the planters, and did not traffic with the islands on their own account; the merchants of Liverpool and Lancaster were on the contrary, exporters and importers of goods, at their own risk.'[12] With fewer rigid commitments these general traders were freer to take advantage of new openings wherever they arose and to withdraw or switch to other enterprises or destinations when those prospects dried up. As such they were well placed to capitalise on opportunities offered from the 1780s, particularly by the British acquisition of 'ceded islands' from other countries and by the emergence of free ports such as St Thomas and St Eustatia licensed by the Danish and Dutch governments respectively to trade with other colonies in the region without the imposition of tariffs. Some of this would have been funded by credit and this left them vulnerable to financial crises during war. They were equally exposed when commodities prices fell dramatically, as after 1799 when Liverpool and Lancaster merchants sought and obtained a government loan to tide them over what they hoped would be a temporary phenomenon.

Success depended not only on the business acumen of merchants based in Britain but on the hiring of reliable captains and on establishing and sustaining networks of agents, factors and planters in the West Indies who could find markets for British products, supply the necessary return cargoes and make secure financial arrangements. Since there were no commercial institutions and little hard currency in the West Indies, these arrangements regularly involved British merchants extending credit through their agents in anticipation of future receipts from the sale of planters' produce. In some cases, they also provided loans for the purchase or lease of properties or slaves. Some of these agents were longstanding members of the white communities in the islands, but others were young men born in England, often relations of home-based merchants, who spent some years there building up their own contacts and, hopefully fortunes, before returning home.

Lancaster's merchant community

By the 1780s Lancaster's merchants had developed an extensive network of contacts throughout the West Indies. Most of those involved in the port's trade had been born in the town or its immediate rural hinterland, which included Furness and Westmorland to the north, the valley of the Lune into the Yorkshire hills to the east and the agricultural region to the south. Trade offered younger sons of local yeomen and farming families, or others engaged in retailing and small scale manufacturing, a chance to diversify through speculative investments as part-owners of ships, suppliers to merchants, as members of trading partnerships or as agents based in the West Indies. The earliest voyages in the seventeenth century had been funded by combinations of small businessmen and this pattern was still evident in the large numbers of names listed as owners of some vessels until the demise of the trade in the early nineteenth century.[13] Trade, however, also laid the foundations for several important commercial dynasties, including the Quaker Rawlinson family.

Lancaster's connections with the New World have been traced to a voyage of 1687. William Stout's autobiography charts the growing involvement of local men in business consortia involved with both the West Indies and North American continent over the next half century.[14] During this period between four and six vessels left the port each year but by the 1750s the number had risen to over 30 and the number of ships 'of this port' virtually doubled again by 1800, although by this date not all those which had initially been registered in Lancaster sailed from the port. Some ships were engaged in the triangular trade which transhipped slaves from the African coast to the colonial plantations,[15] but, as both Schofield and Elder have shown, even in its heyday in the 1750s and 1760s, the number and size of slaving vessels were overshadowed by those engaged in direct transatlantic trade with the West Indies. The absolute and relative importance of Lancaster's slave trade dwindled over the next two decades and by the end of the 1780s it had all but ended. As Elder has shown, major slave traders like the Hindes had transferred their operations to Liverpool and only a 'handful of die-hard slave merchants' who were reluctant to give up their local base remained in the town. For the majority of Lancaster's younger potential investors, the African slave trade had become both 'unnecessary and unattractive' given the lucrative prospects which the thriving West Indian colonies offered for direct trade, although those colonies were, of course, slave economies and remained so for over a quarter of century after the abolition of the British African slave trade itself in 1807.[16]

Direct trade with planters and merchants in the West Indies was both more reliable than, and potentially just as profitable as, the African slave trade. Receipts of the Seamen's Sixpence – a levy on all sailors over 18 years old on vessels involved in overseas trade to support the Greenwich Hospital and merchant seamen – list over 100 voyages to the West Indies between 1750 and 1754, the overwhelming majority of them to Barbados and Jamaica.[17] Ship numbers and sizes virtually doubled by the end of the century contributing to a virtual fivefold increase in trade by volume and even more in terms of value.[18] Over this period imports of sugar, cotton, rum, tobacco, dyes and various hardwoods fuelled an expansion of processing and manufacturing industries in the town, such as Lawson's sugar refinery and Gillows' high-quality furniture making.[19] During the boom years from the 1780s water-powered textile spinning mills were established in the surrounding countryside, virtually all of them financed by members of merchant families engaged in the West Indian trade.[20] Even less exotic trade with other parts of the world, such as Baltic timber for John Brockbank's shipyard and flax and hemp for the town's sailcloth and rope manufacturers, depended heavily on Lancaster's West Indian trade. Local grocers and farmers in the district also benefited from sale of basic provisions in the West Indies and small scale producers supplied a wide range of necessities such as furniture, woollen and linen goods, hats, nails, barrels, bricks, building materials and, particularly, candles.[21] The local area, however, was never able to provide all the commodities for export or to market imports, and merchants developed wide-ranging contacts with manufacturers and wholesalers throughout the North West and beyond.

Lancaster's West Indian trade peaked between 1798 and 1801, when its ships accounted for eight per cent of the British vessels bound for the Caribbean. Around 30 per cent of the ships registered in the port and consequently listed as paying the Seamen's Sixpence at Lancaster traded with Jamaica, Dominica, St Kitts and Barbados, although reports in the *Lancaster Gazette* suggest that a large proportion of these vessels returned to Liverpool or London. Other merchants had moved into new, if sometimes precarious, markets. The 'ceded islands' accounted for 11 per cent of destinations, but nearly 60 per cent of ships were calling either at free ports or territories which the British had occupied during the war including Trinidad and the ex-Dutch colonies on the South American mainland. By far the most common initial destinations (ships frequently journeyed on to other ports) were Martinique, occupied by the British since 1793, and the Danish free port of St Thomas, reflecting its increased importance after the abandonment of St Eustatia in 1795.

The terms of peace agreed in the Treaty of Amiens in March 1802 severely disrupted this trade since most of the colonies taken during the war were returned to the European powers. Lancaster merchants, particularly those dependent on credit, suffered badly as their lucrative West Indian markets and sources of supply were denied them. Commodity prices fell. Ships owned by local merchants continued to frequent the port but they did so in much reduced numbers. By the time *Abram* was launched, Lancaster's West Indian trade had virtually evaporated. In 1807 although 21 ships paid the Seamen's Sixpence at Lancaster, only a handful, including *Abram*, actually traded from the port.

The Virgin Islands

The key to *Abram*'s origins and her successful career as a Lancaster-based West Indian trader, lie in her first advertised destination – Tortola, at 21 miles long, the largest of the British Virgin Islands.

The Virgin Islands had not featured prominently in early British strategy and trade in the Caribbean. Despite being nominally under British control since 1672, historians and contemporaries, particularly those viewing the Caribbean from a metropolitan perspective, have generally dismissed them as 'frontier communities' or 'marginal colonies'.[22] They rarely feature in standard accounts of British expansion and activity in the region or are only referred to in passing as an insignificant backwater. Reasons advanced for their apparent neglect include their perceived isolation from major trade routes in the region. They lay well to north of other British possessions. Ships bound for Jamaica passed far to the south and returned via the Florida Straits or Windward Passage to the west and east of Cuba respectively. British colonies in the Windward and Leeward Islands lay to the south-east; St Kitts was the nearest important British island but was 140 miles away, against the prevailing winds. Vessels returning home from the Leeward Islands sailed home windward of the Dutch island of St Eustatia which helped to sustain its role as a major entrepot, and left the Caribbean via the Anegada Passage to the east of the Virgin Islands.[23] To the west they had potentially hostile neighbours in the form of the French and Spanish colonies of Santo Domingo (or Hispaniola or Saint-Domingue) and Puerto Rico. The British government consequently conceived of their value primarily in strategic terms during war and established an Admiralty Court in Road Town, the only safe harbour on the east coast of the island, with the powers to seize, detain and 'condemn' (i.e. confiscate) enemy shipping and their cargoes as 'prizes'. The absence of any civil authority until the late eighteenth century, their isolation from other British colonies and their proximity to Danish, Spanish and French possessions, meant that they were regarded as haunts of pirates and smugglers.[24]

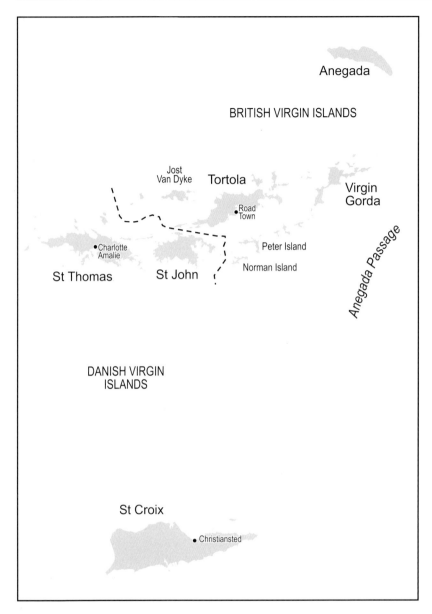

2.4. British and Danish Virgin Islands

There were other reasons why the islands were shunned by larger capitalist planters. Many of the soils are thin and poor and not conducive to intensive cultivation. Apart from the outlying island of Anegada to the north, they are hilly with Tortola itself rising to nearly 2,000 feet within a mile or so of the shore. The islands lack rivers and streams. They also lie in the path of the periodic hurricanes which sweep across the region from September. Until well into the century, therefore, the settlers were predominantly smaller farmers, sometimes displaced from other islands by the development of plantations, who eked out a precarious living growing food and exporting cotton. Their settlements were largely concentrated on smaller lower-lying islands rather than on Tortola itself.

The Virgin Islands prospered, however, in the last third of the century as prices for both cotton and sugar increased and wars boosted their strategic significance. In 1783 the islands' government, first established ten years earlier, was put on a more stable footing. From 1786 the monthly packet boat from Falmouth called at Tortola bringing regular mail, news and commercial information. During the French and Napoleonic Wars the waters off the island were a rendezvous for homeward-bound convoys. Tortola also benefited from the proximity to the free port on the neighbouring Danish Virgin Island of St Thomas and, after 1802, from the granting of free port status to Tortola's only harbour, Road Town.

Whilst metropolitan and Bristol merchants' energies and investments had been directed elsewhere, those in Scotland and the provinces of England, particularly those in the North West, had established a foothold in the Virgin Islands.[25] In 1770, the islands were reported to be second only to Jamaica in terms of sugar imported into Liverpool and third behind Jamaica and Grenada in terms of cotton. The islands also exported rum, staves (for making barrels and hogsheads) and fustic. In return they received a wide range of produce and merchandise from Britain.[26] Much of this can

2.5. View of Tortola and Road Town from Ruthy Hill by J. Johnson, from *Series of Views in the West Indies* (Messrs. Underwood, 1827). (© The British Library Board, General Reference collection 1299.m.1.)

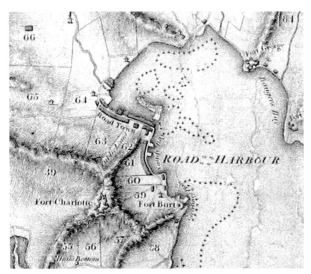

55 Heirs of D.ʳ West. *Cotton.*
56 Robᵗ Fanfset, *Cotton.*
57 Willᵐ Slaney, *Cotton.*
58 Heirs of B. Hodge.
59 Michˡ Macnamara |
  & Jacob Pasea, | *Sugar.*
60 Revᵈ Mʳ Wynne.
61 John Macnamara.
62 Public Land.
63 Heirs of B Hodge. *Sugar.*
64 Dᵒ   *Sugar.*
65 W.R.Hodge. *Sugar.*
66 Isaac Pickering of Tortola. *Sugar.*

2.6.1 and 2.6.2. Plan of Tortola 1798 by George King, detail showing Road Town with part of estates key: TNA, CO 700/VIRGIN ISLANDS5. (Reproduced courtesy of The National Archives, London.)

be attributed to the activities of three generations of the Rawlinson family, leading Quaker merchants in Lancaster and later Liverpool who traded regularly with the islands from at least the 1740s. James Birkett, a Lancaster merchant based in Antigua, was also pivotal in establishing the Society of Friends (Quakers) in the islands in 1738. Lancaster port records from the 1750s record several vessels trading with Tortola and the minutes of Lancaster Friends' Meeting at that time confirm personal contacts between the meetings on the island, and those in Lancaster. William Thornton, later the architect of the first Capitol buildings in Washington, was born on Jost Van Dyke in the islands in the 1750s, but his father was a Lancaster

2.7. Abraham Rawlinson (left) and Thomas Hutton Rawlinson (right), merchants of Lancaster and Liverpool, by George Romney, Lancaster Maritime Museum, LANLM.2009.12.1, LANLM 1934.45.9. (Reproduced courtesy of Lancaster Maritime Museum, part of Lancashire Museums.)

Quaker who had married the resident governor's sister-in-law and settled there in the 1750s. Thornton and his brother were consequently sent back to Lancaster on one of Rawlinsons' ships for their education.[27] One of Rawlinsons' captains, and later in-law, William Lindow, was responsible for bringing the young John Coakley Lettsom, born on the tiny Virgin Island Little Jost Van Dyke, to Lancaster where he was consigned to the care of the Rawlinsons.[28] By the 1770s the Rawlinsons and their in-law and partner John Chorley were responsible for a large proportion of the islands' trade with the North West. Reporting the arrival of the Leeward Island fleet in July 1778 *Williamson's Liverpool Advertiser* records four ships unloading sugar from Tortola, all of them owned by Rawlinsons and Chorley.[29] In 1783 Henry Rawlinson, then MP for Liverpool but whose estate was at Grassyard (or Gresgarth) Hall, Caton in the Lune Valley, became the Colonial Agent for the Virgin Islands, the only West Indian agent outside London.[30]

Richard Hetherington, whose family home was at Burrow in the Lune Valley, acted as an agent for the Rawlinsons on Tortola. After the death of Henry Rawlinson in 1786, his vessels were re-registered in Liverpool with Hetherington as one of the co-owners. By 1798, when an estate map of the island was published, Hetherington had acquired five plantations.[31] In 1801 Chorley advised Captain Thomas Walters of *Mercury* that 'On your arrival at Tortola consult Richard Hetherington Esq. on each Affair relative to the

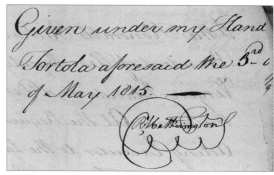

2.8. Richard Hetherington as a young man; an 1872 copy of the original then in the possession of the family, by the Durham-based artist Clement Burlison. (Reproduced by courtesy of Lancashire County Council's Museum Service.)

2.9. Richard Hetherington, President of the Virgin Islands, signature, 1815: TNA, CUST 34/812 Tortola correspondence, 1811–1819. (Reproduced by courtesy of The National Archives, London.) Hetherington was then 78 years old.

Mercury, acting conformable to his wishes'.[32] By 1811 he had been appointed President of the Council for the Virgin Islands, a post he retained till his death ten years later. Despite living permanently on the island, however, Hetherington clearly retained close connections both with Liverpool, from where his son William later traded, and the Lune Valley, where he owned Hill House, an imposing residence in Burton in Lonsdale where his first wife died and several of his children were baptised.[33]

In 1802, in the wake of the Treaty of Amiens, the government sought to protect Road Town's new prosperity by granting it temporary free port status, enabling merchants there legally to import produce in foreign vessels from other European colonies for export to Britain. This privilege was made permanent in 1805 and further legislation the following year allowed foreign sugar and cotton to be imported and exported freely through the port without payment of duty. The following year the President of the Council of the Virgin Islands was authorised to grant licences to British colonial vessels to trade with Santo Domingo.

Tortola's attraction as a destination was further enhanced by its proximity to the free port on the neighbouring Danish Virgin Island of St Thomas. Although it had failed to develop a plantation economy, indeed, its production dropped steadily from the 1750s, the island's port of Charlotte Amalie had been granted free port status in the mid-1760s. After the French occupation of St Eustatia in 1795 this became a major destination for British and foreign merchants and the granting of free port status to Road Town was specifically intended to capture its trade after the islands had been returned to Denmark in March 1802, and to reduce the smuggling between the islands which local merchants were, probably correctly, reputed to engage in. The fertile island of St Croix (or Santa Cruz), 40 miles to the south, had long attracted foreign investors and

2.10. Hetherington family graves in Tunstall churchyard, Lune Valley, Lancashire. (Author's photo.) The grave on the left is of Elizabeth Robinson, daughter of Richard Hetherington and wife of Charles Robinson, Customs Collector in Demerara.

developed as one of the foremost producers of sugar in the West Indies with exports rising from one million pounds (lbs.) in the 1750s to around 12–16 million by the 1780s. In contrast to its policy adopted on St Thomas, however, the Danish government prohibited foreign ships from calling and restricted the export of St Croix sugar and cotton directly to Denmark, although it is likely that this stipulation was more honoured in the breach than in the observance by planters, merchants and officials on the island, some of whom were British. Only during periods of British occupation could its produce be legally exported 'British plantation'.[34]

By the 1800s planters on islands which had been settled earlier were beginning to suffer from over-cropping and soil exhaustion and were complaining about heavier sugar duties levied to pay for the expenses of war, and the limitations on the re-export trade imposed as a result of Napoleon's continental blockade.[35] Business confidence in Lancaster was also depressed in the wake of the financial crisis of 1801–2 which led to the failure of local firms, and a fall in shipping using the port. But there were still opportunities for men who had developed trading links with the British Virgin Islands and St Thomas, especially since the Rawlinsons and Chorley were no longer the force on the islands they had been 20 years earlier; indeed John Chorley was declared bankrupt in November 1805.[36]

But just who were Thomas Burrow, Thomas Mason and Abram Chalwill Hill, after whom *Abram* was named, and what were their connections with the Virgin Islands?

2.11. View of St Thomas from Havensicht by Louis Jean Pierre Vieillot, dated January 1809. (© The British Library Board, George III's topographical collection, Maps, Top K.123.70.)

References

1. Dalziel, 'Trade and Transition', pp. 93–95; M.M. Schofield, *Outlines of an Economic History of Lancaster from 1680 to 1860: Part I Lancaster from 1680 to 1800*, Lancaster Branch of the Historical Association, 1946, p. 24ff. Schofield remains the most comprehensive treatment of the town's shipping.

2. David Ross and Andrew White, *The Lancaster Custom House,* Lancaster City Museums, Local Study, no.9, 1988; Lancs. Archives, DDLPC, Lancaster Port Commission records. The Custom House now (2013) houses Lancaster Maritime Museum.

3. Andrew White, *The Buildings of Georgian Lancaster,* Lancaster, Centre for North-West Regional Studies, Lancaster University, 1992, rev. ed. 2000.

4. George Howson, *The Making of Lancaster: People, Places & War, 1789–1815,* Lancaster, Carnegie Press, 2008, provides a succinct overview and vivid picture of the town during this period.

5. Richard B. Sheridan, 'The Formation of Caribbean Plantation Society, 1689–1748', in P.J. Marshall (ed.), *The Oxford History of the British Empire, vol. 2 The Eighteenth Century*, Oxford University Press, 1998, p. 395.

6. J.R. Ward, 'The British West Indies in the Age of Abolition', in Marshall (ed.), *British Empire*, pp. 422, 427.

7. Ward, 'Age of Abolition', pp. 417, 421.

8. M.M. Edwards, *The Growth of the British Cotton Trade, 1780–1815,* Manchester University Press, 1967, pp. 76–79. Some of these imports, however, were foreign grown and imported through 'free ports' in the Caribbean. Eve's innovation, dated to 1788, and those of earlier inventors, has largely been ignored by historians who have concentrated unduly on Eli Whitney's cotton gin invented five years later which opened up possibilities of using short-staple cotton, the only crop which could be grown in the southern United States. Not until the 1820s did Whitney's invention really displace Eve's. See Angela Lakwete, *Inventing the Cotton Gin: Machine and Myth in Antebellum America*, Baltimore, John Hopkins University Press, 2003.

9. Edwards, *Cotton Trade,* pp. 250–51; Thomas Ellison, *The Cotton Trade of Great Britain,* London, 1886, rpt, Frank Cass, 1968, p. 86.

10. TNA, CO157/1. St Kitts, return of shipping.

11. Coconuts provided all year round work on plantations and were often used to fill the gaps between hogsheads of sugar in the hold to stop them being thrown about during the voyage. They also had uses in candle and soap production and for cables and ropes.

12. Schofield, *Economic History Part II*, p. 18.

13. R. Craig and M.M. Schofield, 'The Trade of Lancaster in William Stout's Time', in J.D. Marshall (ed). *The Autobiography of William Stout of Lancaster, 1665–1752,* Manchester University Press, 1967, esp. pp. 58–60.

14. Marshall, *William Stout of Lancaster, passim.*

15. The victims of this trade are commemorated in the STAMP project which erected a memorial on St George's Quay in 2005. http://www.uclan.ac.uk/schools/journalism_media_communication/literature_culture/abolition/stamp.php last accessed 6 October 2012.

16. Melinda Elder, *The Slave Trade and the Economic Development of 18th century Lancaster,* Halifax, Ryburn Academic, 1992, esp. p. 178, charts and pp. 196–97.

17. Seamen's Sixpence records, 1747–1851, photocopy in Lancaster Central Library, LL58/Por. Peter Skidmore, 'The Seamen's Sixpence: a study of payments made by merchant

seamen to two pension funds and their contribution to the history of maritime trade in the period 1750–1850' unpublished MA dissertation, Lancaster University, 2004; 'New light on seamen, ships and trade of the port of Lancaster in the late eighteenth and early nineteenth century', *Transactions of the Historic Society of Lancashire and Cheshire*, 159, 2010, pp. 63–81.

[18] Schofield, *Economic History* Part I, p. 21.

[19] *Sugar Refiners and Sugarbakers* created by Brian Mawer, http://www.mawer.clara.net/loc-lanc.html last accessed 12 June 2012; Susan E. Stuart, *Gillows of Lancaster and London 1730–1840,* Antique Collectors' Club, Woodbridge, 2008; K.E. Ingram, 'The West Indian trade of an English furniture firm in the eighteenth century', *Jamaican Historical Review*, 3.3, 1962, pp. 23–37.

[20] Michael Winstanley (ed.), *Rural Industries of the Lune Valley*, Lancaster, Centre for North-West Regional Studies, Lancaster University, 2000, pp. 7–9.

[21] Dalziel, 'Trade and Transition', pp. 94–95; C. Workman, 'The Hat Industry' in Winstanley, *Rural Industries*, pp. 105–6.

[22] F.W. Pitman, *The Development of the British West Indies, 1700–1763,* Yale University Press, 1917, rpt. London, Frank Cass, 1967, p. 384; Ward, *West Indian Slavery*, p. 433.

[23] P. Crowhurst, *The Defence of British Trade, 1689–1815,* Folkestone, Dawson, 1977, chapter 6.

[24] Isaac Dookhan, *A History of the British Virgin Islands, 1672–1970,* Caribbean Universities Press, 1975, chapters 2 and 3. Norman Island, at the southern tip of the archipelago, is considered by some to be the inspiration and setting for R.L. Stevenson's *Treasure Island.* Whether or not this is the case, treasure was certainly buried there in 1750. Dookhan, *British Virgin Islands,* p. 48.

[25] Crowhurst, *Defence of British Trade,* p. 195; K. Morgan, 'Bristol and the Atlantic trade in the eighteenth century', *English Historical Review,* 424, 1992, p. 644.

[26] William Enfield, *An Essay towards the History of Liverpool,* 1774, p. 73ff.

[27] George W. Paulson, *William Thornton, M.D., Gentleman of the Enlightenment* published privately 2007, chapters 1–3 is the best account of his early life and Lancaster connections. http://upload.wikimedia.org/wikipedia/commons/b/b2/Thorton_book.pdf, last accessed 12 June 2012.

[28] C.J. Jenkins, *Tortola: A Quaker Experiment of Long Ago in the Tropics,* London, Friends Bookshop, 1923, especially pp. 43, 47–50; Elder, *Slave Trade,* pp. 119–20. Lettsom was educated at the Quaker academy at Warrington under Samuel Fothergill and later became renowned as a protégé of John Fothergill, a prominent physician of the period. The Fothergills were in-laws of the Chorleys.

[29] *Williamson's Liverpool Advertiser,* 10 July 1778. The ships included one called *Hetherington.* Rawlinson and Chorley also had consignments of sugar on two ships from Antigua.

[30] Lillian M. Penson, *The Colonial Agents of the British West Indies* London, 1924, rpt. Frank Cass, 1971, p. 171. Henry was the only named agent whose main residence was not in London. His cousin Abraham was MP for Lancaster at the same time.

[31] Elder, *Slave Trade,* pp. 81, 119 and footnotes; TNA, CO 700/Virgin Islands5, Plan of Tortola 1798 by George King.

[32] *British West Indies (BWI) Study Circle Newsletter,* 80, 1974, pp. 16–17, http://www.bwisc.org/50_bulletins/b080_197403/b080_197403.pdf last accessed 12 June 2012.

[33] Thornton in Lonsdale parish registers. Several of the family are buried or commemorated in Tunstall church gravestones. Those in St Mary's in Lancaster also record the names of members of local families who died on Tortola.

34   Isaac Dookhan, *A History of the Virgin Islands of the United States,* Kingston, Jamaica, 1974, 6th impression, 2006 pp. 81–82.

35   L.J. Ragatz, *The Fall of the Planter Class in the British Caribbean 1763–1833,* London, 1929, rpt. Octagon, New York, 1977, p. 340.

36   *London Gazette,* 9 Nov. 1805.

CHAPTER THREE

Abram's owners: merchants and ship-owners

Who, then, were the men who purchased *Abram*? Clearly they had access to capital: £4,100 was a considerable outlay in 1806. Not surprisingly, the individuals involved were not inexperienced novices; they were well acquainted with the risks, likely returns and the destinations to which *Abram* was to venture.

Thomas Burrow

Thomas Burrow was in his mid-fifties and an established and successful member of the Lancaster mercantile and civic communities when he purchased *Abram*. His origins and early career were

3.1. Thomas Burrow's signature and seal, 1815: Lancs. Archives, DDX 70/acc 881/ box 29. (Reproduced with permission from Lancashire Archives.)

similar to many other shipowners and merchants in the town at the time. He was a migrant, having been born up the Lune Valley at Westhouse, a settlement of scattered farmsteads nestled below the slopes of Whernside, just over the county border in Yorkshire. He was baptised at the church of Thornton in Lonsdale on Christmas Day 1753.[1] His father, also Thomas, was a substantial yeoman farmer. When he died in June 1768 the eldest son Robert (born 1743) inherited the family farm and married Ellen Thornton, daughter of William Thornton of Roeburndale six months later. With no prospects of acquiring land of their own, the younger brothers all left to pursue a career in trade. George (born 1747), had already been apprenticed in 1761 to his uncle, Paul Jackson, a tallow chandler in Lancaster; John (born 1756) was apprenticed to William Bruce, cabinet maker in the town in 1771; and by the 1780s, the youngest, Christopher (born 1761) had also followed his brothers into trade.[2] At the age of fourteen, and on the day his father's will was proved, 21 June 1768, Thomas was dispatched by his guardian uncle to serve under yet another uncle in the town, George Jackson, a grocer and linen draper.

Bailey's directory of 1784 listed over 30 merchants in Lancaster but Thomas was not among them; he was simply returned as a linen draper.[3] A couple of years later, however, he and his brothers were taking advantage of the varied commercial opportunities which were opening up in the West Indies and North American continent in the wake of the cessation of hostilities with France and the United States. Robert sought to capitalise on the situation by constructing a cotton spinning mill on the family's estate at Westhouse and later acquired another at Austwick, near Settle.[4] John moved to Kingston, Jamaica where he imported furniture for William Bruce.[5] In 1784 Richard Gillow, proprietor of the leading firm in Lancaster, sought his advice about the purchase of mahogany in Jamaica, having been alerted to his existence by his brother Thomas back in Lancaster. Thomas also sold Gillows' furniture to a Boston merchant, Thomas English, in 1785.[6] Christopher, too, had established himself as a merchant in Jamaica and on 7 November 1787 he and his brother Thomas, along with the master, William Walker, and William Parke, another merchant of Kingston, registered the 143-ton *Two Friends*. She was described in the shipping registers as a 'prize' captured during the war, which had been legally 'condemned' in New York in 1782.[7] Over the next few years she plied between Lancaster, London and Jamaica but was wrecked off Jamaica in November 1790, although most of her cargo was salvaged. The shipping returns for Jamaica and papers relating to the salvage of her cargo confirm that the Burrows at this stage were general traders, with no apparent access to plantation sugar. *Two Friends* exported soap, candles, hampers, cheese and dry goods and returned with rum, cotton, logwood, mahogany, hides, old iron, pewter and brass, but no sugar.[8]

Thomas rapidly established himself as a member of Lancaster's trading community, joining the Port Commission in 1793 and becoming a member of the town council three years later. He did so, however, not by continuing his business with Christopher in Jamaica but by collaborating with other local men and trading with the smaller Leeward Islands and with the free ports of St Eustatia and, later, St Thomas. In September 1793 Burrow purchased *Aurora,* a 217-ton brig built at Brockbank's yard and armed with six guns. *Aurora* was to cross the Atlantic eleven times under the experienced Captain Thomas Greenwood. For the first two years her destination was St Eustatia, which suggests that Burrow did not at that stage have established contacts on the neighbouring British colonies of St Kitts, Antigua and Grenada. In July 1795, however, when Greenwood arrived in the islands he found that St Eustatia had fallen to the French and he sailed immediately for the free port of Charlotte Amalie on St Thomas. Charlotte Amalie and the neighbouring British island of Tortola were destined to become the major ports of call for all of Burrow's ships for the next half century.[9] Meanwhile, however, Burrow sought to expand into more established markets by partnering James Cort of Lancaster and William Cort of Grenada. In August 1795 he, along with Greenwood and the Corts, registered the 22-year-old, Lancaster-built, 132-ton snow *Chatsworth*, which Greenwood had captained on four voyages to St

Eustatia before 1793. Over the next three years Lloyds Registers record five voyages under various captains to Grenada, Antigua and Dominica with her owners variously given as James Cort and Co., Thomas Burrow and James Cort, and Burrow and Co.. Unfortunately, this venture was to prove short-lived. Despite being armed with six guns she was captured by the French in July 1798.

Burrow's transfer of *Aurora*'s operations to the Virgin Islands of St Thomas and Tortola, therefore, rather than his venture into the established British possessions to the east, provided the foundation on which he and his partners were to build. This, however, was not to be without its setbacks. In November 1796 he acquired the 130-ton brig *Dolphin*, a prize taken in the Virgin Islands, but fortunately transferred her the following May to Thomas Jackson, who was to see her taken by the French on her first voyage to Tortola two months later when she became separated from *Aurora*. The reason for her quick sale may have been that in February 1797 Burrow had acquired another partner, George Danson, and together they registered *Helen*, a larger 207-ton brigantine, armed with six guns, built in Liverpool in 1789. Trading as Danson and Co., she made several voyages to Antigua and Tortola under a variety of captains, but Danson's finances collapsed in June 1801 and Burrow was obliged to re-register her with Danson's assignees, a consortium of Lancaster and Manchester merchants, before she was sold to Whitehaven in August for the Jamaican trade.[10]

TO BE SOLD BY AUCTION,
At the MERCHANTS COFFEE-ROOM, in LAN-
CASTER, on TUESDAY the 18th of August, 1801,
at one o'clock ;

THE GOOD BRIGANTINE
HELEN,
With all her MATERIALS, as
lately arrived from Antigua. Bur-
then, per register, 207 tons; Liverpool built; mounts
14 carriage guns, nine and six pounders; is well
found, shifts without ballast, of an easy draft of water, and suitable for any trade, where a vessel of her
burthen is required.
Said vessel is lying in Glasson-dock ; and inventories or further particulars may be had by applying to
the Assignees of GEORGE DANSON, of Lancaster,
a bankrupt.
LANCASTER, JULY 24, 1801.

3.2. The brigantine *Helen* for sale: *Lancaster Gazette*, 8 August 1801.

In July 1799 *Aurora* was taken by the French on her first voyage under a new master and Burrow acted quickly to replace her with an even larger ship for his trade with the Virgin Islands. In November 1799 he was registered as sole owner of the new ship, *Mars,* which he had purchased from Brockbank's yard for £4280. At 394 tons she was not only far and away the largest vessel he had owned but also the best armed with twelve 24lb. and twelve 12lb. guns. Over the next five years she was described as a 'constant trader' making regular voyages to Tortola and St Thomas, including at least two voyages in which she also called at the captured French island of Martinique.

Mars was initially captained by the experienced Thomas Greenwood who considered her 'not as snug' as *Aurora*, and then by Thomas Wilson, before being sold in October 1804 to a merchant from Greenock for the Jamaica trade. Lloyd's Register of Shipping, however, records the owner throughout not as Thomas Burrow but as T. Mason and Co., while other sources refer to Burrow and Mason.[11]

Thomas Mason

3.3. Thomas Mason's signature, 1806: Lancs. Archives, DDX 2874 MS 5179. (Reproduced with permission from Lancashire Archives.)

Thomas Mason was baptised on 25 October 1767 in Beetham parish, which contained Sandside, the port for Milnthorpe and Kendal in Westmorland. His father, Anthony, was a retired naval man who died while Thomas was still a child.[12] From at least 1793 he was an agent in the West Indies, almost certainly acting for Thomas Burrow. Thomas Greenwood refers to him as a passenger on *Aurora*'s maiden voyage in October 1793 to St Kitts, St Eustatia and French Martinique, which was already under British jurisdiction. For the next couple of years he was probably based at the free port of St Eustatia. *Aurora* returned there in the summer of 1794 and on 11 October 1794 Mason dispatched a letter via *Maria*, informing Burrow of the 'disagreeable news of the French having full possession of the Island of Guadaloup'.[13] The following year news reached St Eustatia that Holland had fallen to the French and *Aurora* sailed post haste to the relative safety of the British Virgin Island of Tortola. Mason returned home on the ship from neighbouring St Thomas in January 1796. Less than two months later, however, he was on his way back to St Thomas and Tortola where he was to stay for several years.[14] In his absence, his sister Nancy married William Swainson, then Quay Master in Lancaster, but previously a captain of *Chatsworth* which the Burrows then owned. By June 1799, Thomas Mason had returned to Lancaster and consolidated his contacts with the trading community by marrying Elizabeth Wildman, whose sister Ellen had married Abraham Zimon Doncker Cuvelje, the son of Mr Peter Cuvelje, Council Lord of the Parliament of St Eustatia, and who later entered into unsuccessful partnerships with George Danson and other merchants.[15] The following year Mason joined Burrow on the Port Commission and in 1801–02 became a freeman of the town.

General traders

Burrow and Mason clearly benefited from the boom years and high prices for West Indian produce around the turn of the century. Not only were they well placed to take advantage of the wide range of produce on offer in St Thomas, the most important trading entrepot in the region, but they would have become aware of the huge potential of the sugar-rich island of St Croix when the British temporarily took control of the Danish Virgin Islands in March 1801. *Mars,* then a Letter of Marque licensed to act as a privateer to take enemy shipping, called at St Croix that year returning to Lancaster with a cargo of sugar.[16]

Between 1802 and 1804 while the fear of French invasion was at its height and sugar and imported commodity prices were low, Burrow and Mason restricted their operations to just one ship, *Mars.* Newspaper reports of the ship's cargo suggest that they only derived part of their income from trading as merchants on their own account. Not only did they frequently advertise for outward cargo, they also brought back consignments for a wide range of Liverpool and Lancaster merchants. When *Mars* arrived in the Lune from St Thomas on 4 June 1802, for example, she carried cargo for her owners and captain, William Noble, but also for 20 other individuals and partnerships, many of them Lancaster-based. Her cargo included cotton, coffee and tortoise shell for Burrow and Mason. Cotton was the sole or major commodity for 14 other merchants. Seven merchants imported tortoise shell, three coffee, one hides, and only one imported a small amount of sugar. Although Burrow speculated in the boom of 1799, he escaped the worst of the depression which set in from late 1801 as prices fell after the Treaty of Amiens brought a cessation in hostilities. Mason, with Burrow's financial backing, established the first spinning cotton mill in the town at White Cross on the recently-

---

SHIP NEWS.
LANCASTER, August 11.

We have to congratulate our readers on the safe arrival of the West-India fleet, with the exception of one Liverpool vessel.---The Eliza, L'Harmonie, Mars, and Eliza (brig) arrived here on Monday.--- Their cargoes are as follow :

ENTERED.

August 6.—Eliza, J Moon, from St. Christophers and St. Bartholomews, with 9 punchs lime juice 11 bales cotton 65 hides 5 calf skins J Sowerby; 70 ox hides 2 calf skins J Thorley, 21 bags cotton 50 casks coffee T Burrow, 2 do 7 bags cotton T Robinson, 2 bls tortoise shell 67 bags cotton 22 hides 1 cask old copper 10 punchs lime juice 348 pieces fustic Worswick & Allman, 11 bags cotton 1 cask coffee G Cooper, 12 bags cotton T Coulston, 19 do 30 punchs lime juice Danson & Walmsley, 9 bags cotton T Cowperthwaite, 300 bags cotton 1 log mahogany 591 pcs lignum-vitæ R Owen, 2 bls tortoise shell 8 bags cotton J Fearenside, 2 do E Blackburn, 7 do 1 box tortoise shell 3 casks 15 bags coffee J Moon, 3 casks coffee Samuel Mather and co.

— L'Harmonie, W Fryer, from Demerara, with 295 bales cotton 120 casks 281 bags coffee Ridley & Dodson.

7.—Mars, T Wilson, from Tortola, with 50 hhds sugar A Worswick & co. 79 hhds 1 tce 3 bls sugar 140 bales cotton 50 logs mahogany 52 tons fustic 40 casks coffee 19 bags cotton 1 box tortoise shell Burrow & Mason, 10 hhds sugar E B Threlfall, 50 bales cotton 10 bags do 103 casks coffee T Burrow, 9 serons indigo J Parker, 43 bags 86 serons cotton 50 logs mahogany Danson & Walmsley, 10 casks coffee 55 bags cotton 37 tcs annotta R Owen, 2 bags cotton D Eccleston, 81 logs mahogany 13 bags cotton J Moore, son & co. 30 serons do 4 casks coffee J Moore, 19 logs mahogany Blount & Kirkham, 20 serons cotton T Lister, 10 do J Smith, 139 do 50 casks coffee Mullion & Bibby, 30 serons cotton R Wallace, 15 bags do 1 bl tortoise shell 10 elephant teeth R Mashiter, 8 bags cotton Robinson & Nickinson.

9.—Eliza, D Macarty, from St. Thomas's, with 148 bales cotton 110 bags coffee 108 hides 2 bls tortoise shell 46 tons fustic J Cumpsty & co.

3.4. Ships entering Lancaster, August 1804, including Burrow and Mason's ship *Mars*, with details of cargoes: *Lancaster Gazette,* 11 August 1804.

opened canal in 1802.[17] Thomas Burrow was also a partner in Thomas Robinson and Company's cotton mill at Halton, further up the Lune.[18]

In April 1804, in partnership with three other Lancaster merchants, Burrow and Mason purchased the new 275-ton *Aurora* from Brockbank's yard.[19] She sailed from Lancaster's outport of Glasson Dock in June but by September she was stranded off St Kitts and sold the following month.[20] Two months later Burrow and Mason alone agreed to pay £4,000 in four instalments to Brockbank for the new 276-ton *Neptune* which sailed for Tortola and St Thomas the following January under Thomas Wilson, the captain previously engaged by them on *Mars*.[21]

Around this time, Thomas Burrow's elder son Edward (born 1783) replaced Mason as his father's agent in the Virgin Islands. During his stay he contracted a relationship with a free, mulatto woman on St Thomas, Catherine Schaltenbrand, by whom he had at least three children after c.1804: Thomas, Mary and Catherine. It was only after his final return to Lancaster that he eventually married her on 28 September 1819 in St Mary's parish church, where his children were also baptised.[22]

3.5. Edward Burrow's signature, 1815: Lancs. Archives, DDX 70/acc 881/box 29. (Reproduced with permission from Lancashire Archives.)

Abram Chalwill Hill

Edward was well-placed to foster relationships with planters and merchants on the neighbouring British Virgin Islands, especially those who owned the small vessels which plied between the islands. Prominent amongst these was Abram Chalwill Hill, a merchant and later planter on Tortola.[23] Hill had close connections with Lancaster and Liverpool merchants, including the influential Rawlinsons and Chorleys, and it feasible that Burrow and Mason benefited from the trading vacuum created after the death of Abraham Rawlinson the younger in 1803 and the subsequent bankruptcy and death of John Chorley two years later. In 1801 Chorley had recommended Hill to the captain of *Mercury,* Thomas Walters, as someone who could be trusted with credit, and linked him to Richard Hetherington, the Rawlinsons' longstanding agent on the island. Chorley cautioned Walters that if he was 'under the absolute Necessity of selling on Credit, let the same be done to no Person whatever, unless of undoubted Solidity' and advised him, if he were unable to dispose of his cargo for cash while he was in the Caribbean, that 'in such case it will be most prudent to place what may remain of them under the care of Abraham Chalwill

3.6. Abram Chalwill Hill's signature, 1815: TNA, CO 152/105 Leeward Islands Correspondence. (Reproduced by courtesy of The National Archives, London.)

Hill Esq. if at Tortola.'[24] Hill was the owner of several small 'droghers', vessels engaged in regional trade. Customs records for St Thomas between 1808 and 1814 record him as the owner of *Sally*, an 83-ton sloop initially registered in Bermuda, plying primarily between St Thomas and Tortola but also venturing to New York, and *Mary*, a 36-ton sloop described as a 'prize' which also traded largely with Tortola but additionally sailed to Curacao. Hill was clearly in a position to furnish potential traders with cargoes for their homeward journey, dispose of their inward produce, and provision planters with basic necessities.[25]

Hill was not named as an estate owner on King's map of the island in 1798,[26] but by 1818 he owned three plantations – Northside, Long Bush and Cappoon's Bay – and 450 slaves on Tortola,[27] as well as properties in Road Town, the only port and settlement on the island. He also owned the whole of Norman Island,[28] and part of Peter Island, both to the southeast of Tortola. In 1811 he acquired various estates on the Danish island of St John, which lay between Tortola and St Thomas, later amalgamating them into one called Abraham's Fancy, and in 1819, just before his death, purchased the late William Ashton's estate at La Vallee on St Croix.[29]

Hill was clearly a prominent and active member of Tortola's small community. In 1811, when he sat under Richard Hetherington to take depositions against Arthur Hodge, a white plantation owner, convicted for the murder of six of his slaves several years earlier, he was a justice of the peace and member of Tortola's Legislative Council, a position which was only open to substantial landowners, and described as the 'Honorable Abraham Chalwill Hill Esq.'[30] Hugh Elliot, General Governor of the Leeward Islands, stayed with a Mr Hill on the island during the trial and Philip Heydinger, Elliot's secretary, writing to Elliot's daughter Harriet, portrayed a bleak picture of the island but also provided some clues as to the probable location of Hill's plantation:

> The place seems miserable enough – there is but one long street, which constitutes the town, and the whole country is mountainous. We are lodging in a very good house, belonging to a Mr Hill, about a mile from the town – and nearer heaven than ever I have lived before.[31]

Hill also supported Christian missionaries' work among the slave population, leaving £500 in his will to the Rev. Joseph Taylor, secretary of the Wesleyan Methodist Missionary Society, and to the Danish church on St John.[32] He also campaigned for the appointment of an Anglican minister on Tortola.[33] In 1815 he presented a petition to Commissioners for Trade and Foreign Manufacturers in London from 'the free negroes, Indian mustees and mulattos' of the island requesting legislation to give greater freedoms for the free coloureds of Tortola,[34] a campaign which was ultimately successful since they were granted the right to own land on the same terms as whites in 1818. Hill's support for this action was not purely altruistic. His six 'reputed and acknowledged' children by his longstanding partner and later wife, Sally, a freed mulatto slave born on Antigua, were all described in official documents as 'free coloureds'. His close associates and executors of his will, George Martin, planter, and William Henry Smith, merchant of Road Town, his nephew, son-in-law and one of his major business partners at the time were also 'coloureds'.[35]

When they purchased and named *Abram* in December 1805, therefore, Burrow and Mason had reliable personal and commercial contacts in the Virgin Islands and good reason to feel confident about their hefty investment despite the continued risks of war.

Over the next nine years they were not to be disappointed.

References

[1]   Thornton in Lonsdale parish registers. Much of the information on the family's residence and background was provided by the late Geoff Brown of Westhouse.

[2]   Lancaster apprentice registers. It has not been possible to verify the claim in some accounts that Christopher joined the East India Company. Another Christopher Burrow was director of the company 1758–61.

[3]   *Bailey's British Directory*, 1784, vol. 2, pp. 557–60.

[4]   Geoff Brown, 'The Cotton Mill at Westhouse', *North Craven Heritage Trust Journal*, 2006, pp. 3–4. Also online at http://www.northcravenheritage.org.uk/nchtjournal/ Journals/2006/CottonMillLowWesthouse/ThecottonmillatLowWesthouseME.html last accessed 10 Jan. 2013. *Lancaster Gazette*, 22 Jan. 1814 – sale of Austwick cotton mill.

[5]   Lancs. Archives, DDX 2743 MS 239, Voyage Book no 3, A. and J. Rawlinson.

[6]   Gillow's Letter Book 1782–1786, 344/170, 3 April 1784 microfilm Lancaster University Library; Susan E. Stuart, *Gillows of Lancaster and London 1730–1840*, Woodbridge, Antique Collectors' Club, 2008, vol. 1 pp. 118–19.

[7]   Lancs. Archives, SS5/1 Lancaster Shipping Register.

[8]   Lancs. Archives, DDX 2743 MS 8171 Letter Book etc., ships and goods, salvage insurance, 1783–93; TNA, CO 142/20, shipping returns for Jamaica, 1787–88.

[9]   Lancs. Archives, SS5/1; Lloyds' Shipping Registers; Thomas Greenwood's memoirs, Lancaster Central Library Scrapbook 2 (2) printed extracts from *Lancaster Guardian*. The whereabouts of the original manuscript memoir is not known.

[10]   The assignees were Robert Inman, Thomas Giles with Alexander Worswick, John Dilworth, James Tinning, all of Lancaster, merchants, and John Philips, Joseph Blair,

James Hanson, Lawrence Peel, all of Manchester. Details of last voyage and sale are given in *Lancaster Gazette*, 11 July, 8 Aug. 1801; see Lloyds Register for details of new owner.

[11] Lancs. Archives, SS5/1; TNA, BT 98/31 Lancaster Muster Rolls; *Lancaster Gazette*, 19 Sept. 1801; Thomas Greenwood's memoirs.

[12] Beetham parish registers. Mason was a common name in the area at the time but this identification is based on Margaret Bainbridge's research.

[13] W. Hewitson, *Memoranda relating to Lancaster and District*, c. 1906, 2 volumes of cuttings from *Manchester Mercury*, Lancaster Central Library microfilm, vol. 2 , p. 201. Guadaloupe had been a French colony until 1791 when it declared independence. The British briefly occupied it in 1794.

[14] Thomas Greenwood's memoirs; Howson, *Lancaster*, pp. 53–60 provides a full summary of their contents.

[15] Cuvelje was made a freeman of Lancaster in 1797. Dutch by birth, he was naturalised in 1799 by Act of Parliament. By 1800 he had established himself in Lancaster as a merchant and shipowner and was a broker in 1800 in partnership with George Danson but was bankrupted in 1802. Cuvelje was also a Port Commissioner. His wife died in 1807 and he married Anna Maria Armstrong in 1811 in St Croix. By 1820 he and his wife established themselves in Puerto Rico by virtue of the Royal Decree of 1815 issued by H.M. King Ferdinand VII of Spain. He died there in 1830 and his second wife died in 1855. *London Gazette*, 2 Feb. 1802; *Lancaster Gazette*, 6 Nov. 1801, 25 July 1807; *Leeds Intelligencer*, 1 Dec. 1800; Antony Maitland's Armstrong genealogy website, http://www.antonymaitland.com/irisharm.htm last accessed 10 Jan. 2013.

[16] *Lancaster Gazette*, 22 June, 9 July 1803 records Burrow and Mason loading provisions at Cork, where West Indian convoys gathered, prior to *Mars* sailing for Tortola.

[17] Schofield, *Economic History*, Part I, p. 111. It has not been possible to confirm this date from original sources. Mason and Co, cotton spinners are first listed in *Holden's Triennial Directory* 1809.

[18] *London Gazette*, 30 July 1814.

[19] Thomas Robinson, George Danson, John Walmsley. The announcement in *Lancaster Gazette*, 14 April 1804 referred only to Burrow and Mason.

[20] TNA, BT 98/30 Lancaster Muster Rolls.

[21] Lancs. Archives, DDX 2743 MS 8127 John Brockbank's ship book; SS5/1.

[22] St Mary's Lancaster parish register. She was described as 'of the Island of St. Thomas in the West Indies, spinster'.

[23] Hill's origins and background remain obscure, although he was clearly descended in some way from the prominent Chalwill (or Chalwell) family who had been present in the Virgin Islands since at least the early 18th century, one of whom captained a small trading vessel. An Abraham Chalwill is also mentioned as Judge of the Vice-Admiralty Court of Tortola in 1763 responsible for deciding the fate of ships taken as prizes by privateers from the islands during the war with France and as owner of a sloop, *Eliza*, trading with St Thomas. A William Chalwell owned an estate on Tortola in 1798. Hill, however, was a common name in the West Indies and it has not been possible to link Abram to any particular family with any degree of certainty. David Hill was listed as master of the sloop *Wild Daniel* in 1765 shipping sugar and rum from Anguilla to Virginia: Anguillan Archaeological and Historical Society, http://www.aahsanguilla.com/readings.html last accessed 30 Jan. 2013. It is possible that he was related to Daniel Hill of Antigua, a member of the Leeward Islands Council, where

Abram's partner Sally hailed from and where Lancaster merchants had longstanding trading links; House of Commons papers 1803–04, *Correspondence with British W. India Colonies on Slave Trade*, 1797–1800, Leeward Islands, p. 227. A 'Mr Hill' was resident on the Danish island of St Croix, where he introduced and supported a touring repertory company in the early 1770s. Another was customs controller on St Thomas. Intriguingly, Edward Burrow's granddaughter later married Charles Hill, a partner in a ship owning firm and grandson of a Bristol sugar refiner, but no evidence has yet been found which connects the family to the Hills of Tortola.

[24] Letter from John Chorley to Captain Thomas Walters of *Mercury*, 25 April 1801, *British West Indies Study Circle Newsletter* vol. 80, 1974, http://www.bwisc.org/50_bulletins/b080_197403/b080_197403.pdf last accessed 28 March 2010. Walters was later a passenger on the *Neptune* in 1809 with Edward Burrow when it was temporarily taken by the French.

[25] TNA, CO 259/2 (1808–1810); CO 259/3 (1811–14) Naval Officers' Returns for St Thomas.

[26] TNA, CO 700/Virginislands5 Plan of Tortola from actual survey by George King.

[27] The estates were still in the hands of his executors in 1823 when 'A.C. Hill's heirs' were described as owning 431 slaves in the British Virgin Islands including 126 at Northside, 95 at Long Bush and 77 at Cappoon's Bay. House of Commons papers, 1825 *Reports by Commissioners of Inquiry into State of Africans apprenticed in W. Indies*.

[28] The site of pursuit of buried pirate treasure in 1750 and allegedly the inspiration for Robert Louis Stevenson's *Treasure Island*; A. Boyd, *Where's Where?*, Eyre Methuen, 1974.

[29] Information on estates from Camilla-Marlene Jensen (personal correspondence 7 April 2007) and David W. Knight, *A Documentary History of the Cinnamon Bay Plantation 1718 – 1917,* Virgin Islands Historical & Genealogical Resource Center, 1999, http://www.friendsvinp.org/archive/cinnamon_history.pdf last accessed 12 June 2012. A.C Hill's heirs are listed as free coloureds in returns of 1825 and 1831.

[30] Arthur M. Belisario, *A Report of the Trial of Arthur Hodge ... on the Island of Tortola, 25th April 1811,* Middleton, 1812. Hodge was condemned for the murder of Prosper, one of these slaves, in April 1811.

[31] Quoted in John Andrew, *The Hanging of Arthur Hodge: A Caribbean Anti-Slavery Milestone*, Xlibris Corporation, 2000, p. 124. Original letter in National Library of Scotland.

[32] TNA, PROB 11/1636 Abraham Chalwill Hill's will, 1817.

[33] TNA, CO 152/104 Colonial Office and predecessors: Leeward Islands, Original Correspondence.

[34] TNA, CO 152/105 Colonial Office and predecessors: Leeward Islands, Original Correspondence.

[35] House of Commons papers, 1828, *Reports by Commissioners of Inquiry into State of Slaves in H.M. Colonies under Acts abolishing Slave Trade: (Tortola)*, pp. 241–42; *London Gazette*, 25 May 1818 for dissolution of partnership between Hill, W.M. Glover and W.H. Smith.

CHAPTER 4

For Tortola, St Thomas and St Croix

For Tortola

Abram's maiden voyage was prominently and, as it turned out, rather optimistically advertised to local merchants in *Lancaster Gazette* throughout January 1806 (Figure 4.1). 'The new ship *Abram*', burthen 320 tons would sail 'For Tortola' by 1 February and 'proceed with the first convoy after that time, from Cork.'[1]

4.1. Advert for *Abram*'s first voyage. This appeared in *Lancaster Gazette* throughout January 1806.

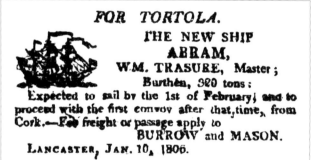

FOR TORTOLA.
THE NEW SHIP
ABRAM,
W.M. TRASURE, Master;
Burthen, 320 tons:
Expected to sail by the 1st of February, and to proceed with the first convoy after that time, from Cork.—For freight or passage apply to
BURROW and MASON.
LANCASTER, JAN. 10, 1806.

Abram finally received clearance to sail on 18 February 1806, nearly three weeks after her advertised expected departure. On board was a crew of just twenty. Captain William Trasure, at 64, was oldest member with a long career which had incorporated dozens of voyages to the West Indies. First and second mates were Thomas Watson, a 30-year-old and previously a mate on *Eliza*, who had been described in 1802 by William Swainson, treasurer of the Mariners' Society, as 'a healthy young man', and 21-year-old Edward Postlethwaite.[2] The rest of the complement consisted of a boatswain, carpenter, cook (the last man to be hired before she was cleared from Lancaster), nine seamen, all bar one aged between 18 and 26, and six apprentices aged between 14 and 16.

Things did not go well initially. In early March she was reported to have been at Milford Haven and hoping to join the next convoy from Cork, but this had departed by the time she arrived there a week later. Although cleared from Lancaster in February 1806, *Abram* did not leave home waters until 4 April when she sailed from Cork in one of the regular transatlantic convoys instituted by the Royal Navy to provide protection for the vulnerable merchant shipping. The only other vessel in the convoy which had been cleared from Lancaster was *Isabella*, for Antigua.[3] The rest were drawn from a variety of ports and were sailing to a wide range of destinations. There were twelve ships from Liverpool bound for Trinidad, Dominica, Jamaica, Surinam and one for Tortola; five from London, four of them for Jamaica; fourteen from Greenock; ten from Whitehaven; several from Bristol and Dublin and one each from Carmarthen, Scarborough, Jersey, Workington and Poole, the last bound for Newfoundland (Figure 4.2).[4]

Having taken further provisions on board, the convoy headed south for Madeira, where the trade winds would take them across the Atlantic. They were escorted by HMS *Anson*, a 44-gun frigate under Captain Lydiard and the 18-gun sloop HMS *Cygnet*. The frigate HMS *Aeolus* under Lord William Fitzroy joined them as far as Madeira. *Anson* could boast a distinguished naval career dating back to 1781 but was clearly nearing the end of service; *Cygnet* had been launched from Yarmouth less than two years earlier. Both were to engage in action against the enemy later in the year in the West Indies. As it turned out, however, *Abram* would have a much longer life than either of her initial protectors. *Anson* went down in a storm in Mount's Bay off the Cornish coast with a loss of over 120 lives less than two years later, while the HMS *Cygnet* was wrecked off Guiana within weeks of war finally ending in May 1815.[5]

Those who had invested in the ship or contracted to send cargo waited anxiously for news of her progress. It was not until 30 June that the *Lancaster Gazette* could report that a ship returning from Tortola had sighted her there on 11 May. The entries in her muster roll suggest that her crew were far from settled. Five seamen and the second mate left the ship on its arrival, followed a few days later by the carpenter and another seaman a month later. It was late June before Trasure succeeded in recruiting four seamen for the return journey, possibly from other ships arriving to wait for the convoy to Britain, making her complement up to just sixteen.[6] While waiting for the return convoy home she was joined by Burrow and Mason's other ship, *Neptune*, which had left Lancaster for Tortola in early May.

The West Indies were dangerous waters for merchant vessels and the men who crewed them. The crew could be pressed into service into the Royal Navy and were susceptible to disease and even death. Ships not only had to clear the Caribbean before the hurricane season started in September, they were liable to be attacked by privateers and enemy naval vessels. Despite the French navy's defeat at Trafalgar the previous October, her ships continued to harass British merchant ships in the West Indies. A letter written in Falmouth on 8 July 1806 by a merchant who had left St Thomas in mid-June, which was published in the *Lancaster Gazette* on

4.2. Ships, including *Abram,* sailing with the convoy from Cork, April 1806: *Lancaster Gazette,* 19 April 1806.

SHIP NEWS.
LIVERPOOL, APRIL 14.

The ship George Washington, with a cargo of sugar, cotton, coffee, &c. from the Isle of France, at Falmouth, sent in there by the Ainsley, Capt. Little, belonging to this port.

The following are the vessels that sailed from Cork, on the 4th inst. to the West Indies ; under convoy of his Majesty's ship Anson, Captain Ledger ; and sloop Cygnet, Campbell ; who would accompany them to the West Indies. The Eolus, Lord Wm. Fitzroy, would proceed with them to Madeira :—

The Castor, Paul, from hence for Trinidad : Mary Ann, Hutchinson, and Richard Boyle, from ditto to Dominica : Africa, Saunders ; Lady St. John, Whittle, John Bull, Lea ; Neptune, Holliday ; Cambridge, Catterall ; and Mary, Oswald, from ditto to Jamaica : Jane, Davis, ditto to Surinam : Henry, Ritson, ditto Tortola : Hopewell, Warden ; St. George, Palmer ; John & Thomas, Clark ; and Rashleigh, Melville, from London to Jamaica : Marquis of Huntley, Hart, ditto to Nevis : Catharine, Poole, from Dublin to Jamaica : Ivies, Atkinson ; Bristol, ——— ; and Kingston, Dove, ditto to St. Vincent : British Queen, Shilston, ditto to Demerara : Commerce, Godfrey, ditto to Dominica : Venus, Phillips, ditto to St. Kitts : Eliza, Bulpin, ditto to Grenada : Maria, Summers ; Martha Brae, Thomas ; Vulcan, Gardner ; Diana, Weeks ; Hope, Gibbs ; and Severn, Etheridge, ditto to Jamaica : Catharine, Williams, ditto to St. Thomas's : Rosetta, Currey, ditto to Nevis : Mercury, Reed, do. to Barbadoes : Abram, Trasure, Lancaster to Tortola : Isabella, Collins, ditto to Antigua : Atlas, Stockdale, Whitehaven to Jamaica : Druid, Wilson ; Mary Ann, Bell ; and Ranger, Atkinson, ditto to Antigua : Three Sisters, Mounsey, do. to St. Vincents : Ann and Eliza, Greaves, ditto to Trinidad : Wiliam, Sinclair ; and Edward, Stewart, ditto Baroadoes : Lady Cremorne, Aikin, from Liverpool to Antigua : Carmarthen, Richards, Carmarthen, to Jamaica : Countess of Crawford, Moore ; Britannia, Miller ; and Hope, Gilkinson, Greenock to Grenada : Jason, Morris, do. St. Vincent : Gathland, M'Echrin ; Mariana, Ewin ; Union, Bruce ; and Emerald, Franklin, ditto Jamaica : Active, Gourley, ditto St. Thomas's : Boyd, M'Kenzie ; and Oughton, Beard, ditto to Trinidad : Highlander, Ingles, ditto Demerara : William Patterson, ditto Tobago : Lucretia, Craig, ditto St. Kitts : Union, Arundell, Cork to Barbadoes : Henry, Clarke, Scarborough to Surinam : Eliza, Lloyd, Whitehaven to Barbadoes : Venus, Tozer, Topsham to Jamaica : Industry, Durvell, Jersey to Honduras : Ardent, Campbell, Workington to Jamaica : and Swallow, Allen, from Poole to Newfoundland.

The Mary, Crosby, and Otway, Hackney, from hence at Africa.

19 July, raised fears by describing how two French vessels had attacked British ships at Martinique and warned that four other French warships were at Puerto Rico. Others reported that the French fleet were lying south of Tortola and had only retreated when challenged by British vessels.[7] Although there were reports that the convoy was scheduled to leave at the end of June, the 300-strong contingent did not sail until 3 August, escorted by two aged naval vessels under Admiral Cochrane, who had commanded the Leeward Islands fleet since 1805. These included HMS *Agamemnon*, Nelson's old ship, which had been posted to the West Indies after Trafalgar where she pursued and engaged a French fleet off Santo Domingo in February. From mid-September newspapers all over the country reported any fragments of information they could glean. Towards the end of the month they began to report the safe arrival of individual ships which had run ahead of the convoy and then, in the last weekend of the month, welcomed home the bulk of the convoy. But it was not until early October that the *Lancaster Gazette*, with a palpable sense of relief, was finally able 'to congratulate' its readers on the safe arrival from St Thomas of *Neptune, Abram* and another Lancaster vessel, *Speculation*.[8]

While in port, Seward and Brockbank would have made good any damage to the ships and just over a month later in early November both vessels cleared Lancaster again.[9]

Over the next twelve years *Abram* was to undertake a further two round trips to the West Indies virtually every year, a shorter one leaving in spring or early summer and returning between August and October with the bulk of the season's crops; and a longer voyage departing in October or November and returning the following spring or early summer. All of her voyages were to the Virgin Islands and with similar outward cargoes, but there were distinct changes over time in terms of the crew who manned her, the specific islands she called at, the vessels she sailed with and the return cargoes she carried for her owners.

Captains and Crews

Trasure would appear to have had difficulty recruiting able-bodied men for the second voyage; nearly half *Abram's* complement of 20 was made up of teenage apprentices and a landsman who had never sailed before (Figure 4.3). Seven experienced seamen were recruited in the West Indies for the return journey but *Abram* still docked in Lancaster with a crew just two more than she had left with. Three apprentices had died on Tortola in early February and the captain himself perished at sea before the end of the month, followed a few days later by the boatswain. It was left to the first mate, Thomas Watson, to bring her into Lancaster in early April.

Watson assumed command for the next eight years. Unlike Trasure he successfully recruited an enlarged ship's complement of 27 to 29 men until

4.3. Muster Roll for *Abram*'s second voyage, October 1806, showing crew's lengths of service: TNA, BT98/30 Port of Lancaster Muster Rolls, 1800–50. (Reproduced by courtesy of The National Archives, London.)

1814 when hostilities with United States and France ended. As well as first and second mates, the ship always sailed with a carpenter, a post filled for most of Watson's captaincy by John Rumilly. Under Watson, she also sailed with a specialist gunner, hired to take care of the ten guns which were installed on the ship after the maiden voyage. Edward Bradshaw, a man in his late 40s, filled the role of gunner for five of the early voyages before being replaced by a younger man, Thomas King, who had previously sailed as gunner on *Neptune,* and then a quick succession of other men of various ages.[10] On most occasions she also carried a boatswain, cook and occasionally a steward. Up to 14 seamen were engaged, supplemented by occasional landsmen and as many as nine youthful apprentices, a few seemingly as young as twelve. James Greenwood, son of Thomas, one of Burrow and Mason's captains, sailed on two trips in 1809.[11] (Figure 4.4) The ages of these men were not always accurately recorded, their geographical origins were not given and their surnames were not always consistently spelt. While there were names which were clearly local such as Bleasdale, Allston (or Alston) and Gornall, and a few of foreign origin, there are indications, not unexpectedly, of possible links with Merseyside, London, the Humber, Tyne and West Country, all areas with strong maritime connections. Lancaster crews were not all necessarily Lancaster men.

4.4. Apprenticeship of James Greenwood, son of Captain Thomas Greenwood, to Burrow and Mason 1806: Lancs. Archives, DDX 2874 MS 5179. (Reproduced with permission from Lancashire Archives.) Greenwood sailed as an apprentice on *Abram* in 1809 and 1810.

After the first two voyages the scale of desertions and deaths witnessed under Trasure were not repeated, but Watson nearly always returned with fewer men than he left with. Philip Lovel, the cook, died on the way home in April 1810. Robert Willson, landsman, drowned in June 1807 as did Joseph Wynn, seamen, just over a year later on 3 September 1808. Even more men were pressed into the service of the Royal Navy and a few probably left in the West Indies to try to avoid this fate. The boatswain and two seamen were pressed on 25 June 1808 and this may explain why the cook 'ran' the following day and another seaman departed just over two weeks later. The carpenter, Timothy Bainbridge, was pressed in Santo Domingo less than a year later. Three men were taken just before Christmas 1809 and another fled the ship on Boxing Day. The following December the ship's gunner, 32-year-old William Harrison, was pressed followed in April 1811 by a further seven seamen. Even in the closing stages of the war, on 13 November 1814, the second mate and a seaman were lost to the Royal Navy.

Perhaps not surprisingly, crew members other than the captain rarely served on consecutive voyages during the war although several had longer, if occasionally broken, service and some went on to sail on other Burrow ships. Joseph Smith, second mate in 1809, sailed again as first mate from July 1816, while Thomas Dawson, first mate on several of the voyages in 1807 and 1808, later became captain of *Neptune* and part owner of *Thomas Burrow*, eventually going down with his ship on 29 August 1833 as he tried to save some of his papers in his cabin when she foundered off Sunderland Point, within sight of home. The return of peace, which also probably reduced opportunities for alternative work, witnessed more stability in the crew, with eleven men serving on both of the last two voyages.

Cargoes

Outward-bound *Abram*'s hold contained goods and provisions necessary to maintain life on board and in the colonies; homeward-bound it was filled with more exotic and potentially valuable produce. The log of another ship, *William Ashton*, owned by Thomas Burrow and James Barton Nottage, and named after a planter on St Croix, gives some idea of the diet the crew survived on during her maiden voyage in April 1810: beef, pork, tripe, ling fish, cheese, butter, potatoes, oatmeal, barley, flour, bread, peas, water and, of course, rum.[12] They would have had access to poultry which were regularly carried on board ships; Brockbank's day book includes references to work on 'hen coops' for *Abram* in 1808.[13]

Colonial port records for Lancaster ships unloading at St Thomas during this period, including *Neptune*, provide detailed breakdowns of the huge variety of products which were assembled in Britain for shipment to the islands at this time (Table 4.1).

Table 4.1: Imports into St Thomas on *Neptune*, 1808[14]

Textiles and clothing	linen, haberdashery, bunting, silk stockings, silk handkerchiefs, silk and other hats, stuffs, calicoes, woollens, boots, shoes, thread, bunting.
Household items	earthenware, glassware, tinware, stationery, saddlery and tanned leather, paper, soap, candles, brushes, umbrellas, quills, curled hair, combs, perfumery, hand trunks, apothecary's wares, violins.
Furniture	furniture (in cases), sofas, mattresses.
Vehicle	six crates containing a phaeton.
Ironmongery and hardware	hardware, paint, pumps, pipes, nails, tiles, matchets, sheets of copper, iron pots, iron girdles, sieves, bricks, blacking, glue, linseed oil, twine.
Minerals	brimstone, coal, lime.
Equipment	grindstones, pumps and pump brakes, fishing lines.
Ships' goods	anchors, sail canvas, mast hoops
Food and drink	potatoes, cheese, butter, groceries, mustard, pickled beef, tripe, hams, pork, lard, rum, flour, oats and oatmeal, maize, peas, barley, garden seeds, refined sugar, ling fish, porter, beer.

The surviving manifests for three voyages of *William Ashton* to St Croix in 1810 and 1811 are rather less varied, consisting mainly of provisions, earthenware, candles, lime and 'sundries', but on her first voyage she also carried sugar boilers, hewn stone and fire bricks for the plantations on the island.

Although *Abram*'s owners were responsible for the bulk of the shipments, other merchants also placed cargo with her. The Liverpool newspapers regularly advertised sailings of Burrows' ships from both Lancaster and Liverpool in the hope of attracting business and the firm employed an agent in Liverpool, John Cawson, initially of 14 Brunswick Street but from 1814 of 41 Lancelot Hey, who was described as broker, dealer and chapman in 1816.[15] In most cases cargoes were dispatched to named individuals in the islands. Hill and Edward Burrow would have been major recipients on Tortola and St Thomas, although it is likely that a much larger number of merchants were involved in the latter. The vast majority of *William Ashton*'s cargo for St Croix was destined for just one partnership, Ashton and Smith, who took significant quantities of lime, readily available from Lancaster's rural hinterland and a vital ingredient in early stages of sugar refining,[16] along with large consignments of oats, earthenware, and various sundries. On the maiden voyage, other merchants on the islands, many of them Danish, received smaller quantities of household goods, clothing and foodstuffs including dairy produce and cereals. Butter was sent to both Edward Burrow on St Thomas and Abram Chalwill Hill on Tortola via St Croix.[17]

4.5.1 and 4.5.2. *William Ashton*'s Log Book, 1810–11 showing cargoes and merchants they were destined for, including A.C. Hill, Edward Burrow and Ashton & Smith. Lancs. Archives, DDX 2743 MS 5084. (Reproduced with permission from Lancashire Archives.)

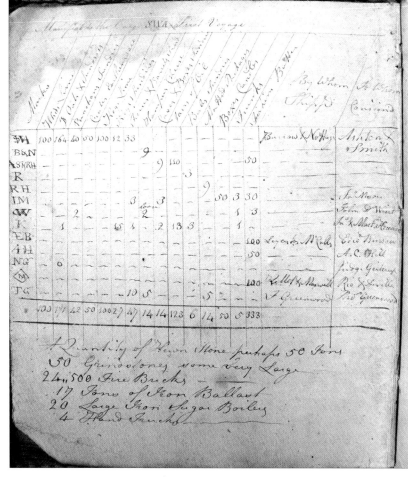

Cargoes destined for free ports such as Road Town and Charlotte Amalie could be sold on and distributed to other islands, or even the American mainland, either by other foreign ships which called there or smaller vessels owned by local merchants. Hill's 36-ton sloop, *Mary*, captained by John Dunlop, sailed from St Thomas on 29 October 1808 with butter, flour and rum for Curacao while the larger *Sally* sailed the following March with flour, lumber, copper sheets, oats and cotton for Tortola and again in 1810 with Catalonia wine, soap, trunks, British maize, cordage, tar, pitch, oil paint, tallow, cotton bagging, wrought iron, nails, lime, paper and hoops.[18]

The precise composition of *Abram's* return cargoes depended on which ports she called at in the Virgin Islands and where and when they were unloaded back in England. Cargoes from the entrepot of St Thomas, where Edward Burrow was based, were more diverse than those from Tortola and reflected the range of produce available throughout the Caribbean region: cotton in considerable quantities, rum, fustic, mahogany, indigo, succades, arrowroot, satin wood, Nicaragua wood, tamarind, tortoise shell and cow and ox hides. Although sugar featured in her cargo from Tortola from the outset, it only dominated her trade from late 1808 and never to the total exclusion of other products, unlike other vessels the firm owned from 1810 which traded primarily with St Croix (see below p. 51ff).

As well as trading on their own account, Burrow and Mason continued to act as carriers for other merchants, some of whom were shipowners in their own right. *Neptune* returned from Tortola in October 1806 with cotton, indigo, tortoise shell, mahogany, staves and sugar for nine named merchants. Although sugar comprised a much larger proportion of the commodities imported by her owners than on earlier voyages, cotton was still the major component of her cargo, possibly reflecting Mason's interest in textiles. Returning from her maiden voyage to Tortola in the same month, *Abram* also carried a mixed cargo but with more sugar. On board were 230 hogsheads and 12 barrels of sugar, 260 bales of cotton and 10 tons of fustic for Burrow and Mason but also sugar for the Lancaster merchants Worswick and Allman, 50 bales of cotton for the Liverpool firm

4.6 Shipping reports for *Abram* and other vessels owned by Burrows and Nottage: *Lancaster Gazette*, 14 Aug 1813 and 24 June 1814.

of Falkner and Mawdsley, mahogany for two other merchants and a small consignment of sugar for William Trasure.[19]

Although many of the earlier shipments on *Mars* had been for Lancaster traders, *Abram* initially carried for merchants based elsewhere. Some had their headquarters in Liverpool, such as David Tyson, and Venables, Stanniforth and Bailey who imported sugar, Lowndes and Bateson for whom she brought indigo in September 1808, and Falkner and Mawdsley, who were Liverpool brokers with interests in sugar and cotton plantations in the Virgin Islands. Yet others were London-based. L.B. Cohen, who imported 355 bags of coffee from Santo Domingo in April 1808, was a relative of the Rothschilds, trading in commodities, textiles and diamonds; Blake, Hobson and Allfrey were London underwriters; Inglis, Ellis and Co. were London merchants and plantation owners; Thellusson Nephew and Co. were subscribing members of Lloyds and descendants of an important Swiss/French banker with estates in the West Indies and a base in London.[20] Reports in the Liverpool and Lancaster press suggest that *Abram,* like other Lancaster vessels, not only sought outward cargo in Liverpool but also returned to the port if the cargo merited it.[21]

St Croix: the sugar island

From late 1808, however, *Abram's* destinations and return cargoes began to change, as did the range of the merchants they were intended for, and this presaged a major departure in Burrow's pattern of trade from 1810.

In October 1807, *Abram* cleared from Lancaster for Tortola, but exceptionally returned the following April with a cargo of coffee and cotton from Santo Domingo bringing news of another merchant ship's engagement with a French squadron in early March.[22] This opportunistic venture can be explained by the British government's decision to grant licences to ships trading through Tortola to import coffee and other produce from Santo Domingo at normal levels of duty.

On her next voyage she returned in September 1808 from Tortola with a cargo of sugar, cotton and indigo for 12 different merchants but in company with *Thomas,* owned by the Lancaster firm of Worswick and Allman, which carried nearly over 500 hogsheads of sugar, virtually twice as much as that on *Abram* and *Neptune* combined. *Thomas* had sailed not from St Thomas or Tortola but from the nearby Danish island of St Croix. For the next five years St Croix was to become a major port of call for more Lancaster ships.

The emergence of the sugar-rich St Croix as a major destination lay in Britain's deteriorating relationship with Denmark. In 1807 hostilities between the two countries resumed and the British fleet bombarded Copenhagen harbour. On 9 February 1808 the *London Gazette* reported

that a British force had retaken the Danish Virgin Islands the previous December. Rejecting the Danes' request to keep the ports open to all-comers, the terms of the surrender insisted that 'The Colony must trade subject to the British Laws, as in force in the British West India Islands' but that it 'shall have whatever Advantages are allowed to the most favoured British colony.' This meant that sugar and cotton plantations of St Croix could theoretically draw in necessary provisions and sell either to America or to Britain and her possessions. However, because of the United States' Embargo Act of December 1807, which prohibited American ships from trading with Europe, and the subsequent Non-Intercourse Act of 1809 and open warfare with Britain three years later, British and colonial merchants had a stranglehold on trade with St Croix for over six years. For as long as the islands remained British there were rich pickings to be had but there was no guarantee that this bonanza would last if the experiences of 1802 were repeated and the islands were handed back to Denmark as part of a future peace settlement.

Production of sugar on St Croix rose dramatically from just over 32 million lbs. in the early 1800s to 46 million lbs. by 1812, making the island second only to Jamaica in terms of its contribution to the British sugar trade (Table 4.2).[23] From being insignificant marginal colonies, the Virgin Islands now accounted for nearly one-eighth of the entire British sugar trade and a similar proportion of its rum imports. Much of this was due to merchants like Burrow and Mason who were already trading with

4.7. The port and the shipyards of Christiansted in Saint Croix in the Virgin Islands in the 19th century. (© De Agostini, The British Library Board Images Online 11093843.)

the Virgin Islands, and who were consequently well placed to establish relationships with resident planters and merchants such as William Ashton.

Table 4.2: British sugar imports, 1807 and 1812.[24]

| | 1807 | | 1812 | |
	cwts	%	cwts	%
Jamaica	1,780,757	50.7	1,453,954	41.0
Other British colonies (exc. Virgin Islands)	1,233,542	35.1	1,160,845	32.7
Virgin Islands (British and Danish)	21,847	0.6	422,901*	11.9
Ceded French and Dutch colonies	474,082	13.5	510,655	14.4
Total	3,510,228		3,548,355	

* St Croix accounted for 353,285 cwts.

William Ashton and William Smith of St Croix

William Ashton and William Smith, trading as Ashton and Co., were initially merchants on Tortola who established plantations on St Croix. The Ashtons hailed from Risley near Warrington, an area also connected with John Chorley, partner of Henry Rawlinson. Ashton and Co. were exporting sugar from Tortola in the 1770s. In February 1784 William and James Ashton are recorded as merchants on the island and joint owners of *Polly,* a 30-ton schooner which had been seized as a prize during the war and registered at Tortola. James was also sole owner of *Reprisal,* a 20-ton sloop built in Bermuda and also registered at Tortola. Both vessels were officially licensed by the government as 'droghers' or vessels 'at liberty to sail' in the region in search of trade, transporting goods and produce between Tortola and other West Indian islands such as Dominica and Barbados, as well as New York. Both men were also involved in the transatlantic trade. James was co-owner with Thomas Dickinson of *John,* captained by John Ashton, a 70-ton brig originally registered in Liverpool on 28 July 1784, while William Ashton and Co. owned *Planter,* a much larger ship which had been taken as a prize and which cleared Tortola for Liverpool in 1784 with a mixed cargo of sugar, cotton wool, fustic, a box of bread, cloth and coffee from Dominica, all 'legally imported into this island' by the schooner *Polly.*[25] The Liverpool shipping registers for 1786 list them as merchants on Tortola with shares in two ships previously owned by Henry Rawlinson and his partners: the Liverpool-built *Patsey* (329 tons) and *Sally* (459 tons) in both cases with John Chorley, James Grierson, Richard Hetherington and Martha Rawlinson, Henry's widow. William is known to have continued as a ship owner and local merchant trading between Tortola, St Thomas and St Croix until his death in 1814, owning at least three vessels in the 1800s in his own right: *Nelson,* a

REGULATIONS,

FOR THE PORT OF

CHRISTIANSTÆD.

I.

No Vessel of any description, to lay off and on, within the Port after Sun-set, and any Vessel entering the Harbour after that Time must anchor under the Fort till Morning.

II.

Every Vessel on arriving, shall be visited by the Harbour-Master, and a proper place pointed out by him for the same to Moor; every Master will also receive from him a printed Copy of these Regulations, (paying Two Bitts for the same) which he is hereby enjoined and commanded punctually to obey.

III.

All Masters, or Commanders of Vessels shall at the furthest, within one hour after their arrival in harbour, apply to the Wharfinger who will furnish him with a Guide to the Government House, and previous to the said Master, or Commander, having made his report there; no Passengers must be allowed to land. If this Order is not complied with, the Vessel will be fired at every 15 Minutes until it is obeyed. Five Pieces of Eight charged for the first Shot, Ten Pieces for the Second, and so on.

IIII.

Vessels with Guns to have them drawn immediately after Anchoring, and on no account to fire them off, or to fire any small arms of any description, without the previous sanction of the Harbour Master, who will forthwith, report the same to the Governor or in his absence to the Commanding Officer in the Fort.

V.

All Ships or Vessels on arriving (except small Sloops or Schooners) shall be Moor'd directly, and Rig in their Jib-Booms without any out-rigger, and in such cases as the Harbour-Master may direct, the Sloops and Schooners above excepted, shall also Moor and Rig in their Jib-Booms, &c.

VI.

No Boats except those of the Pilot, Harbour-Master, Health Officer, or Custom-House, are under any pretence to board a Vessel before she is Anchored, and the Master made his report at the Government House, or after she has made Sail to go out.

VII.

Masters of Vessels who sail, warp, moor, or drift foul of others, shall pay what Damage they thereby do.

VIII.

No Goods or Passengers to be landed without directions from the Wharfinger, who will point out the Proper Place on the Wharf for so doing.

IX.

Masters or Commanders of Vessels are to be mindful not to allow any Ballast, whether, Sand, Gravel, or Stone to be thrown over board, but shall be obliged to have the same conveyed and deposited at such place as the Harbour-Master, shall point out to them, under a penalty of Fifty Pieces of Eight for the first offence, and double that sum if repeated.

X.

No Vessel to take Ballast, any where in the harbour, or outside thereof, without the permission of the Harbour-Master, nor are any Rocks or Stone to be taken or removed from the Reef on any account without the special permission of Government.

XI.

No Person to be received on Board, any Ships, Vessels, or Craft as Passengers, without producing their Pass to the Inspector of Passports for Signature.

XII.

All Spanish Boats to be entered and cleared at the Custom House by the Broker, who is also to aid them in the Disposal of their Cargo, for which, he is to charge One Dollar, any Persons whose Vessels are Decked, and above 15 Tons, choosing to employ the Broker, for the sale of their Cargo, are to pay 5 pr. Cent Commission.

XIII.

All Boats and Vessels to quit the Wharf, so soon as their Cargo is out, and to haul off from the shore at Sun set, until Sun rise.

XIV.

No Vessel to heel, scrub or burn, without permission from the Harbour-Master, and on the place by him appointed.

XV.

No Hulks are permitted to be in the Harbour, but in such places as the Harbour-Master, shall point out.

XVI.

No Seamen belonging to Vessels in the Harbour shall be allowed to remain on shore after Eight o'Clock at Night.

XVII.

No Pitch or Tar to be boiled on board under penalty of the Law in that case made and Provided.

XVIII.

Lastly be it made known, that the Masters and Commanders of Vessels, disobeying any of the foregoing articles, for the transgression of which, no punishment or penalty has been prescribed, judgment shall be passed by the Governor, or the Polity Master, except in cases subject to the common course of Law, which shall be subject to the Cognizance of the proper Judges,

Government-House, St. Cruz, 8th December 1813.

By Command,
S. R. JARVIS,
Government Secretary.

GEO. WILL. RAMSAY,
Governor.

4.8. British regulations for the port of Christiansted, 1813: TNA, CUST 34/793. (Reproduced by courtesy of the The National Archives, London.)

95-ton sloop seized as prize during the war and registered at St Croix; *Tom*, a vessel of 91 tons built at Liverpool and, jointly with his business partner, William Smith, *John* (91 tons) which had been built in Lancaster.[26] By 1795 he had settled on St Croix and obtained citizenship there. When trade with the Danish Virgin Islands briefly became feasible in 1801 as a result of the British occupation, John Chorley advised Captain Walters of *Mercury* to consult 'Abraham Chalwill Hill if at Tortola' but 'William Ashton Esq. if at St Croix ... it is very probable that Mr. Ashton and others of my Correspondents may think it really prudent that the Mercury should load at St Croix.'[27]

William Smith, Ashton's partner, had direct connections with Lancaster and the Burrows so it may have been through him that they made initial contact with Ashton. In January 1803, Smith had been described as 'merchant, late of Lancaster' when he conveyed land in Romalkirk, County Durham, to Thomas Burrow which he had inherited from his uncle James.[28] At the time he was resident on the French island of Martinique which was controlled by the British until the Treaty of Amiens in March 1802, which may explain why the Burrows twice instructed *Mars* to call there. At some stage soon after, however, he, too, transferred his interests to the Danish island of St Croix and entered into partnership with William Ashton and another local man, Thomas Hughes Hill. Between them they acquired several plantations on the island.

Burrows and Nottage

4.9. George Burrow's and James Barton Nottage's signatures, 1815: Lancs. Archives, DDX 70/acc 881/box 29. (Reproduced with permission from Lancashire Archives.)

In January 1809, just as St Croix was opening up for British trade, Burrow and Mason terminated their trading partnership, although Mason retained his part-share in the *Abram* and *Neptune* and remained a member of the Port Commission until 1821 and Burrow retained his share in Mason's cotton spinning enterprise.[29] When *Neptune* docked in September of that year, therefore, she brought sugar for Mason alone, cotton and fustic for Burrow and Mason and sugar for a new partnership, Burrow and Nottage.

James Barton Nottage had previously operated as an independent merchant, first recorded as importing cotton and mahogany on *Abram* in April 1807.[30] He came from and married into maritime families. He had lived in Lancaster virtually all his life but his mother Mary originated from the Quaker Bartons near Scarborough while his father was born in Essex.

He was in the West Midlands around 1786 since he and his widowed mother were first mentioned in the Lancaster Quaker records of 1787 when they moved from the Warwickshire meeting. Within a year she had contracted what was described as an 'irregular marriage' (i.e. Anglican) with the Quaker John Lawson, son of Lancaster's prominent and successful sugar refiner, who lived in a large detached house on St Leonardgate adjacent to the refinery which was later to be occupied by Thomas Burrow and his son George.[31] It may have been Lawson who provided the young James with his entry into trade but his acceptance within Lancaster circles was cemented in June 1807 when Nottage, by then a lapsed Quaker, married the 19-year-old daughter of Captain Thomas Alston who, unbeknown to them, had died at sea en route from Port au Prince earlier that month.[32] The partnership of 'Burrow and Nottage' first appears in the press in July 1809.

Burrow and Nottage's new partnership did not get off to an auspicious start. The average price of sugar dropped by 20 per cent between December 1808 and April 1809, although the varied nature of their cargoes continued to shelter them from the worst impact of this. Then, on 22 April, barely a week out from Lancaster for St Croix, *Neptune,* under Captain Thomas Wilson and with four passengers including Thomas Burrow's son Edward and Captain Walters on board, was captured by the French corvette *La Mouche.* With just six guns Wilson's vessel was no match for a 16-gun adversary with a crew of 145. Plundered of her cargo and with the crew taken off into captivity, *Neptune* and her passengers headed for Corunna with a French prize master and small Spanish crew but, by exploiting divisions among their captors, the four passengers succeeded in retaking her and Captain Walters sailed her to Madeira and from there headed for St Thomas where Edward Burrow, then described as 'of Tortola', re-registered her in his own name. Thomas Wilson himself was not so fortunate. He finally returned to Lancaster nearly five years later on 12 January 1814 having escaped with some other prisoners of war from the fortified town of Verdun where they had been held.[33]

On 16 September 1809 *Abram* and *Neptune,* now under a new master, docked at Lancaster laden with sugar from St Croix and smaller quantities of Madeira wine and cotton and fustic from St Thomas and Tortola, all of it destined for Burrow and Nottage's warehouse. Over the next three years, the partners embarked on a major expansion of trade with St Croix. On 9 October 1809 they contracted to pay John Brockbank £6,230 for a new ship, the 366-ton *William Ashton,* which was delivered to them on 6 April 1810. Thomas's younger son George joined the partnership around this time, first appearing as one of three purchasers of the 166-ton *Flora* (built 1792) in March 1810, which had previously only plied from Lancaster as a coaster. She sailed to the West Indies under her existing captain, a young Thomas Rogerson. All three were also named as owners of *Neptune* when she was re-registered in Lancaster in October 1811. In January 1812 they purchased *Eliza* (214 tons) from Worswick and Allman; she joined *Abram* in her voyages to Tortola and St Thomas, freeing up the larger *Neptune* to concentrate on bringing sugar from St Croix.[34]

In 1812 therefore, Burrows and Nottage, as they now called themselves, owned five ships which made eight voyages to the Virgin Islands, most of them 'well manned and armed'. They accounted for nine of the twelve vessels arriving in Lancaster from the West Indies (Table 4.3). By this date they were operating very differently from Burrow and Mason's initial forays into the trade or the other firms trading from the port. Whereas *Pusey Hall* from Jamaica, *Thomas* from Antigua and *James* from St Thomas and St Croix, all returned with mixed cargoes for their owners and other merchants in Lancaster and Liverpool, Burrows and Nottage's vessels from St Croix were laden predominantly with sugar, exclusively destined for their owners. The quantities dwarfed the 250 hogsheads carried by *Abram* from Tortola just five years earlier. By 1812, Lancaster's pattern of trade had been transformed from that which prevailed a decade earlier and was totally different from its larger rival to the south (Table 4.4).

Table 4.3: Imports of sugar, Burrows and Nottage's ships 1812.[35]

Port	Ship	Hogsheads	Tierces	Barrels	Origin
Lancaster	*Abram*	358	34	177	Tortola and St John
Lancaster	*Eliza*	240	20	100	Tortola and St Thomas
Lancaster	*Flora*	225	12	40	St Thomas and St Croix
Lancaster	*Flora*	108			St Thomas and St Croix
Lancaster	*Neptune*	440	2	140	St Croix
Lancaster	*Neptune*	no details available			St Croix
Lancaster	*William Ashton*	606	20	133	St Croix
Lancaster	*William Ashton*	572		37	St Croix
Lancaster	*James**	41			St Thomas and St Croix
Liverpool	*Abram*	370	112	5	Tortola and St Croix
Liverpool	*Mercury**	100			Tortola
Liverpool	*John**	693		124	St Croix
Liverpool	*Mercury**	109			Tortola

* These vessels also carried cargoes for Burrows and Nottage but were not owned by them.

Table 4.4: Ships arriving at Liverpool and Lancaster 1812.[36]

Liverpool		Lancaster	
Jamaica	39	St Croix	3
Demerara	27	St Croix and St Thomas	4
Antigua	13	Tortola and St Thomas	1
Barbados	12	St Thomas	1
St Croix	8	Tortola and St John	1
St Lucia	5	Jamaica	1
Berbice	4	Antigua	1
Surinam	3		
Tortola	3		
Bahamas	2		
Honduras	2		
St Thomas	2		
Trinidad	2		
Bahia	1		
Barbados/Berbice	1		
Dominica	1		
Grenada	1		
Guadaloupe	1		
Havana	1		
Madeira, Demerara, Berbice	1		
Montserrat	1		
St Croix and Tortola	1		
St Vincent and St Lucia	1		
St Vincent	1		
Total	133	Total	12

All their vessels made two journeys to and from Lancaster that year except *Abram* which exceptionally docked at Liverpool in May with some sugar and indigo for two of the major Liverpool merchants, Bolton and Littledale, and Duff, Findlay and Co. *Abram* also differed from the other ships in bringing sugar from the Danish island of St John almost certainly from the plantations which Abram Chalwill Hill had acquired in 1811. In addition, the partnership also brought in smaller consignments of sugar on other vessels from the Virgin Islands.[37]

In early 1813 they expanded their operations still further. In December 1812 they and Edward Burrow registered the 383-ton *Sterling* (frequently *Stirling*), built in Montreal, which was to be captained by Thomas Rogerson whose much smaller *Flora* had been advertised for sale the previous month. In February 1813, they acquired the new 354-ton *Lancaster* to be captained by William Dennison who had previously sailed as a mate on *Neptune*.[38] These sailed to St Croix and returned with even larger cargoes of sugar. In May *William Ashton* docked with 580 hogsheads on board; in June, the smaller *Neptune* with 364 hogsheads and some rum and fustic; *Sterling* arrived in August with a record 935 hogsheads, rum, cotton, coffee, hides and fustic, accompanied by *Lancaster* with 548 hogsheads, rum, cotton and nicaragua wood. The purchase of these ships, however, allowed *Abram,* now joined by *Eliza,* to concentrate on the longer-established trade with Tortola.[39]

4.10. Advertisements for sale of sugar in Burrows and Nottage offices: *Lancaster Gazette*, 29 September 1810.

TO BE SOLD BY AUCTION,
At Burrow and Nottage's office, Market-street, Lancaster, on Thursday the 11th October, 1810, at twelve o'clock;
400 Hogsheads
TORTOLA AND ST. CROIX
SUGARS,
NOW LANDING.
§ For particulars apply to
BURROW and NOTTAGE.
Lancaster, Sept. 18, 1810.

These were to prove golden years for the partnership which now dominated Lancaster's West Indian trade. Deprived of access to many North American provisions and supplies after war broke out between Britain and the United States, the prices of materials which planters imported from British merchants rose, as did the freight and insurance charges they had to pay. In Britain, too, sugar prices were rising. Official average prices for brown or muscovado sugar sold at London and Lancaster fluctuated wildly over the years depending on sugar supplies and the activities of speculators but, apart from a dip in early 1811, prices displayed an upward trend from mid-1809. In the summer of 1811 they hovered around 35 to 39 shillings per cwt., exclusive of duty. A year later they had risen to the mid-forties. By July 1813 they were over 60 shillings and from November they rose again to peak in Lancaster at 97 shillings in March 1814. Although they fell back by the summer, they rose again towards the year and only began a slow decline from late 1815.[40]

For ST. CROIX, TORTOLA, and ST. THOMAS.
The following Vessels, well manned & armed, viz
For ST. CROIX,
The Ship NEPTUNE,
JOHN JOHNSON, Master,
Burthen 500 tons, and will sail from Lancaster about the 20th June.
For TORTOLA,
The Ship ABRAM, Thos. Watson, Master,
Burthen 500 tons, and will sail from this port about the 10th June.
For ST. THOMAS,
The Brig FLORA, Thos. Rogerson, Master,
Burthen 170 tons, and will sail from Lancaster about the 20th June.
For freight or passage apply to Messrs. Burrows and Nottage, Lancaster, or to
JOHN CAWSON, Broker, 14, Brunswick-street.
May 26. (*One property.*)

For ST. CROIX,
The new Ship STIRLING,
Thomas Rogerson, Master,
Burthen 383 tons, and intended to join the next Convoy from Cork.
For ST. THOMAS,
The Ship NEPTUNE, John Johnson, Master,
Burthen 500 tons, and will sail in a few days from Lancaster, to join the next Convoy from Cork.
For TORTOLA,
The Ship ABRAM, Thomas Watson, Master,
Burthen 500 tons, and will sail from Lancaster, in company with the Neptune, to join the next Convoy from Cork.
For freight or passage apply to Messrs. Burrows and Nottage, Lancaster, or
JOHN CAWSON, Broker.
Dec. 1. (*One property.*)

4.11.1 and 4.11.2. Advertisements for Abram and other Burrow and Mason ships sailing from Liverpool and Lancaster, 1812: *Liverpool Mercury* 5 June, 1812 and 11 December 1812.

The *Lancaster Gazette* reported equally dramatic rises in the prices obtained at auctions and private sales in the town. In May and November 1811 St Croix sugar sold at 66–67 shillings per cwt., inclusive of duty. A year later it had risen to 76 shillings and the year after to nearly 90 shillings. In February 1814 St Croix sugar sold for 123s. 6d. per cwt. and a consignment of Jamaican sugar sold by private sale for a staggering 140 shillings, the highest price ever recorded in the town.[41] Although prices fell from 1815, sugar auctioned in Lancaster at Burrows and Nottage's offices in 1818 continued to fetch prices which were significantly higher than those which prevailed a decade earlier.

Until 1814, however, these were still dangerous waters. Although there is no record of *Abram* engaging enemy ships, *William Ashton,* returning on her maiden voyage under Thomas Greenwood, was badly damaged whilst repelling an armed French privateer. She arrived in Lancaster on 3 September in company with *Abram* and sailed with her throughout the subsequent voyage which commenced a month later but there is nothing to indicate that *Abram* had been involved in the affray.[42] Just over two years later Thomas Dawson, captain of *William Ashton,* was issued a letter of marque by the British government for 'apprehending, seizing and taking the Ships, Vessels, and Goods, belonging to the United States of America or any Persons Inhabiting within the said United States of America.' The warrant described her as carrying 14 carriage guns, with shot of 24 and 9 pounds, 18 small arms, 12 cutlasses, 12 barrels of powder and 20 pounds of great shot, and crewed by 25 men and boys including a gunner and surgeon, and carrying enough provisions for six months.[43]

Post-war contraction

War may have increased the dangers but it had also been responsible for the dramatic expansion of Burrows and Nottage's trade. When war ended in 1814–5, so too did their golden years.

The declaration of peace with the United States in 1814 meant that the West Indies could again draw supplies from there. The first Treaty of Paris in May 1814 ended war with France and outlined possible terms of an agreement to be finalised at the Congress of Vienna in September of that year. The most important element of the peace treaty as far as Burrows and Nottage were concerned, however, was the agreement in December 1814 to hand back the Danish Virgin Islands on 1 January 1815. The riches of St Croix were now 'foreign' not British sugar.

The summer of 1814 consequently saw Burrows and Nottage preparing to scale down their operations, a decision no doubt strengthened, if not precipitated, by the death of William Ashton that year. In July *Neptune,* which had visited St Croix regularly over the previous five years, sailed instead for Quebec, returning with a cargo of timber.[44] She never returned to St Croix; her destinations from then on until she was sold in 1822 being returned in official records exclusively as Tortola and St Thomas. Also in July they disposed of *William Ashton* and in October they sold the recently purchased *Lancaster*, which had only succeeded in completing two round voyages, followed a year later in October 1815 by *Sterling*. By 1815, therefore, they had resumed their earlier pattern of trade with Tortola and St Thomas now supplemented by Abram Chalwill Hill's acquisition of further plantations on Tortola and St John. These activities were capable of supporting the three remaining smaller ships *Neptune, Eliza* and *Abram,* which was captained on the last five voyages by Thomas Rogerson, previously of *Flora* and *Sterling*.[45] Commodity prices began to slip after 1815, but this was partially compensated by the lower costs involved in trade. Insurance and freight rates dropped. With the need to man the guns eliminated, *Abram's* crew contracted from 27–29 to around 17–18, falling as low as 14 on occasions. Few apprentices were attracted, or needed, and the number dropped to just three on the final voyage in 1818.

Abram's last voyage

Abram cleared Lancaster for the West Indies for the final time on 13 June 1818. Her owners had probably already decided to dispose of her before she set sail although the precise reason for the sale remains unclear. The sugar trade had clearly been declining for several years, as had the carriage of cargo for other Lancaster merchants, a reflection of the moribund state of trade in the town. In June 1817 she had brought some wine for Thomas Worswick and Co. from Madeira and the following May returned with a few bales of cotton for the same firm, but these were the exceptions.[46] She had returned to her initial pattern of trade, bringing in a mixed cargo for her owners, but the rest of her cargo, rather inconveniently, was destined for Liverpool merchants. The ship was probably also in need of some further repair. Lloyd's registers reported that there had been some repairs in 1814, but until 1817 had still classed her as A1, a first class vessel in first class state of repair. At the time of her inspection in May 1818, however, she had been downgraded to E1, second class. This may have prompted Thomas Mason's decision to sell his share of the ship to Burrows and Nottage that month and this in turn may have propelled them to sell.[47] After discharging her last cargo of sugar and mahogany from Tortola and cotton from St Thomas at Lancaster in October 1818, she made her way to Liverpool where the remainder of her cargo of mahogany, fustic and coffee were consigned to brokers in the town and where she was advertised for sale.[48]

Over the next forty-four years she was to voyage into new, still largely uncharted waters. The future for the men who had owned her was equally uncertain.

Port of Tortola

In Pursuance of an Act made *anno decimo nono* GEORGE II. intituled *An Act for the Encouragement of the Trade of His Majesty's Sugar Colonies in America.*

An Account of the Names, Stations, Ages, and Descriptions of the Men belonging to the *Ship Abram* of *Tortola* Burthen *245* Tons, *British* Built, whereof *Thomas Rogerson* is Master, and bound for *Liverpool*

Nº	Men's Names.	Station.	Age.	Stature.	Complexion.
				9 in. 8 in.	Ground O. Will
1	Thomas Rogerson	Master	39	——	4.3
2	James Wilson	1 Mate	23	——	4.3
3	John Benson	2 Do	23	——	4.3
4	Robert Alton	Boasman	31	——	4.3
5	Joseph Nixon	Carpenter	26	——	4.3
6	Daniel Brown	Seaman	51	——	4.3
7	James Cooper	do	46	——	4.3
8	Wm Wilson	do	48	——	4.3
9	J McCarthy	do	25	——	4.3
10	Wm Phillips	do	26	——	4.3
11	John Brewer	do	29	——	4.3
12	James Harries	do	25	——	4.3
13	John Higham	do	16	——	4.3
14	Edward Davis	Apprentice	18	——	4.3
15	William Bannister	do	16	——	4.3
16	Tho Butler	do	14	——	4.3
17	John Page	Seaman	30	——	4.3
18	Robert Kitchman	do	25	——	4.3
					64.10
			120.0	10 Men	£1.12.4

THESE are to certify, That the above is a true List of Men belonging to the aforesaid Vessel, attested by the Master thereof.

Given under my Hand, this 15 Day of *August* 1818

4.12. Muster Roll for *Abram*'s last voyage, 1818: TNA, BT 98/30 Port of Lancaster Muster Rolls (Reproduced by courtesy of The National Archives, London.)

References

[1] *Lancaster Gazette*, 18 & 25 Jan. 1806.

[2] Watson later captained *Abram* but nothing is definitely known of his subsequent career. He may have been the Thomas Watson, master of the new ship *Jonathan*, sailing out Liverpool in the 1820s for Calcutta, although there is a Thomas Watson of Dexter Street, Liverpool, whose wife Margaret died in 1826: *Liverpool Mercury*, 22 Sept. 1826. A report in the *Liverpool Mercury*, 6 March 1835, noted the loss of Thomas Newton Watson (born 1811 Lancaster), eldest son of Captain Thomas Watson 'late of Lancaster', second mate of the brig *Norah*, along with the captain of the vessel on East Hoyle Bank on 22 Feb 1835.

[3] *Isabella* was a 168 ton Whitehaven vessel owned by her Captain which plied from Whitehaven, Lancaster and Liverpool to a variety of ports. She returned to Lancaster in mid-August with a cargo of sugar for Atkinson and Willocks.

[4] *Lancaster Gazette*, 15 April 1806.

[5] *Anson* was built in 1781 and was involved in several naval engagements before coming to grief off Mount's Bay, Cornwall on 29 Dec. 1807; the *Cygnet*, 18 guns, was built in Nathaniel Parker's yard in Yarmouth and launched on 6 Sept. 1804. She was wrecked in the Courantine River, Berbice, Guiana, on 7 March 1815.

[6] TNA, BT 98/30 Lancaster Muster roll.

[7] *Jackson's Oxford Journal*, 13 Sept. 1806.

[8] *Lancaster Gazette*, 4 Oct. 1806.

[9] Lancs. Archives, DDX 2743 MS 242; MS 3726; *Lancaster Gazette*, 15 Nov. 1806.

[10] TNA, BT 98/30 Muster Rolls. All details of crews are taken from this source, which has a virtually complete run of papers for *Abram.*

[11] Lancs. Archives, DDX 2743 MS 5179, Apprenticeship of James Greenwood son of Thomas of Lancaster to Thomas Burrow and Thomas Mason as a mariner for 5 years.

[12] Lancs. Archives, DDX 2743 MS 5084 William Ashton log, 1810–11.

[13] Lancs. Archives, DDX 2743 MS 242, John Brockbank's day book.

[14] TNA, CO 259/3. St Thomas shipping records. These port records date from 1808 when Britain occupied the islands and contain details of cargoes unloaded from a number of Lancaster vessels including *St Anna, John, James* and two vessels owned by Burrow and Mason, *Flora* and *Neptune.*

[15] *Liverpool Mercury*, 12 Feb. 1813, 1 July 1814, 27 Dec. 1816. He possibly had Lancaster origins since the surname appears in parish registers.

[16] I am grateful to David Johnson for information and references about the use of lime in the West Indies. Milk of lime (i.e. very watery hydrated lime) was added to the raw sugar juice as the first step in the purification process. It was also used for soil improvement: M. Day, 'The karstlands of Antigua, their land use and conservation", *Geographical Journal*, 173, 2007, pp. 170–85. On some islands, lime was present and could be burnt, but elsewhere it had to be imported.

[17] Lancs. Archives, MS 5084, William Ashton's log.

[18] TNA, CO 259/3 St Thomas shipping records.

[19] *Lancaster Gazette*, weekly 'Ship News' reports, particularly, 5 Dec. 1803, 4 Oct. 1806.

[20] Sources of information on merchants drawn from a variety of sources including *London Gazette, Lancaster Gazette, Liverpool Mercury*, trade directories and catalogues of the Guildhall Library Sun Fire offices.

[21] See for example *Liverpool Mercury*, 15 May 1812; 9 July 1813; 26 August 1814; 3 May 1816; 28 Jan. 1820; 30 June 1820.

22   *Lancaster Gazette,* 16 April 1808.

23   Dookhan, *Virgin Islands of the United States,* p. 82; House of Commons Papers, 1812–13, *Account of Quantity of Sugar imported into Great Britain,* 1812.

24   Adapted from House of Commons Papers: 1808 *Select Committee on Distilleries; 1812–13 Account of Quantity of Sugar imported into Great Britain.*

25   TNA, CO 317/1 Tortola shipping returns, 1784–86.

26   R. Craig and R.C. Jarvis, *Liverpool Registry of Merchant Ships, 1786–1789,* Chetham Society 3rd series, vol. 15, 1967.

27   John Chorley to Captain Thomas Walters of *Mercury,* 25 April 1801, *British West Indies Study Circle Newsletter* 80, 1974.

28   Durham County Record Office, D/HH 3/1/5/12, 4 Jan. 1803, Hanby Holmes, solicitors, collection. Thomas Hughes Hill and William Smith were joint executors of Ashton's will in 1814.

29   For some reason this was only published in *London Gazette,* 30 July 1814.

30   *Lancaster Gazette,* 11 April, 24 Sept. 1807; 15 Sept. 1808.

31   Lancs. Archives, FRL/2/1/15/189; FRL/2/1/33/44, Lancaster Society of Friends.

32   *Lancaster Gazette,* 25 July 1807; Lancs. Archives, ARR 11, James Barton Nottage marriage bond, 30 June 1807.

33   *Lancaster Gazette,* 15 Jan. 1814; Howson, *The Making of Lancaster,* pp. 43–44.

34   Lancs. Archives, SS5/1, Lancaster shipping registers.

35   *Lancaster Gazette,* Ship News, *Liverpool Mercury,* Vessels Arrived.

36   *Lancaster Gazette,* Ship News, *Liverpool Mercury,* Vessels Arrived.

37   *Lancaster Gazette,* 16 May, 23 May, 25 July, 29 August, 19 Sept., 10, 31 Oct. 1812. *Liverpool Mercury,* 18 Sept. 1812.

38   Lancs. Archives, SS5/1, Lancaster shipping registers. Also Lancaster City Library collection, MS 8127 *William Ashton* purchase.

39   *Lancaster Gazette,* 29 May, 2 July, 14 August 1813.

40   Figures are taken from the *London Gazette* and *Lancaster Gazette.* John Brockbank noted prices from 1811 in his daybook, Lancs. Archives, DDX 2743 MS 242.

41   *Lancaster Gazette,* various reports.

42   *Lancaster Gazette,* 8 Sept. 1810. Lancs. Archives, DDX 2743 MS 5084 William Ashton's log.

43   TNA, HCA 26/111/ no 27 A full list of letters awarded can be viewed at http://www.1812privateers.org/Great%20Britain/index.html last accessed 13 Sept 2012.

44   *Lancaster Gazette,* 14 Jan. 1815.

45   A Thomas Rogerson had been part-owner and master of the 173-ton brig *Flora* since 1792 and a man of that name continued to captain it after the Burrows had purchased it in March 1810. The same name appears as master and shared owner of other Lancaster vessels: *Rose* (93 tons brigantine, 1786); *Myrtle* (136 tons, brig, 1788); *Laurel* (154 tons, brig, 1789). These are probably father and son since Thomas Rogerson junior is mentioned as a master in 1806 and he is recorded as being in his late thirties in the crew lists.

46   *Lancaster Gazette,* 14 June 1817, 16 May 1818; *Gore's Liverpool Advertiser,* 12 Nov. 1818.

47   Lancs. Archives, SS5/1 Lancaster shipping registers; *Lloyds Register,* 1814–1819.

48   *Lancaster Gazette,* 17 Oct. 1818, *Liverpool Mercury,* 20 Oct. 1818.

CHAPTER 5

'The uncertain nature of West Indian property'

Reaping the rewards

West Indian trade made wealthy men of Thomas Mason, the Burrows and James Barton Nottage, all of whom became prominent businessmen and leading figures in their home town. Thomas Burrow was honoured in February 1821 with the presentation of 'an elegant piece of plate' by tradesmen in Lancaster 'in testimony of their regard for his character and the high sense they entertain of the eminent services he has rendered the town' in the 'honourable character of a British merchant.'[1] Just over a month later, on 9 April, he was dead. Since his eldest son Edward, only 36, had predeceased him, his will made provision for his four daughters but his sole surviving son George inherited all his properties and business interests. Meanwhile, Christopher Burrow, Thomas's brother, had also made his fortune from the West Indies, although he had retained his interest in Jamaica and traded not with Lancaster but with London and Liverpool. By the 1820s he had retired to Buckstone House, a new mansion he had erected near Burton-in-Kendal.

George Burrow continued to live in an imposing house on St Leonardgate adjacent to the sugar house, and was actively involved in local political affairs, social activities and business ventures. As a freeman of the borough, he was elected bailiff of the brethren in October 1823, chamberlain in 1830 and mayor in 1828, 1833 and 1836, the first under the reformed, democratically-elected corporation. He was appointed a Justice of the Peace for Lancashire in 1829 and for the municipal borough in 1836. He was prominently involved in the Society for the Promotion of Christian Knowledge and the Lancaster Auxiliary Bible Society, the local Temperance Society and campaigns to enforce better observance of the Sabbath. He diversified his business activities, promoting the Lancaster Steam Navigation Company and its steamship, *John O'Gaunt*, which plied between Liverpool and Lancaster after 1825. He was one of the directors of the new joint stock bank established in the town in July 1826. From the 1830s he was director and chair of the Lancaster and Preston Railway Company and was involved in promoting the Lancaster and Carlisle and the Caledonian Railways. He chaired a meeting at which a company was established to prospect for coal in the region. With his brother-in-law, Thomas Housman Higgin, he established a worsted manufactory adjacent to the canal on Moor Lane in 1819 and together they took over and extended Mason's cotton business after his death.[2] With William Chorley and Lawrence Nunns he even ventured into silk spinning.[3]

James Barton Nottage also achieved office as port commissioner, bailiff in 1819, alderman in 1821 and mayor the following year. Like George, he also invested in the Lancaster Steam Navigation Company and by the

5.1. Textile mills on Lancaster canal, showing White Cross and Cotton Manufactory on the north side of Moor Lane, owned by Burrow and Higgin. Ordnance Survey, 6 inch, 1845. (Reproduced by courtesy of Ordnance Survey and Old Maps www.old-maps.co.uk)

mid-1830s, although still described as a merchant, his offices in Market Street doubled as an agency for the Imperial Life Insurance Company. By the time of the 1841 census he had moved from his house on the prestigious Queen Square to a rural residence at Claughton in the Lune Valley.

But all was not well. Although Burrow and Nottage had diversified into other activities these did not always thrive, and events on the other side of the Atlantic conspired to leave them inextricably entangled from the 1820s in the problematic and increasingly unprofitable West Indies, not just as merchants, but as plantation and slave owners.

Ashton and Hill

William Ashton, merchant and planter of St Croix, died in Liverpool in 1814. His will, drawn up in May of the previous year, generously bequeathed £10,000 for the poor of Risley in south Lancashire. His financial affairs, however, were disastrous and the money was never paid.[4] It transpired that he and William Smith owed Burrows and Nottage £39,638; Smith and Thomas Hughes Hill were in debt to the tune of £36,095.[5] Whether these debts had been incurred as part of their normal trading relationship or, as seems likely, in the form of loans to assist in the purchase and development of estates on St Croix is not clear. What was clear at the time was that in the changed circumstances which now prevailed Smith and his surviving partner had little hope of paying these debts off. With the return of St Croix to Denmark the island's sugar no longer qualified as 'British' so sugar from there was liable to much higher excise duties, making it uncompetitive precisely at a time when prices were falling. The buoyancy in Tortola's sugar exports in the two years after the peace settlement could well have been accounted for by smuggling between the Danish and British Virgin Islands; certainly the British government suspected that Abram Chalwill Hill and his partners were smuggling Danish sugar into the island.[6] In July 1815 William Smith signed over two estates, Enfield Green (300 acres) and La Vallee (150 acres) in settlement of the debt. Although they succeeded in disposing of La Vallee estate to Abram Chalwill Hill, within a few years events again transpired to return it to their ownership and by the 1840s, whether by intention or default, Burrows and Nottage had acquired three additional estates on the island, Hope, Annaberg and Anguilla.[7]

Events in Tortola were also to take a dramatic turn for the worse. On 25 September 1819 Abraham Belisario, an agent on the island, in a letter to a one-time resident of the island, Henry Gent, originally of Cheshire but then in Philadelphia, described 'the fatal effects of the most awful and destructive visitation which it pleased the Almighty to punish us with on Tuesday and Wednesday last'.[8] The island had been devastated by a hurricane. Seven-eighths of the houses in Road Town had been levelled, not a stick remained of the President's house and there was 'not a Negro

House in the whole Island remaining'. The loss of life was considerable, nearly 100 people perishing. Among the dead were Mrs Hetherington, wife of the President, and two prominent members of the council, 'The Hon'ble Andrew Anderson and the Hon'ble Abraham C. Hill.'

Abram's sale and the death of the man after whom she was named did not end Burrow and Nottage's relationship with either Tortola or the Hill family. Rather, as on St Croix, the partners were dragged deeper into the island's affairs. Hill had already made arrangements for the disposal of his estates and effects after his death. Like Ashton's, however, these were complicated since he also had estates on St Croix and St John which came under the authority of Denmark. His will, dated 10 November 1817, confirmed that he had entered a marriage bond in 1815 with Sally Urlin, his long-time partner and mother of his children, and she was to be provided for with lands and an annuity. He also made provision for his sister Ann and her children and for Elizabeth, who had married William Henry Smith, his partner and captain of his sloop, *Sally*. All his estates in the British Virgin Islands and Danish island of St John he bequeathed to his 'reputed and acknowledged children', Henry Jennings and Ruth Ann then on Tortola, and Mary and George 'now in England' where his eldest son, named after himself, had died in 1812.[9] He named as his executors his children, as they variously reached the age of 21, and three 'esteemed friends': two planters on Tortola and St John, and 'George Burrow of Lancaster in the kingdom of Great Britain merchant', who were also to act as his children's guardians during their minorities. Codicils were appended, drawn up before Richard Hetherington four days after Hill's death, in which the witnesses confirmed under oath that they were present and that the wills were true representations of Hill's wishes.[10] Copies were dispatched to England and George Burrow appeared personally before the prerogative court on 20 November 1820 to swear that he did 'verily and in his conscience believe that such copy is a true copy from the original will' which was still held in Tortola. Burrow requested, and was granted, probate 'for the preservation of the said deceased's personal estate and effects within the province of Canterbury'. Over the next few years George Burrow became embroiled in legal cases in the courts in Tortola in attempts to sort out his ex-trading partner's affairs.[11]

Burrow had a vested interest in collecting debts owed to Hill since it transpired that Hill himself owed Burrow and Nottage over £19,000 at the time of his death, some of it possibly incurred as a result of advances to purchase properties in the islands. The partners agreed to reduce the debt to £17,000 to be paid in half yearly instalments from 1 January 1826 and to facilitate this gave a £12,000 mortgage on various estates. It was also agreed that 'all Sugars made on the said estates of the said Abraham Chalwill Hill ... should be shipped and consigned to the said George Burrow and James Barton Nottage' until such time as the sum has been paid off.

The agreement was signed in the Chancery Court on Tortola on 12 May 1826 whereby the sum owing was to be paid off at 5 per cent over a ten year period to 1 January 1836, payments to be made every six months. In return and until such time as the sum was paid, Burrow and Nottage took possession of the family's extensive estates on the island: the plantations Long Bush (120 acres), Ronan Hodges (100 acres), Todmans (84 acres) and Cappoons Bay (90 acres); a pasture estate called Whim (120 acres); some plots of land in Road Town and Wickham's Quay 'opposite to the Road Town of Tortola' and various lands on the island of Spanish Town.[12]

These were not inconsiderable holdings. In the first slave registers of 1818 Hill had been returned as the owner of 450 plantation slaves on Tortola. Sixteen years later in 1834, his coloured son Henry and two of his sisters still owned 83 and George and Elizabeth (now remarried) 264.[13] Two years later, however, in the wake of the emancipation act of 1833, the British government paid compensation for the freeing of 360 slaves not just to the Hills but to their creditors, Burrow and Nottage. The partners by then also had claims on other estates on the island, making them second only to the banking, trading and insurance house of Reid, Irving and Co. in terms of compensation for the ending of slavery on the island.[14]

5.2. Burrow and Nottage's claim for compensation due as a result of the emancipation of slaves on Cappoons Bay Estate, TNA, T 71/883 Register of claims and counterclaims (Reproduced by courtesy of The National Archives, London.)

'The uncertain nature of West Indian property'

On 9 October 1835, Francis Johnson, lawyer of Aykley Heads, Durham, composed his will. As the son-in-law of the late Richard Hetherington, planter and President of the Council of Tortola, he had inherited shares in two estates on the island – Road Town Estate (c.160 acres) and Hetherington's Spring Gut estate (c.100 acres) – together with all the mills, stills, coppers, and other plantation implements and utensils, horses, mules, cattle etc.. He was also aware that he or his heirs could be entitled to compensation paid or payable by the government on the emancipation of slaves but instead of giving one of his daughters a share of the income from these estates as he had initially planned, he noted ruefully that 'the advantage of having such estates was unknown' due to the 'uncertain nature of West Indian property' and opted instead to provide her with a fixed annual sum.[15] George Burrow and James Barton Nottage would have appreciated his concerns as they sought to extract income from their West Indian estates and those of the planters they dealt with. The Hills still owed them money in the early 1840s.

In the decade and a half after Abram's death, they gradually disposed of their shipping interests. Their ship, *Eliza,* under Captain Miller, plied between Liverpool, Tortola and St Thomas, carrying a mixed cargo of sugar, cotton, rum and other Latin American products before she was sold in November 1821.[16] The following year George Burrow disposed of his late father's shares in *Neptune* to James Dickson and John Curry of Liverpool to finance the purchase in October 1822 of the new, but smaller, 227-ton *Thomas Burrow*, with the captain, Thomas Dawson, taking one eighth of the shares.[17] This traded primarily with Tortola and returned to her home port of Lancaster although she occasionally ventured into new regions, returning from Trinidad in February 1825 with cargoes for Liverpool merchants.[18] *Lavinia*, built at Napan in New Brunswick in 1826, captained and initially jointly owned by George Burrow's brother-in-law, James Higgin, also traded from Lancaster and Liverpool to Tortola and St Croix. Higgin, however, transferred his share to James Nibbs of Tortola the year after and died on St Croix from yellow fever in April 1831 and the ship was sold the following year.[19] Nottage died in 1845 but George Burrow continued to sell sugar in Lancaster into the 1840s (Figure 5.3). In 1845 he was described as the last of the old West Indian merchants still using the port. As late as November 1847, he was still auctioning Tortola sugar from his Lancaster offices in Market Street.[20]

> ## To be Sold by Auction,
>
> On Friday, the 12th day of November, 1847, at One o'clock, at the office of George Burrow, in Market-street, Lancaster,—
>
> **140** HOGSHEADS, 28 TIERCES, 500 BARRELS, Good and Fine Tortola, St. John's, and St. Croix SUGAR, recently landed.
>
> For particulars apply to GEORGE BURROW.
> Lancaster, 4th November, 1847.

5.3. Sale of sugar from Tortola, St John and St Croix in Lancaster: *Preston Chronicle,* 6 Nov. 1847.

But sugar was an increasingly unprofitable trade.[21] Average sugar prices, which had peaked at over 90s. per cwt. in early 1814 and were still over 50s. per cwt. in early 1818, had fallen back to just 35s. at the end of 1820. By the end of the decade they were barely above 23s. Burrow and Nottage's Danish connections offered no respite. John Dunlop, their agent in Copenhagen, reported in July 1824 that sugar prices there were 'very low', and he refused to take a bill of exchange which their agent, Luke Greenwood, had sent him from St Croix because 'I have made so many debts in St Croix for these few years past from accepting liberally which I find extremely difficult to recover'. He would 'accept only such as are moderately drawn.'[22]

Tortola was in serious decline. With the Danish reinstatement of St Thomas as a free port and the disappearance of the wartime convoys from Road Town's harbour, its days as an entrepot of free trade (which had never fully lived up to the high expectations), vanished.[23] In 1819, with Road Town destroyed by the hurricane, the regular packet boat service was terminated. Contemporary accounts of the islands portray a colony in freefall with sugar works in ruins and plantations devastated. Sugar exports never again came close to the levels achieved during the wars. A description of the island in 1827 claimed that much of it had reverted to scrub or was used as grazing for the black population's animals, that many estates had been abandoned and that 'Road Town bespeaks every thing allied to depopulation and poverty ... the ravages of the hurricane are still conspicuous in every direction' and there were only 'two or three ships which visit[ed] the harbour annually to carry away the scanty produce of the island's impoverished soil'.[24] By the mid-1830s when the government paid compensation to slave owners under the terms of the emancipation act of 1833, the amount paid per slave on Tortola was the lowest in the Caribbean, reflecting the lack of demand for labour in the island.

Not surprisingly, Burrow and Nottage's West Indian affairs became increasingly precarious. Correspondence from Crabb and Isaacs on Tortola, frequently refer to having to draw money on Burrow's account to cover their costs and offset shortfalls, potential lessees' refusal to accept valuations, the low price of sugar, the difficulty of obtaining supplies, the lack of adequate containers for rum, and a plague of rats infesting the island (Figure 5.4).[25] As the price of the sugar continued to fall Burrow and Nottage mortgaged *Thomas Burrow* with some Liverpool brokers in 1826, transferring this liability in 1831 to John, Jacob and Edward Wakefield, bankers of Kendal. At the same time they also took out a further loan using *Lavinia* as security. In 1832 *Lavinia* was sold to repay the loan and in June 1832 she sailed for Hobart and Sydney under new owners. On the evening of 29 August 1833, within sight of her home port, *Thomas Burrow* foundered off Sunderland Point. Although the crew were rescued, Dawson went down with his ship as he tried to save some papers from his cabin.[26]

When Nottage died in 1845 his personal estate was valued at less than £300. George Burrow hit even harder times as several of his investments faltered. In 1841 he withdrew from the cotton business with Thomas Housman Higgin owing money to the Kendal bankers Wakefield and Crewdson, who claimed the mortgages he had on the West Indian estates.

5.4. Letter from Crabb and Isaacs, attorneys on Tortola for Burrow and Nottage, outlining problems caused by rat infestation, 11 July 1831: Lancs. Archives, DDX 70/acc 881/box 29. (Reproduced with permission from Lancashire Archives.)

In 1846, despite being freed of these liabilities, Higgin's business still went into liquidation.[27] Burrow was also clearly unable to pay off the debts. His other investments failed to thrive. Although he continued to import sugar from Tortola, he did not do so on his own ships; *Governor*, a 148-ton ship which brought in sugar from the island in 1845 was owned by a Liverpool firm.[28] The shareholders of the struggling Lancaster and Preston forced the resignation of all bar one of the directors in 1846 when they proposed a merger with the Lancaster and Carlisle Railway.

The late 1840s witnessed the irretrievable collapse of the sugar economy and sealed Burrow's fate. Prices dropped to barely 20 shillings at the end of the decade in the wake of the opening up of the British market to foreign sugar. In 1847, the finance house Irving and Reid, which owned a third of Tortola's remaining plantations at the time and had leased others from Burrow and Nottage, were declared bankrupt, although the immediate cause of their problems would appear to have been unwise speculation in Mauritius and other ventures and not just their involvement in the West Indies. E.H. Drummond Hay, the governor of the British Virgin Islands, reported to the government in 1848 that 'There are now no properties in the Virgin Islands whose holders are not embarrassed for want of capital or credit sufficient to enable them to carry on the simplest method of cultivation'. A meagre 610 hogsheads, or just over 8,000 cwts. of sugar had been exported in 1847. Although this represented an improvement on previous years, it was a fraction of the 21,000 cwts. exported half a century earlier and barely enough to fill the hold of one of the larger ships Burrow and Nottage had operated at that time.[29] On 6 June the same year, A. Macgregor, when asked about the state of Tortola by the Select Committee on Sugar and Coffee Planting in East and West Indies and Mauritius, replied bluntly that the island was 'abandoned'.[30] Ten years later it was unique in being the only British possession unable to supply the home market with any produce whatsoever. What remained of Cappoon Bay, one of the Hills' estates which had been worth thousands half a century earlier, was sold for as little as £30 in 1864 under the Encumbered Estates Act of that year.[31]

Burrow and Nottage were still recorded as owners of Annaberg, Anguilla, Hope and La Vallee estates on St Croix as late as 1846 and the census of that year shows that 37-year-old Thomas Nottage, James' eldest son, had been sent to the island to manage their affairs.[32] But to no avail. On 16 December 1848 George Burrow transferred all his assets to two trustees. The following October the *London Gazette* reported that he was detained in the debtors' prison in Lancaster Castle. He was discharged in November 1849.[33] The census for St Croix in 1851 recorded the new owner of the partners' three estates as 'J. Wakefield', the Kendal banker. By this time George's 'capital mansion' on St Leonardgate, along with twenty other properties he owned, had all been auctioned and he had moved into a more modest (although still impressive) rented residence on Fenton Street.[34] The census for 1851 describes his status as 'magistrate for this borough and formerly West Indian merchant'. When his sister Jane died in 1850 her will displayed clear signs of concern over George's finances; when another sister, the widowed Elizabeth Inman, died in 1858 she left him only a lifetime interest in her properties which were entailed to her nephew (Edward Burrow's son), the Reverend Thomas Burrow, then curate of Pinner.

5.5. George Burrow's house on St Leonardgate, Lancaster advertised for sale after his bankruptcy: *Lancaster Gazette,* 16 March 1850.

VALUABLE FREEHOLD PROPERTY
In Lancaster, for Sale.

TO BE SOLD BY AUCTION,
BY MR. HODGSON,
AT THE KING'S ARMS HOTEL,
IN LANCASTER,
On *MONDAY, the 8th day of APRIL,* 1850,
At Three o'clock in the Afternoon,
(Either altogether or in various Lots, and the Land divided for the Erection of Dwelling-houses),

THE CAPITAL MANSION,

Many years the Residence of George Burrow, Esquire,

SITUATE in St. Leonard Gate, in Lancaster, with the Coach-house, Stable, Offices, Ornamental Summer-house, and other Buildings belonging thereto, together with the Garden and Pleasure Grounds, extending from St. Leonard-gate to Cable-street. The site of the Buildings and the Garden contain 8346 square yards, or thereabouts.

In the autumn of 1861 George Burrow and his nephew Thomas both passed away. Against all the odds, *Abram,* the ship which Thomas Mason and George's father had bought nearly 56 years earlier, was still on the high seas, despite spending the last 43 years in some of the most treacherous waters on the planet.

References

[1]   *Liverpool Mercury,* 9 March 1821; *Lancaster Gazette,* 10 March 1821.

[2]   Biographical details are taken from *Lancaster Gazette* and *Lancaster Guardian* (from 1837).

[3]   *London Gazette,* 16 Sept. 1823.

[4]   House of Commons papers, 1829, *Commission of Enquiry into the Charities of England and Wales,* pp. 218–20.

[5]   For Ashton's and Smith's transfer and debts see Lancs. Archives, DDX 2743 MS 4689, Release of two plantations on St Croix, 22 Nov. 1815.

[6]   TNA, CUST 34/814, Board of Customs: Papers Relating to Plantations actions brought by Customs Controller against A.C. Hill owner of the sloop *Sally* and the shallop *Abraham* and their captains, 1 Feb. 1819.

[7]   Lancs. Archives, DDX 70 Messrs. Swainson and Satterthwaite of Lancaster, solicitors, 'Tortola package'; Census returns for St Croix, 1841, 1846. http://stx.visharoots.org/db.html last accessed 12 June 2012.

[8]   A.M. Belisario, letter to Henry Gent, 25 September 1819, Gent Family Papers, http://fjgent.zxq.net/henrygent/index.htm last accessed 12 June 2012.

[9]   *Liverpool Mercury,* 3 Jan. 1812.

[10] TNA, PROB 11/1636. Unfortunately Hill's will was not witnessed. A codicil was necessary after his death in which two of the witnesses named swore to the validity of his signature. Hill also had a grant from the Danish government dated 20 September 1814.

[11] House of Commons papers, 1826–27, *Third report of the Commissioner of Inquiry into the Administration of Civil and Criminal Justice in the West Indies,* pp. 240–41, 252–57. Hill's wishes with regard to his properties in the Danish and British Virgin Islands were implemented. The younger family members continued to reside on Tortola until the 1840s when they would appear to have moved to Hill's extensive estates on the Danish island of St John. Abram's namesake and grandson, Abraham Chalwill Hill was born on Tortola in 1825 to George Hill but on his father's death he joined the rest of the family on St John and became one of the most successful planters there by the 1850s. David W. Knight, *Cinnamon Bay Plantation, 1718–1917.*

[12] Lancs. Archives, DDX 70, 'Tortola package'.

[13] TNA, T 71/370 (1818); T 71/375 (1834) Office of Registry of Colonial Slaves and Slave Compensation Commission, Virgin Islands.

[14] House of Commons Papers, 1837–38, *Return of Sums awarded by Commissioners of Slave Compensation,* pp. 109–10 (Virgin Islands); TNA, T 71/883 Register of Claims; T 71/1040 and T 71/1238–40, Claims and Counterclaims certificates. Burrow and Nottage had also acquired interests in other mortgaged estates; Lancs. Archives, DDX 70, 'Tortola' package' correspondence regarding Brewer's Bay East Plantation on Tortola. See also University College, London, Legacies of Slave Ownership, online database, http://www.ucl.ac.uk/lbs/ last accessed 3 March 2013.

15 TNA, PROB 11/1909 Francis Johnson will, proved 20 April 1839.

16 *Liverpool Mercury,* 9 June 1820; 7 Sept. 1821.

17 Lancs. Archives, SS5/1, Lancaster shipping registers.

18 *Liverpool Mercury,* 11 Feb. 1825; TNA, BT 98/31 Muster rolls.

19 Lancs. Archives, SS5/1 *Lancaster Gazette* for sailings.

20 *Preston Chronicle*, 6 Nov. 1847.

21 J.T. Danson, 'Some particulars of the commercial progress of the colonial dependencies of the United Kingdom during the twenty years 1827–46', *Journal of the Statistical Society of London*, 12.4, Nov. 1849, pp. 349–439.

22 Lancs. Archives, DDX 70, 'Tortola' package', Dunlop to Burrow and Nottage, 11 July 1824.

23 Dookhan, *British Virgin Islands*, pp. 63–65.

24 *Series of Views in the West Indies,* London, Underwood, 1827. British Library, General Ref. 1299.1. Image available on British Library Online Gallery, http://www.bl.uk/onlinegallery/index.html last accessed 3 March 2013.

25 Lancs. Archives, DDX 70, 'Tortola' package', Crabb and Isaacs to Burrow and Nottage, letters, 1828–40.

26 Lancs. Archives, SS5/1; *Times*, 2 Sept. 1833; *Liverpool Mercury,* 15 June 1832. Captain Grey donated two opossum to Liverpool Zoological Gardens on his return, *Liverpool Mercury,* 27 Sept. 1833.

27 *London Gazette,* 4 Aug. 1846.

28 *Lloyds Register,* House of Commons papers, 1847–48, *Third report from the Select Committee on Sugar and Coffee Planting*, p. 280.

29 House of Commons papers, 1847–48, *The reports made for the year 1847 to the Secretary of State having the Department of the Colonies: report on the Virgin Islands by E. Drummond Hay*, pp. 136–38; 1847–48, *An Account of the Imports into the United Kingdom for the years 1831 to 1847.*

30 House of Commons Papers, 1847–48, *Third Report from the Select Committee on the Slave Trade*, p. 648.

31 House of Commons papers, 1866, *Reports showing the present state of Her Majesty's colonial possessions for the year 1864, Part I: West Indies and Mauritius*, p. 136.

32 Census returns for St Croix, 1841, 1846, http://stx.visharoots.org/db.html last accessed 12 June 2012.

33 *London Gazette*, 22 Dec. 1848, 16, 26 Oct. 1849; *Liverpool Mercury*, 13 Nov 1849.

34 *Lancaster Gazette*, 16 March 1850; Census returns, 1851.

Part II
Hull and Kirkcaldy and the Northern Whale Fishery, 1819–62

Rob David

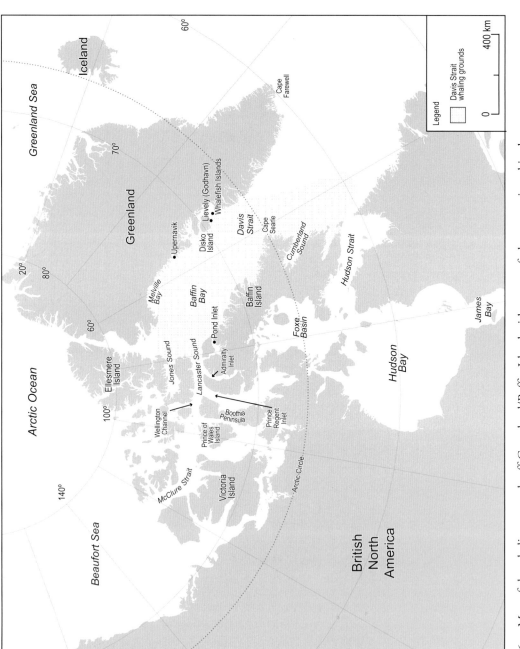

6.1. Map of the whaling grounds off Greenland/Baffin Island with names of places mentioned in the text.

CHAPTER 6

The whaling industry

In November 1818 *Abram* was 12 years old when she was purchased by John Tidd and William Mercer, co-partners of the firm Tidd, Mercer and Co., oil and seed merchants of Gainsborough in Lincolnshire. She was first registered in Hull on 11 January 1819 when she was listed as 'Built: Lancaster' (Figure 6.2). For 44 years she was to sail as a whaling ship, initially from Hull and after 1855 from Kirkcaldy in Fife, to the Northern Whale Fishery. In 1862 she was wrecked in the Arctic.

Hull and the Northern Whale Fishery

The peace which followed the defeat of Napoleon in 1814 enabled the British whaling fleet to expand rapidly. Between 1814 and 1817 an average of 143 ships were sent each year from British ports to the Northern Whale Fishery, and catches were at their highest in the entire history of the industry. At Hull the fleet returned annually with, on average, 5,223 tuns of oil and 5,320 cwts. of bone. In 1818 25 companies in Hull sent 64 ships (out of a national total of 154) to the Northern Whale Fishery. The average value of a ship's catch was £4,323, so there was clearly considerable profit to be made.

Tidd, Mercer and Co., like the other Humberside companies, recognised the financial opportunities offered by this whaling boom. The company would have been well aware of the government bounty, initiated in 1732, which had been designed to encourage the conversion of merchant ships into whalers. Since 1794 it had been set at the rate of 20 shillings per ton of shipping on vessels over 200 tons, so *Abram* would benefit. As oil merchants they would have seen the advantage of acquiring a fleet of their own which would help to secure their supplies of whale oil. By 1818 they were already part-owners of the Hull whaler *Cherub* (1817–19), and two years later they acquired another whaler, *Mercury*.[1] They would also have heard that in the autumn of 1817 William Scoresby, the leading whaling master of the time, had brought news of open seas along the east Greenland coast, and that two Scottish whaling captains had reported a similar reduction in ice cover to the west of Greenland. This latter discovery was particularly significant because it would enable ships to access new hunting areas in the ice-free 'North Water' in Baffin Bay and along the Baffin Island coast.

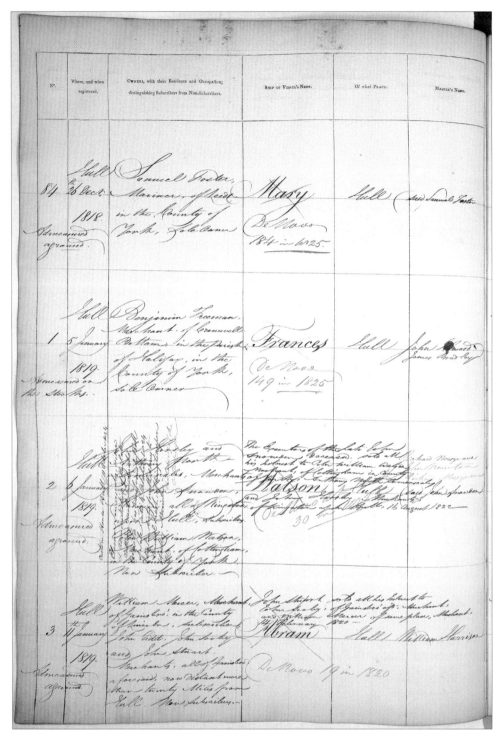

6.2. Registration of *Abram* at the port of Hull on 11 January 1819: Hull History Centre.
C DPC/1/2/3 (1819). (Reproduced by courtesy of Hull History Centre.)

When and where built, or (if a Prize) made free; with Circumstances of Capture, and Date of Condemnation.	Name and Employment of the Surveying Officers.	Whether British, Foreign, or British Plantation Built.	Number of Decks.	Number of Masts.	Ship's extreme Length a well.	Ship's extreme Breadth, at the broadest Part, distinguishing whether taken above or below the Main Wales.	Height between Decks.	Depth of Hold.	Tons Burthen.	Kind of Vessel.	Whether any or no Gallery.	Kind of Head.
At Leeds aforesaid, and Launched 27 January 1812 as ff Certificate of Registry granted here 16 April 1812 No 36. now delivered up and cancelled, property changed.	Michael Welburn Coster Selby	British	1	1	56.9	16 2½	—	7.0	50 46/94	Round sterned Sloop flush Deck	None	None
At Mirfield, in the County of York, and Launched 7 December 1818 as ff Certificate of Registry granted to William Patrick the Builder dated same day	Michael Welburn Coster Selby	British	1	1	56.5	14 1¾	—	6 2½	49 22/94 Sloop flush Deck	—	None	None
On the River Hull, the 4th January 1819, as ff Certificate from Thomas Stemson the Builder dated this day.	Nicholas Osbourne	British	1	3	97.6	24 10½	—	—	263 13/94	Square sterned Ship flush Deck	None	None
At Lancaster, in the County of —, in 1806 as ff Certificate of Registry granted there 14 January 1806 No 1. now delivered up and cancelled, property changed to this Port	William Lace Liverpool at Liverpool	British	1½	3	100.11	26·9	—	5·1	306 77/— Ship	None	Man's figure

This was important because more than a century of commercial whaling by Dutch, British, Danish and German whalers had substantially reduced the population of bowhead or Greenland right whales (*Balaena mysticetus*) in the North Atlantic, so there was a need for new unexploited whaling areas.[2] Gone were the days when Captain Sadler of *Molly* of Hull had been able to return from the Greenland Sea with a full ship on 11 June 1799, a mere 87 days after sailing.[3] The company was also able to take advantage of the whaling infrastructure at Hull. The 'Greenland yards' on the River Hull were able to equip and repair the whaling vessels, and the port had its own whale oil processing plant. Scoresby had remarked that the years after 1814 were 'uncommonly prosperous',[4] and Tidd, Mercer and Co. would be well aware that their investment had the potential to be very profitable.

Unfortunately for the whaling fleet the boom years proved to be short-lived. Whaling, like the sugar trade in which *Abram* had previously participated, was prone to violent fluctuations in fortune. A dearth of whales in the traditional fishing grounds, and the difficulties associated with whaling in the more distant waters of northern Baffin Bay, resulted in reduced catches, and the uncertainty of supply meant that during the mid-1820s the customers for whale oil began to seek alternative products. The industry was dealt yet another blow in 1824 when the government, influenced by Adam Smith's views on the importance of free trade,[5] refused to renew the whaling bounty. Not surprisingly these developments reduced the size of the fleet. However, an expanding market for whale bone was some compensation for the reduction in demand for oil, and for those vessels such as *Abram,* which continued to sail to the fishing grounds, there were still profits to be made. Hull whalers did not follow the lead of those from Peterhead, who turned to sealing in the Greenland Sea as an alternative source of oil. Between 1824 and the early 1850s Peterhead alone took nearly 750,000 seals as well as nearly 1,600 whales.[6] In time sealing was to become as unsustainable as whaling. As Hull's prosperity was based on trading in a variety of commodities the decline in the number of whaling ships, although significant, was not catastrophic for the fortunes of the town.

By the 1830s whaling in the Greenland Sea had all but ended (see Table 6.1) and the concentration was increasingly on the more northern waters of Davis Strait and Baffin Bay. Although ship owners were reluctant to admit as much, it was already becoming clear by the end of the 1820s that voyages to these distant whaling grounds were reaching the limit of their crews' physical endurance. The greater distance meant that ships were often at sea from March until October or even November. Not only did it now take much longer to reach the whaling areas and to return from them in the autumn, thereby squeezing the whaling season into the short summer of the High Arctic, but the ships were also forced to 'rocknose' through uncharted waters and cope with more unpredictable and dangerous ice and icebergs. Hull, like all the whaling ports, was badly affected by several years of harsh weather conditions during the 1830s which resulted in unforeseen over-wintering and many wrecked ships. The dangers of High Arctic navigation were highlighted during the epic voyage of John Ross and his nephew James Clark Ross when they were trapped in the ice of the Gulf of Boothia for four winters (1829–33), while searching for the North West Passage. They were rescued by a whale ship, *Isabella*, an event noted by the Admiralty, and the potential for the whaling fleet to support the explorers was again recognised in the late 1840s during the search for Sir John Franklin when *Abram*, amongst others, became involved.

Table 6.1: The Northern Whale Fishery, 1815–34.[7]
Numbers of whalers (five-yearly averages)

	Greenland Sea – all British ships	Greenland Sea – Hull ships	Davis Strait/Baffin Bay – all British ships	Davis Strait/Baffin Bay – Hull ships
1815–19	97	31	54	27
1820–24	66	25	67	22
1825–29	11	3	84	29
1830–34	7	2 (1830–33)	75	28 (1830–33)

Although the 1830s were a difficult period for the whaling fleet, there was a hint of recovery by the end of the decade. One of the most experienced of Peterhead's whaling masters, William Penny, raised the possibility that there might be new whaling opportunities further south in Baffin Bay around Cumberland Sound on Baffin Island. Although the idea for a whaling station on the east coast of Baffin Island was stillborn, the fleet began to exploit this new area over the next few years.[8]

At Hull whaling was revived on a smaller scale in the 1840s, but by the middle of the decade Peterhead had displaced Hull as Britain's leading whaling port.[9] *Abram* remained part of the Hull fleet although she did not sail to the fishery in every year.[10] In the early 1850s whaling from Hull declined still further and trading difficulties during the Crimean War had a significant short-term impact on the town's fortunes, so the sale of *Abram* to Kirkcaldy in 1855 was not surprising given the industry's move northwards to the ports of the Scottish east coast.

Kirkcaldy and the Northern Whale Fishery

When Thomas Barkworth of Hull sold *Abram* to George Turnbull of Kirkcaldy in January 1855, Kirkcaldy was 'the most thriving town on the north coast of the Firth of Forth'[11] (Figure 6.3), but as at Hull, the town's whaling industry was much diminished from its heyday during the 1820s.[12]

Kirkcaldy had expanded during the eighteenth century with the development of a number of industries including linen manufacture, cotton spinning, coal mining, salt panning and shipbuilding, to which was added brewing, distilling, iron founding and whaling at the beginning of the nineteenth century. During the 1830s the port flourished with flax, timber and whale oil the largest imports, and linen yarn and coal the main exports.[13] At this time the town's whaling fleet was small (Table 6.2). The poor weather conditions in the Arctic during the 1830s created difficulties for some of the vessels in the Kirkcaldy fleet: *Egginton* was one of 19 British ships lost in Davis Strait in 1830, and in 1835 *Viewforth* was one of the whaling ships trapped in the ice in Davis Strait over the winter. When she was released from the ice at the end of January 1836 her crew was in such grave condition that only seven, of the complement of fifty, were fit to sail the ship back to Stromness on Orkney's mainland. Expansion was also hampered by a lack of infrastructure for processing whale products, and cargoes were shipped elsewhere. In 1834, for example, John Black shipped 40 tons of 'whale oil' on *Albion* to Rotterdam on 22 April 1834, and other shipments were sent to London and Glasgow. The whalebone may have been sold locally to Alexander Balfour, 'Wood merchant, bone manure crusher, and flax spinner' of Kirkcaldy, but in April 1834 David Dougall sent whalebone 'ex *Chieftain*' to London.[14]

6.3. Kirkcaldy from the Top of the Path (1838). Artist unknown. (Reproduced by courtesy of Fife Council Museums: Kirkcaldy Museum and Art Gallery and Antonia Reeve.)

Table 6.2: Kirkcaldy whaling fleet in 1833.[15]

Date of return from the Arctic	Name of ship	Tonnage	Owner	Blubber (tons)	Whalebone (tons)
28 Sept. 1833	*Caledonia*	363	David Dougall	270	15
1 Oct. 1833	*Chieftain*	333	David Dougall	285	14
28 Oct. 1833	*Triad*	287	John Black	139	7
12 Nov. 1833	*Earl Percy*	319	Michael Beveridge	75	3.5

From 1847 the defining industry of Kirkcaldy, the manufacture of linoleum, developed with the opening of Michael Nairn's factory for 'floor cloth' at Pathhead. This development brought a new prosperity which was reflected in the improved streets and the quality of the town's public buildings. The industry's need for whale oil also provided a rationale for a renewed investment in whaling, and by the middle of the century Kirkcaldy had its own whale oil manufactory.

6.4. Etching of Kirkcaldy Harbour by Joseph Swann. From John Leighton, *History of the County of Fife*, vol. 2, 1844. (Reproduced by courtesy of Fife Council Museums: Kirkcaldy Museum and Art Gallery.)

By the 1850s Dundee was rapidly emerging as Scotland's premier whaling port. In 1858 a steam engine was installed in the Dundee whaler *Tay*, creating what was known as an auxiliary-powered ship. It became obvious that the future lay with such wooden auxiliary-powered steam ships, as by 1861 13 per cent of whalers and sealers were steamships, a figure which was to grow to 71 per cent by 1871.[16] In 1860 William Barron returned to his old sailing vessel *Truelove*, after two seasons in a steamer, and noted that 'few men having experienced the great difference between steam and sail, will go hereafter in a sailing ship if they can possibly get into a steamer......It is so disheartening to men towing and tracking at a snail pace, and a fine powerful steamer pass them at the rate of eight or nine knots'.[17] The following year, sailing once again in a Dundee-built wooden hulled steamship *Polynia*, he commented 'that men would cheerfully tow in company with other ships until a steamer appeared in sight, then lost energy, and the ship would not have steerage way, after seeing the easy life those on board a steamer have compared to their own laborious work'.[18] While wooden-hulled ships with auxiliary engines clearly had advantages, Hull and Peterhead's reliance on iron-hulled steamers turned out to be a mistake as iron hulls were much less flexible than wooden ones when ships became stuck in pack ice. Peterhead's iron-plated flagship *Empress of India*, in an incident prescient of the *Titanic* disaster half a century later, only survived four hours after being struck by the first piece of ice which she encountered.[19]

Not only was work harder and conditions more taxing on the sailing vessels, it was also becoming clear that steamers were more successful at catching whales. In 1861, the United Kingdom fleet caught 193 whales, the Dundee fleet being the most successful by far with 121. Although the Dundee fleet consisted of only eight ships (as against Peterhead's twenty-one), all six wooden-hulled UK steamships involved with whaling were registered at that port.[20]

The future for the old wooden sailing vessels such as those at Kirkcaldy was bleak. An historian of whaling has written that 'the next half-century of Scottish whaling was to be dominated by wooden-hulled auxiliary vessels from Dundee'.[21] Had Kirkcaldy's ancient whalers not sunk in 1862, they might well have ended their lives as hulks, slowly rotting in a creek on the Firth of Forth.

Although there were still developing markets for whale oil in the jute and oilcloth industries of Dundee and Kirkcaldy, the Scottish whale industry was becoming centred on Dundee, Peterhead and Aberdeen.[22] In 1855 when *Abram* joined *Chieftain* and *Lord Gambier*, the vessels that formed the Kirkcaldy whaling fleet, the town's whaling industry was already in decline (Table 6.3).

Table 6.3: Comparative performance of Scottish whaling ports and Hull, 1848–57, (average annual catches).[23]

	Seals	Whales	Tuns of oil	Cwts of bone
Peterhead	72,631	24	1,216	321
Fraserburgh	7,970	1	110	4
Aberdeen	1,074	20	192	223
Dundee	169	27	271	373
Kirkcaldy	901	16	151	188
Bo'ness	–	3	47	57
Hull	13,182	20	371	280

Constructing a whaling ship

Few whale ships were purpose built, so it was usual for merchantmen, such as *Abram*, to undergo a significant change of function and be rebuilt and fitted out as whalers. During the winter of 1818 *Abram* was probably in dry dock in Hull, or perhaps Gainsborough, undergoing her refit. A ship built at Lancaster for the West Indian trade would not survive an encounter with the Arctic pack ice without considerable modification. The process of conversion was a task familiar to the shipwrights at the whaling ports. *Abram* was a three-masted ship. She was 101 feet long and nearly 27 feet in breadth, and at 319 tons was, according to William Scoresby, ideal for a whaler.[24] The most important work involved strengthening her hull with a second layer of oak planks, 50 millimetres thick, with a third layer at the bow. In addition the bow and stern would have been fortified with thick oak beams and sheathed on the outside with iron plates. This would not have made *Abram* a beautiful ship to look at, but it would have meant that she was fit for purpose – 'broad of beam to carry a sixty ton animal alongside, thick-skinned to absorb collision with the rock-hard ice, rigged for ease of handling in the unpredictable northern waters when all but a handful of men were away in pursuit of a whale'.[25] She would also have to be redesigned internally to provide space for a ship's company of about 50, more than double the ship's complement when she had participated in the West Indian trade, provisions for a voyage of up to eight months, and the storage of the blubber casks and the whalebone. In addition space had to be found on her decks for six open boats used for the actual whale hunt.

The whaling calendar

The whaling season began in the spring. Departure was in February or March if the ship was destined for Davis Strait, in March or April if the destination was the Greenland Sea. The ship's company signed on either in the home port or in Lerwick in the Shetland Islands, or occasionally Stromness in Orkney. When the ships sailed into Lerwick or Stromness, they embarked islanders who had been hired by the company agents. Generally speaking about thirty signed on in the home port and the rest in the northern isles. Thirty was more than enough crew to sail the ship to Lerwick. Hiring Shetlanders in particular was beneficial, both because it kept the cost of wages down as they were only paid for the time they were on the ship, and also because they were experienced seamen and efficient oarsmen. Many had been haaf fishermen. These men were members of small teams of deep-sea fishermen who rowed their sixareens some forty or more miles into the Atlantic to catch cod and ling. This fishing took place from fishing stations such as Fethaland and Stenness, where the primitive conditions made the potential profit to be made from whaling, despite the privations of life on board the whalers, an attractive proposition for the summer months.[26] Shetlanders called the time spent at Lerwick the 'Greenland time'. In 1830, for example, it lasted from 5 February when the first ship arrived and ended on 7 April with the departure of the last.[27] There were a number of agents operating in the town, but Hay and Co. was the busiest from the mid-1840s. The days spent at Lerwick also provided an opportunity for the crew to equip themselves with specialist clothing, referred to as 'hosiery', and for the masters to acquire further equipment.

The ships then proceeded to the whaling grounds and remained at sea 'fishing' until the late summer or early autumn. Those in the Greenland Sea usually returned in July or August, those in Davis Strait and Baffin Bay between September and November. Once caught, a whale was flensed and the blubber cut into small pieces and stowed in barrels. The whalebone, or baleen, was also kept, and those parts of the animal that had no commercial value were set adrift, or beached. The onset of winter storms and the expansion of the sea ice usually meant that the ships left by October at the latest. Ships that became caught in the ice and were forced to over-winter, as happened to *Abram* in 1835, had left their departure too late.

The ships returned via Lerwick to allow the Shetlanders to disembark and fresh food to be taken on board, and then proceeded to their home port. At Hull the ships were unloaded in the Humber, and the blubber and whalebone loaded onto lighters and taken to the Greenland Yards.[28] The empty whaling vessel followed and the crew, except for the master who was usually retained, was discharged. Over the winter the ships were cleaned by the apprentices, and repaired, and in January and February restocked for the next season. If a ship returned early it was sometimes possible to arrange a further voyage in the autumn. Tony Barrow has suggested that added work as colliers plying between the Tyne and London was essential during the autumn if the owners of whalers at the north eastern ports were to make a profit.[29] For *Abram* there is only evidence that she embarked on a further voyage twice. On one occasion a second voyage was made to Liverpool, and on another to St Petersburg. When such voyages took place the much reduced ship's company consisted of some of the whalers alongside a new crew.

During the winter the whale blubber was rendered into oil, and the whalebone sold for a variety of purposes (Figure 6.5). 'The blubber was emptied into vats which were arranged in succession and as boiling began in the highest one, the oil rose to the top and was drawn off into the one below and so on, until eventually the oil in the lowest vat became quite clear.'[30] The return of the vessels and the process of manufacturing whale oil were the only occasions the general public came face to face with the industry.[31] The filth and the stink were so all pervading that no one wanted to live in the neighbourhood of the boiling houses in which the blubber was rendered. An 1830 tract written to prevent the introduction of a boiling house in the genteel seaside resort of Burntisland, a few miles distant from Kirkcaldy, although probably exaggerated, provides a vivid impression of the filth and noise associated with the industry.

> Besides the blubber in the casks, there is always an immense accumulation of filth in the hold, consisting of large masses of the carcass and tails of the whale, stuffed in between the casks; and often a full ship has even the boats on deck filled with blubber. The whole of these materials being in a rancid and putrid state, generally swarming with maggots, the stench they occasion may be better imagined than described.
>
> The blubber, when moved, gets into a state of fermentation, often bursting the casks, or throwing out the bungs, and dispersing their contents in the ship, or during the removal to the store-houses or boiling places. The process of landing, however goes on accompanied by much bawling and noise, and may be accomplished in the course of a few weeks, if a proper allowance of whisky has been administered, that being deemed necessary to overcome the squeamishness even of those best seasoned to the work…The sickening fumes all the while are widely diffused, even to the distance of miles.
>
> The nuisance does not cease with the act of boiling, which may terminate in six or eight weeks…Not only are the ships themselves in a disgusting state, but the empty blubber casks, and whalebone, or gills, which are stored up in great quantity, and often kept in that state many months, become extremely rancid and offensive; not to mention the refuse from the boilers, which is so highly putrid, and unconquerably bad, that the mere sprinkling or droppings from the carts employed to remove it, pollute the roads and streets through which they pass to such a degree, that they are frequently not purified or divested of the smell for weeks afterwards.
>
> No doubt a great deal of the refuse and garbage is thrown into the sea…a filthy scum is formed upon the surface of the water, and

the sea-shore itself becomes loathsome...In such a state of matters, bathing there is out of the question, and few, walking or riding, would choose to frequent these shores for pleasure, or recreation of any kind.[32]

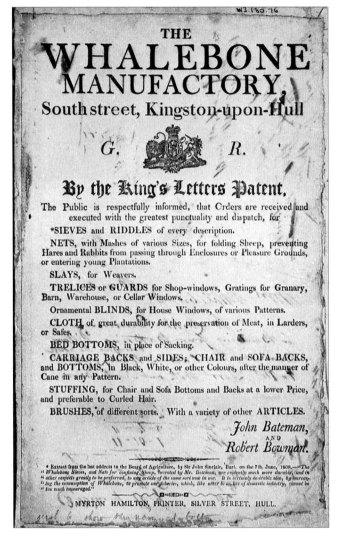

6.5. Advertisement for a whalebone manufacturer, Hull. (Reproduced by courtesy of Hull Maritime Museum: Hull Museums.)

The composition of the ship's companies

The ship's company were known as Greenlandmen. Crew lists provide a wealth of information about their composition (Figure 6.6). They reveal that the specialist skills associated with whaling required a crew that was very different from any other seafaring activity.

The occupational composition of whaling ships' companies, such as *Abram*'s, remained similar throughout the whaling era (Table 6.4).

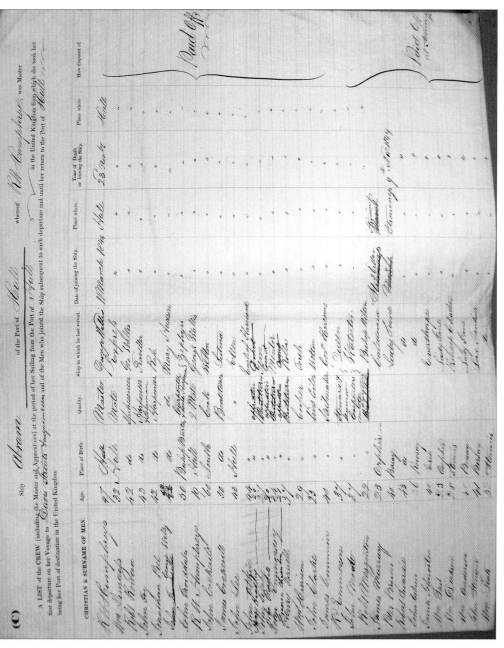

6.6. Part of the crew list for *Abram*, 1844: TNA, BT 98/297. (Reproduced by courtesy of The National Archives, London.)

Table 6.4: Ship's company of *Abram* 1839 and 1855.[33]

	Hull 1839	Kirkcaldy 1855
Master	1 (William Couldrey)	1 (Alexander Hay)
Mate	1 (mate and harpooner)	1 (mate and harpooner)
2nd Mate	1 (2nd mate and harpooner)	1 (2nd mate and harpooner)
Boatswain	1 (boatswain and harpooner)	
Surgeon	1	1
Spectioneer	1 (spectioneer and harpooner)	1
Harpooner	5 (all had more than one role)	4 (+2 who had other roles)
Boatsteerer	5	6
Line Manager	*	8
Loose Harpooner (a harpooner on trial)	1	1
Carpenter	2	2
Cooper	2	2
Sailmaker	1	1
Steward	1	
Skeeman	1 (skeeman and harpooner)	
Cook	1	1
Seaman/Ordinary Seaman	26	21
Boy		1

* The line managers in 1839 were probably counted amongst the seamen.

The master was supported by the mate and the spectioneer. The most skilled whale men were the harpooners, boatsteerers and line managers, of which there were normally six of each. In addition there were skilled sailmakers, carpenters and coopers on board. Payment was based on the level of responsibility, the bounty, and oil and bone money. There was always a surgeon, a requirement of accessing the government bounty. The cook was often the oldest member of the ship's company. Whaling demanded stamina and personal strength as well as a high level of physical fitness, so crews were largely composed of young men. The average age of the crews from the time that *Abram* was registered at Hull between 1848 and 1851 was between 26 and 29. During her time at Kirkcaldy in the late 1850s the average was a little higher, between 28 and 33 years.[34] Most voyages carried one or more 'boys', aged in their mid-teens, as well as some very experienced and more elderly crew in their mid-to-late fifties. As the 'officers', who were more experienced whalers, mostly embarked at the home port, those members of the crew from the mainland tended to have a higher average age than those engaged in Lerwick. The ships' companies which were signed on in the home port tended to come from the town itself and neighbouring communities. Hull crews came from Hull, other east coast ports and east Yorkshire. The

Kirkcaldy crews came not only from the town itself, but from virtually every community along the northern shore of the Firth of Forth, from other whaling ports such as Peterhead, Aberdeen and Dundee, and occasionally from further afield. Most of the Shetlanders came from the 'mainland' (the name given to the largest island, on which Lerwick is situated), but there were always some drawn from outlying islands.

Ships' masters were often re-employed year on year, and were in some cases also shareholders. During the 34 years that *Abram* sailed from Hull, she had only ten masters, one of whom, William Jackson, remained in charge for eight consecutive years (see Appendix 2). Similarly the Kirkcaldy Whale Fishing Company employed Robert Tod, as master of *Chieftain*, on every occasion between 1836 and 1844.[35] From the limited evidence available, it appears that crews, particularly the more skilled seamen, remained loyal to particular masters (Table 6.5). This seems to have been the case on *Abram*. As she had been registered at Kirkcaldy for the first time in January 1855 a new crew had to be engaged that year. A small number signed on again in 1856, but by 1857 a significant proportion of the crew were returnees, including some of those from the Shetland Islands.

Table 6.5: The ship's company of *Abram* who signed on for more than one year, 1855–57.[36]

	1855	1856	1857
	Signed on at Kirkcaldy	*Signed on at Kirkcaldy*	*Signed on at Kirkcaldy*
Alexander Hay	master	master	master
William Horn	spectioneer	harpooner	boatswain
Alexander Horn	harpooner		spectioneer
John Thompson	boatsteerer	harpooner	harpooner
James Dickson	linemanager	boatsteerer	boatsteerer
Alexander Rae	cooper	cooper	cooper
James Mills	cooper's mate	cooper's mate	cooper's mate
James Watson	cook	cook	cook
William Thompson	seaman	ordinary seaman	ordinary seaman
Hebron Nelson		harpooner	harpooner
Thomas Burnett		boatswain	harpooner
Thomas Hay		boatsteerer	boatsteerer
James Wilson		line manager	line manager
Thomas Townley		line manager	line manager
John Robertson		boatsteerer	line manager
James Irvine		boatsteerer	line manager
James Barclay		line manager	line manager
Alexander Allan		sail maker	sail maker
Robert Tirrel		ordinary seaman	ordinary seaman
		Signed on at Lerwick	*Signed on at Lerwick*
Lawrence Bigland		boatsteerer	line manager
John Manson		line manager	seaman
William Halcrow		line manager	seaman

At the conclusion of every voyage the master was required to give grades for conduct and ability in seamanship to every member of the company. This task was performed with varying degrees of thoroughness. In 1857 Alexander Hay, master of *Abram* reported on his crew with some care although the lack of differentiation between the two criteria suggests that he considered this task a chore (Table 6.6).[37] He seems to have been a hard man to please judging by the reports he wrote, so the enthusiasm with which the ship's company signed up to serve under him was perhaps more to do with his success in catching whales than a liking for the master.

Table 6.6: Report on the ship's company of *Abram*, 1857.[38]

Grade	For General Conduct (%)	For Ability in Seamanship (%)
Very Good	4%	4%
Good	36%	36%
Middling	40%	40%
Indifferent	20%	20%

Illness, injury and death

The master was required to report on all cases of illness, injury and death during a voyage. This was done in the Official Log Books. Compared with sailors who worked in warm climates, sailors in the Arctic were exposed to few illnesses. Although many whaling ships were wrecked in northern waters, most ships companies were rescued by other whalers working in the vicinity. The ice floes that often squeezed the ships and caused them to sink were also relatively safe platforms onto which the crew, with much of their supplies, could escape and await rescue.[39] Injuries were common and similar to those found elsewhere. Given the rudimentary skills of the surgeon and limited facilities on board ship, it is surprising that many sailors recovered. The surgeon on the Kirkcaldy ship *Lord Gambier* in 1854 had to deal with crew members suffering from bile, boils, ulcers, a carbuncle, a hernia, constipation, whitlow (an inflammation near a fingernail or toenail), contusion, a sprain, rheumatism, diarrhoea, toothache, pleuritis, vomiting, a lacerated wound from a seal bite, and a puncture wound from a seal club. An accident on 11 October could have had serious consequences had not the surgeon shown some skill. In deteriorating weather, the main topsail mast gave way. While the crew were taking the main topsail down, a heavy sea struck the ship and carried away part of the structure and one of the boats, as well as the master and some of the crew. All got back on deck except James Burton, the cooper, who was never seen again. While the rest of the crew cleared the deck, those that were injured were taken below to be attended by the surgeon. The second mate had 'a head much cut', and others were 'much bruised', but they all recovered. During the voyage of *Chieftain* in 1852 Captain Archibald recorded that there had been three crew members who had been ill – one each with glandular abscess, gastritis and bronchitis and a number of injuries which included a wound of the hand and bruising.[40]

Two crew members died on the 1857 voyage of *Abram*. The spectioneer, Alexander Horn, died of acute bronchitis after having been ill for three days. The surgeon had treated him with purgatives, expectorants and blisters, but none of these remedies helped and he died on 25 April 1857 and was buried at sea the following day. A month later Andrew Cargill, boatsteerer, died as a result of an accident involving the failure of a bolt holding one of the whaling boats in the tackles, which caused one end of the boat to fall into the sea, taking him with it. Although a rescue boat was launched, Cargill was found to be dead.[41] On *Chieftain* in the same year, Thomas Clinker fell ill on 27 June with a disease of the kidney. This became complicated with dropsy and he finally died on 1 October. His treatment had initially included 'regulation of diet; exercise with Tonic medicines and Laxatives as occasion required', but towards the end had involved 'drastic Purgatives and Diaphoretics'.[42]

Personal possessions

A window into the nature and extent of the possessions of whaling seamen in the mid-nineteenth century is provided both by the surviving ledgers of purchases made by the ships' companies at Hay and Co. of Lerwick, and the inventories of the belongings of the deceased that the ship's master was required to make.

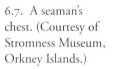

6.7. A seaman's chest. (Courtesy of Stromness Museum, Orkney Islands.)

The whalers were responsible for their own kit. Hay and Co. acted as agents for many whaling companies and the purchases of the crews of *Abram* were recorded for many of her years sailing from Hull, as well as the period during which she was owned by the Kirkcaldy Whale Fishing Company. When *Abram* called at Lerwick in 1859, Hay and Co. sold the Kirkcaldy men items such as mittens, oiled coats, stockings, oiled trousers, socks and sou'westers. One crew member purchased eight pairs of mittens, a frock, a kettle and 'duck' – a strong outer fabric used by sailors. Nineteen Shetlanders had an account with the company. They also made their purchases there, and could borrow money against their wages. Their families could also buy provisions while the men were at sea. Hay's was responsible for paying the Shetlanders' wages and their share of the oil money. Both wages and oil money varied depending upon the role of the individual.[43] In 1862, the year *Abram* was wrecked, the Kirkcaldy men spent £15 17s 9d at Hay's. Alexander Booth, a harpooner from Dundee, was one of the more lavish spenders, purchasing four pairs of stockings, two pairs of hose, a nightcap, six pairs of mittens, two ounces of thread and six needles, two frocks, a sou'wester, one oiled coat and three yards of duck, all for £1 18s 10d. Shetlanders such as John Hunter, a seaman from Bressay, purchased soap, a tin pot, a thimble, a knife, tobacco and 'mess things' (crockery and cutlery) as well as items of hosiery. The fact that he and others also purchased extra items of food such as butter, tea, coffee and sugar, indicates that the officially agreed rations may not always have been adequate.[44]

The contents of the sea chests of the deceased provide a fuller picture of the entire possessions of the sailors on board whaling ships. The inventories of those who died on the Kirkcaldy whalers in 1857 reveal what typical sailors possessed (Table 6.7). Alexander Horn was the most senior of the three, and Thomas Clinker was an ordinary seaman on his first voyage. However, by way of comparison, it is noteworthy that John Thompson, a harpooner on *Chieftain* who died of consumption during the return voyage from Davis Strait the previous year, had more of most kinds of clothing with him.[45]

There were clearly a range of articles which were basic to the needs of whalers, and generally speaking Thomas Clinker, the most junior and least experienced of the three, had smaller numbers of most of them. The items owned by Thomas Clinker, and not owned by the others, may be the result of a novice whaler not being sure what to pack, or may reflect a more assiduous listing of the contents of his chest. It is surprising (and may be the result of an oversight) that no caps or mittens are listed for John Thompson, as these were vital articles of clothing in Arctic seas.

It is clear from contemporary accounts that many of these items of clothing were worn at the same time in an attempt to keep warm and dry:

He has generally as many folds of woollen around his body as a mummy has swathes of sere-cloth; he has two or three shirts of flannel or striped cotton, two pairs of stockings, worsted or flannel drawers, two pairs of trousers, two waistcoats, an under jacket and a pea jacket, two or three pairs of mittens, and a wig of lamb's wool which fits so closely around the head that little more than the face is exposed, and the tar peeps through his bale of clothing like an owl through the scooped out orifice in a five century grown oak.[47]

Table 6.7: The inventories of men who died on Kirkcaldy whalers, 1856–7.[46]

Alexander Horn (1857)	Andrew Cargill (1857)	Thomas Clinker (1857)	John Thompson (1856)
One chest		One chest	One chest and one bag
13 shirts	9 shirts	1 shirt; 3 blue flannel shirts	7 white flannel shirts; 2 blue shirts; 5 striped shirts
3 caps	4 caps	2 caps; 1 nightcap	
3 handkerchiefs	4 handkerchiefs	2 handkerchiefs	3 handkerchiefs
6 pairs of drawers	4 pairs of drawers	3 pairs drawers	4 pairs of white flannel drawers; 4 pairs of blue flannel drawers
3 pairs shoes	2 pairs shoes	1 pair sea boots	1 pair long boots; one pair short boots;
9 pairs stockings	6 pairs of stockings	5 pair stockings	11 pairs of stockings in a net bag
2 jackets	4 jackets	2 jackets	3 pilot cloth jackets; 4 pilot cloth waistcoats
4 vests	3 vests	2 vests	
5 pairs mitts	8 pairs mitts	1 pair mitts	
4 pairs trousers	5 pairs trousers	3 pairs trousers	3 pairs trousers; 2 pairs moleskin trousers
2 frocks	1 worsted frock	1 worsted frock	4 striped frocks
bed and bedding	hammock, bed and bedding	1 pillow case; 1 blanket	1 pair blankets
	1 oil coat	1 oilskin coat; 1 oilskin trousers	1 oilskin jacket
	2 ghavets		
		1 broke pock[?]	
		1 pair cuffs	
		1 pair bluchers	2 pairs Blucher shoes
		1 leather belt	
		1 brush	
		3 jars; 1 mess tin; 1key; 1 Bible; 8 tobacco packets; 2 balls worsted; 1 comb; 1 wig	

Diet

Although some members of the crew purchased extra items of food and drink from Hay's at Lerwick, the provision of food was part of the agreement between the ship's owners and the crew. The diet changed little from voyage to voyage. Typically rations consisted of 1lb. of bread, 8oz. of flour and 8oz. of peas daily, 1lb. of beef four times a week and 12oz. of pork three times per week. They were also given 8oz. of tea, 1lb. of coffee and 3lbs of sugar monthly.[48] In 1819 the cost of these provisions for the whaleship *Exmouth* amounted to £901 19s 0d.[49] When opportunity arose, as was the case on board *Abram* in 1839, this restricted diet could be supplemented by food harvested or hunted during the voyage. The cook, often the oldest member of the crew, had to work with a restricted range of provisions for most of the time, and when tempers became heated it is perhaps not unsurprising that food was often the cause. A line manager on the 1854 voyage of *Lord Gambier* led a small group who lodged a complaint over the quality of the beef, although it was not substantiated by the other officers on board. The complainants had to give in with a bad grace.

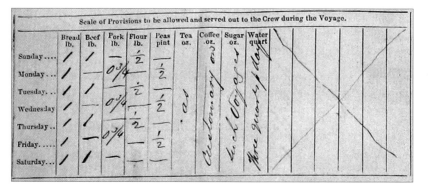

6.8. Diet information included on the crew list for *Abram* in 1849: TNA, BT 98/1905. (Reproduced by courtesy of The National Archives, London.)

The markets for whale products

As with the West Indian trade, *Abram* was to be employed in an industry which was taking advantage of new sources of supply and an expanding market. Whale oil was a vital raw material underpinning many parts of the British economy. Once refined, whale oil, or 'train oil' as it was commonly called, was used to light street lamps where its use has been credited with reducing urban crime, and in soap manufacture which provided the first opportunity for the Victorian public to wash frequently and cheaply.[50] Whale oil also made possible the development of the Dundee jute industry and Kirkcaldy's manufacture of oilcloth and linoleum. It also had other industrial uses in the preparation of leather and coarse woollen cloths, varnish and paint manufacture, and machinery lubrication. In industry it was used to light mines, workshops and factories and in the home it was used in domestic lamps and in candles.

Another valuable product of the whale was whale bone (or baleen) which was used in ornaments, articles of clothing such as corsetry (Figure 6.9), household objects such as sieves, riddles, trellises, umbrella spokes (Figure 6.10), brush bristles, watch springs, tennis rackets and whips, as well as blinds and guards for shop windows.[51] The jawbones were sometimes used as entrance arches and gate posts. Part of the offal was used for glue and a fibrous substance, similar to horsehair, was used for stuffing chairs (Figure 6.5).[52] Any bone remaining could be crushed for manure.

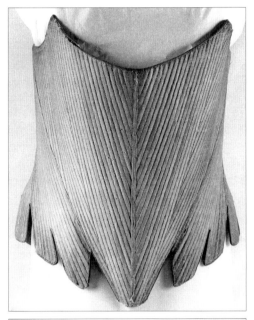

6.9. A whalebone corset. (Reproduced by courtesy of Hull Maritime Museum: Hull Museums.)

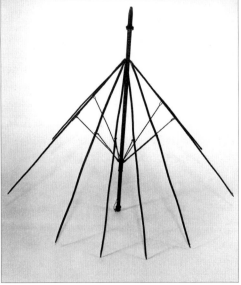

6.10. Whalebone umbrella spokes. (Reproduced by courtesy of Hull Maritime Museum: Hull Museums.)

The difficulty for industries reliant on whale oil was the unreliability of the annual catch which resulted in shortages and wild swings in the price of whale oil. This was such a problem that industrialists sought commodity substitution. For the woollen industry rape seed oil was an alternative to whale oil, and under the influence of Adam Smith and free trading, import duties on rape seed fell in stages from £1 per quarter in 1821 to 1s. in 1827. The resulting increase in imports from 9,000 quarters in 1821 to an average of 58,000 in 1827–30, was achieved at the expense of whale oil. Linseed was another oil seed that could act as a substitute for whale oil, and Hull became a centre for its manufacture with the number of factories increasing from eight in 1831 to thirteen in 1838.[53]

By 1809 gas lighting was already beginning to supplant whale oil as the source of street lighting in the centre of towns and cities. The Gas Light and Coke Company was providing gas lighting for London streets and by 1823 there were 47 gasometers in London, and other cities were busy converting their street lighting to gas. The endorsement of gas as a safe fuel by Humphrey Davy meant that the market for whale oil was likely to decline. The whaling industry retaliated by developing a process that could convert whale oil to oil gas which was able to provide light three times as bright as that provided by coal gas. The equipment to do this could be fitted into larger houses, which proved to be attractive particularly in locations that had not been linked to a coal gas supply. According to William Scoresby oil gas could more than hold its own pricewise 'in places where coal is not very cheap. Gas it seems can be produced from oil, at about the same expense as coal gas; consequently the numerous advantages of the former will render it highly preferable'.[54] In a spirit of optimism oil gas works were built in many towns, including Hull, during the early 1820s. However oil gas proved to be less popular than anticipated and Hull abandoned its oil gas plant in favour of coal gas in 1829. Despite this setback the whaling industry still had one market for their oil gas, and that was where portable gas was needed. The main market was on the railways: the North Eastern Railway Company continued to manufacture oil gas in Hull until the beginning of the twentieth century. The problem for the whaling industry was that there were few industrial processes for which whale oil was uniquely suitable, and as substitutes were produced the key markets for whale oil began to disappear. Consequently the English whaling fleet declined from 158 to 94 ships between 1821 and 1826, and the whaling industry provided about 3,000 fewer jobs.[55]

With the loss of some markets, the reducing demand for whale products during the nineteenth century did not encourage investment. The Northern Whale Fishery increasingly became a backwater: without investment, British whaling companies could not compete on a world stage. The Southern Whale Fishery, which had only been of minor significance for Britain during the first half of the nineteenth century, failed in 1849 because it could not compete in terms of costs with the expanding industries in America, Australia and New Zealand.[56] A reduced fleet based at a number of east coast ports sailed to the Northern Whale Fishery until the 1860s, but after that only Dundee retained an interest, with whalers from that port supplying whale oil for the jute industry as well as exporting oil for the benefit of other users elsewhere in the United Kingdom. This trade ended in the first decade of the twentieth century.

Abram sailed to the Northern Whale Fishery in almost every year between 1819 and 1862. Her story reflects much of the history of nineteenth century British whaling in the Arctic: it is therefore a story worth telling.

References

[1]   A.G. Credland, *The Hull Whaling Trade: An Arctic Enterprise*, Beverley, Hutton Press, 1995, pp. 55–56. It was traditional to divide the ownership of whaling vessels into 64 shares. Usually there was a small group of principal owners who held most of the shares. Subscribing owners formed a larger group who owned a few shares each, and 'non-subscribers' had a very small stake in the enterprise, perhaps owning one share each. Details of *Abram* can be found in the Hull Shipping Registers. After the first registration on 11 January 1819 she was re-registered on many occasions as owners changed or modifications were made. Hull City Archives: DPC/1/2/19 (1820); DPC/1/3/77 (1824); DPC/1/9/15 (1839).

[2]   K. Jamie, *Sightlines*, London, Sort of Books, 2012, p. 97. The Greenland right was 'right for all the wrong reasons'. It was a docile, slow moving giant of up to sixty feet long with a thick layer of blubber and large quantities of baleen in the mouth. Its greatest advantage over many other whale species was that it floated when killed, and thus was relatively easy to tow towards the mother ship for flensing.

[3]   J. Dykes, *Yorkshire's Whaling Days*, Clapham, Dalesman, 1980, p. 49.

[4]   Quoted in G. Jackson, *The British Whaling Trade*, London, A. & C. Black, 1978, p. 118.

[5]   In 1820 a Parliamentary Select Committee reported that 'the time when monopolies could be successfully supported, or would be patiently endured, either in respect of subjects against subjects, or particular countries against the rest of the world, seems to have passed away'. Quoted in Jackson, *British Whaling Trade*, p. 119.

[6]   A.G.E. Jones, *Polar Portraits: Collected Papers*, Whitby, Caedmon, 1992, pp. 188–89.

[7]   Source of British figures: J.R. McCulloch, *Statistical Account of the British Empire* (1834), vol. 2, p. 33. Quoted in Jackson, *British Whaling Trade*, p. 125; Hull figures: T. Sheppard and J. Suddaby, *Hull Whaling Relics and Arctic or Historical Records of 250 Years*, Hull, Hull Museum Publications 31, 1906, pp. 17–18.

[8]   C.A. Holland, 'William Penny, 1890–92: Arctic Whaling Master', *Polar Record*, 94, 1970, pp. 25–43.

[9]   J.M. Bellamy, *The Trade and Shipping of Nineteenth Century Hull*, Hull, East Yorkshire Local History Series, no. 27, p. 37.

[10] *Abram* was laid up in 1842 and 1843 because of the poor outlook in the whaling industry.

[11] *Report on the Burgh of Kirkcaldy, Fifeshire, to Accompany the Reform Act of 1832*. Quoted in E.P.D. Torrie and R. Coleman, *Historic Kirkcaldy*, Edinburgh, Historic Scotland, 1995. (This book provides the most accessible introduction to the history of the town.)

[12] J.Y. Lockhart, 'Kirkcaldy Harbour History', Kirkcaldy, 1940 (a manuscript available at Kirkcaldy Central Library).

[13] TNA, BT/98/320; 'Kirkcaldy Harbour Record' (12 Nov. 1832–20 June 1834).

[14] 'Kirkcaldy Harbour Record'. Alexander Balfour is listed as the recipient of 42.5 tons of 'jawbones' from Aberdeen and Peterhead on 13 Dec. 1833. This consignment, coming from two whaling ports, was almost certainly whale jawbones, some of which may have been sold on as ornamental gate arches.

[15] 'Kirkcaldy Harbour History'. Whaling statistics are extremely unreliable. The statistics for the whole country compiled by William Coltish in Hull at that time record the figures for five Kirkcaldy ships in 1833, and each entry for whale oil and whalebone is slightly different. W. Coltish, 'Whaling Statistics 1772–1842', unpublished manuscript, Hull History Centre.

[16] Jackson, *British Whaling Trade*, p. 149.

[17] W. Barron, *Old Whaling Days*, London, Conway Maritime Press, 1996 [first published 1895], p. 142.

[18] Barron, *Old Whaling Days*, p. 142.

[19] B. Lubbock, *The Arctic Whalers*, Glasgow, Brown, Son and Ferguson, 1978 [first published 1937], pp. 371–72.

[20] Lubbock, *Arctic Whalers*, pp. 375–376, 460.

[21] M. Archibald, *Whalehunters: Dundee and the Arctic Whalers*, Edinburgh, Mercat Press, 2004, p. 30.

[22] Kirkcaldy Central Library, Kirkcaldy Register of Shipping 2:102 (1841–1855).

[23] *Dundee Year Book, 1894*, p. 210. Quoted in Jackson, *British Whaling Trade*, p. 145.

[24] W. Scoresby, *An Account of the Arctic Regions*, vol. 2, Newton Abbot, David and Charles, 1969 [first published 1820], p. 189.

[25] D. Francis, *Arctic Chase: A History of Whaling in Canada's North*, St John's, Breakwater Books, 1984, p. 7.

[26] Samuel Hibbert described Fethaland in 1822 as 'On a narrow isthmus of low marshy land, that connects the peninsula of Feidaland with the mainland, is interspersed, with all the disorder of a gypsey encampment, a number of savage huts named 'summer lodges' and in the centre of them is a substantial booth used…for curing fish'.

[27] Shetland Archives, D25/58/16, Tom Henderson papers.

[28] J.C. Rowley, *The Hull Whale Fishery*, Lockington, 1982, p. 26.

[29] T. Barrow, *The Whaling Trade of North-East England*, Sunderland, Sunderland University Press, 2001, p. 93.

[30] Rowley, *Hull Whale Fishery*, p. 30.

[31] For the uses of whale oil see above, pp. 98–101.

[32] *Statement concerning the Whale-Fishing Trade at Dundee, in reference to its proposed introduction into Burntisland*, 1830.

[33] TNA, BT 98/297; BT 98/4183.

[34] This information is taken from crew lists. However, it should be remembered that at that time age was often remembered and/or recorded inaccurately.

[35] TNA, BT 98/320 (There are no records for 1843 but there is no reason to think that she did not sail that year.) However, masters were not always retained. The Kirkcaldy whaler *Caledonia* had four masters between 1837 and 1844. TNA, BT 98/320; A.G.E. Jones, *Polar Portraits*, p. 235.

[36] TNA, BT 98/4183; BT 98/4508; BT 98/4966.

[37] The criteria for these judgments seem to have been subjective. William Archibald of *Chieftain* assessed his entire ship's company in 1857 as 100% Very Good for General Conduct, and 89% Very Good for Ability in Seamanship.

[38] TNA, BT 98/4966.

[39] For a discussion about captains and crews on Liverpool vessels, including comments on illnesses, injury and deaths, see K. Jordan, 'The captains and crews of Liverpool's Northern Whaling Trade', *International Journal of Maritime History*, 22.1, 2010, pp. 185–204.

[40] Kirkcaldy Central Library, Whale Fishing log of *Chieftain*, 1852.

[41] TNA, BT 98/4966.

[42] TNA, BT 98/4966.

[43] Shetland Archives, D31/6/26.

[44] Shetland Archives, D31/6/29 Hay & Co. records.

[45] TNA, BT 98/4508.

[46] TNA, BT 98/4960; BT 98/4966; BT 98/4508.

[47] Quoted in Lubbock, *Arctic Whalers*, p. 54.

[48] These figures applied on *Abram* in 1851.

[49] Copies of the accounts for *Exmouth* can be found in Hull History Centre.

[50] Archibald, *Whalehunters*, pp. 22–23.

[51] During the first two decades of the nineteenth century numerous patents were taken out for potential new uses for whale bone. See: R. Vaughan, *The Arctic: A History*, Stroud, Alan Sutton, 1994, pp. 85–86.

[52] Bellamy, *Trade and Shipping of Nineteenth Century Hull*, pp. 11–12; M. Archibald, *Whalehunters*, p. 22.

[53] Bellamy, *Trade and Shipping of Nineteenth Century Hull*, pp. 29–30.

[54] Scoresby, vol. 2, p. 428. Quoted in Jackson, *British Whaling Trade*, p. 124.

[55] In 1821 there were 6,000 men directly employed in whaling nationally, with several thousands more employed in shipbuilding and ship repair, sail, rope and barrel making, whale oil rendering and a myriad of other jobs connected to the industry. Archibald, *Whalehunters*, p. 14. For the situation later in the 1820s see *Hull Packet*, 12 Sept. 1826.

[56] For the Southern Whale Fishery see Jackson, *British Whaling Trade*, pp. 132–42.

CHAPTER 7

Abram: the Hull years, 1819–55

Abram was prepared for her first Arctic voyage during the spring of 1819. No account books have survived, but it is possible to gain an idea of what was involved in fitting out a whale ship from surviving accounts of other Hull whalers such as *Exmouth*. In the spring of the same year, £245 15s 10d was spent on re-equipping her for the new season's whaling. Two shipwrights, one joiner and one blockmaker were employed, and materials purchased included timber, iron-work, cordage, sails, paint, boats, casks and general chandlery. A further £445 12s 5d was spent on sundries including coal, bungs, rivets, drugs, cooper's tools, membership of the Marine Bible Association, and insurance. On her return from the fishing grounds in the autumn there was further expenditure including dock and Trinity House fees, duty owed on oil and bone, wages and fish money for the voyage, lighterage, and payments to the blubber boiling factory. In total, expenditure on this one voyage was £2,881 10s 11d. The oil and whalebone was sold to eight customers locally and to other customers in London. This produced an income of £3,090 18s 7d, giving a profit for distribution amongst the owners, shareholders and ship's company of £209 7s 8d. However, not every voyage made a profit. In the same year, for example, *Neptune*, also of Hull, returned 'clean' and made a loss of £367 3s 6d.[1]

As a new whaler *Abram*, under the command of Captain Harrison, was destined for the Greenland Sea, east of Greenland. This was a shorter and less dangerous journey than that to the Davis Strait fishery, so *Abram* was amongst the last of the 65-strong fleet to depart from Hull. During the season she caught nine whales which produced only 57 tons of oil, which suggests that at least some of the whales were immature, the consequence of over-fishing.[2] She was more successful than many of the ships which sailed for Davis Strait, where poor weather and ferocious ice conditions resulted in a number of wrecks, and many ships returned 'clean' or nearly clean. The price of whale oil rose from £28 to £36 per ton which would have gone some way to compensating Tidd, Mercer and Co. for the small catch.[3]

Compared with 1819, 1820 was one of the most successful years on record, with Hull's 59 ships earning £250,588, or over £4,247 per ship.[4] *Abram*, once again fishing in the Greenland Sea, took 13 whales and 147 seals and returned with 118 tons of oil. The resultant glut in whale oil led to its price falling to £18–£19 per ton.

7.1. *Abram* attributed to James Wheldon (1832–1893). (Reproduced by courtesy of Hull Maritime Museum: Hull Museums.)

The 1821 season was unusually well documented (see Figure 7.2). Once again *Abram* fished in the Greenland Sea alongside 30 other Hull whalers. The smaller Davis Strait fleet included the Hull whaler *Harmony*, which had also been built in Lancaster (1798). *Abram* sailed from Hull on 15 March, called in at Lerwick in Shetland, and departed for the Arctic with a crew of 48, nine of whom had sailed with her the previous year.[5] At the beginning of May, she was fishing about 40 miles north of Svalbard (Spitsbergen), right at the edge of the pack ice. However, this was not a particularly good year and *Abram* returned to Hull on 3 September with only three whales, below the average for Hull whalers in the Greenland Sea that year.[6] Even though other Greenland Sea whalers fared better than *Abram*, the consequences of over-fishing in that area were clear when set against the greater success of the Davis Strait fleet. The Hull ships which fished in the Greenland Sea in 1821 caught on average six whales, while those that fished in Davis Strait and Baffin Bay caught on

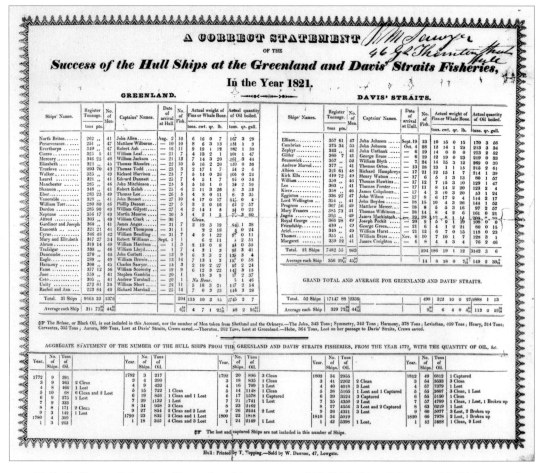

7.2. Hull whaling statistics 1821. (Reproduced by courtesy of Hull Maritime Museum: Hull Museums.)

average 14 whales, which produced nearly nine tons of bone and 149 tons of oil. It was clear that the immediate future lay in these new, more distant, fishing areas, although on this occasion the success of the Davis Strait fleet came at a price. Seven ships of that fleet, including *Harmony*, sank, and consequently the Hull fleet was reduced in size the following year. There were few industries more fickle than that of whaling. 'Prosperity depended upon a number of factors: chance, experience, determined perseverance, the skill of the crew and their confidence in the master, and the ship and equipment and capital that went into the venture.'[7]

Despite the disappointing catches, *Abram* continued to be fitted out for whaling, and from 1822 she was destined for Davis Strait under a new captain, Samuel Couzens.[8] Before the fleet set out from Hull, one of the owners of *Abram*, John Tidd, concerned for the moral welfare of the men he employed, gave the masters of his ships a book of his tracts entitled 'Five Letters to the Officers and Crews of the fishing ships *Mercury*, William Jackson, Master, and *Abram*, Samuel Cousins, Master of the Port of Hull'.[9] These were sermons which were to be read to the officers and crew on the first Sunday of each month. It is probable that these were read at the religious gatherings conducted while the fleet was awaiting the opportunity to proceed across Baffin Bay towards the western shore.

> Thirty ships were in the ice docks, all within a distance of three miles, and though the ships in company had 1,500 men or more, the day was marked with more solemnity than I have often seen in England. Three services were held, and six sailors from different ships joined in praying. It was remarked that the weight of the men who attended sank the *Cumbrian* (a ship of 360 tons) down four inches. Later in the evening a prayer meeting was held on board the *Abram*, of Hull (Captain Cousins).[10]

Contemporaries referred to whaling crews as 'rough tars' and 'curs'd ruffians' and with concerns expressed about the ungodliness of whalers, these sermons, as well as the reference to the payment of a subscription to the Marine Bible Association in the accounts of *Exmouth* in 1819, were clearly part of an attempt to maintain Christian values and worship whilst at sea.[11] Despite these religious observances, 1822 turned out to be another poor season for *Abram* with a catch of only four whales.

Whaling was always unpredictable, and in the following year (1823) *Abram* had her most successful year ever. She returned to Hull on 10 October with 31 whales out of the total of 469 caught by the Hull fleet.[12] The fleet fished off the coast of north east Baffin Island, and with so much slaughter the environment in which the ships worked rapidly deteriorated. The log of *Cumbrian*, another Hull whaler, provides a graphic description of the scene in the killing fields:

On July 27th we were turning to the southward along the land floe nears Ponds Bay. Here and there along the floe edge lay the dead bodies of hundreds of flensed whales, and the air for miles around was tainted with the foetor which arose from such masses of putridity. Towards evening the numbers come across were even increasing, and the effluvia which then assailed our olfactories became almost intolerable.[13]

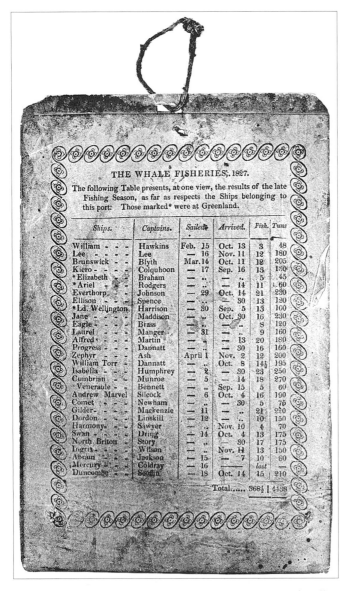

7.3. Hull whaling statistics 1827. (Reproduced by courtesy of Hull Maritime Museum: Hull Museums.)

Whaling ships were usually cleaned and repaired in winter and spring although another voyage was occasionally fitted in. This happened in 1823. After returning to Hull, *Abram* made a further trip to Liverpool. During December advertisements in the *Liverpool Mercury* claimed that 'quick despatch' was anticipated for the return voyage to Hull as the 'great part of this vessel's cargo' was already 'engaged'.[14] Her Hull owners were no doubt hoping to profit from the ship's earlier connections to Liverpool.

By the mid-1820s the rigours of fishing in the more distant Davis Strait and Baffin Bay, the reduced demand for whale oil, and the removal of the bounty, contributed to the decline in size of the whaling fleet. In 1824, the Hull fleet numbered only 13 ships, and *Abram*, skippered by Captain William Jackson, the brother-in-law of William Scoresby Junior, was the most successful of the Hull whalers, catching ten whales. 1825, 1826 and 1829 were all poor years, although the catches for 1827 (Figure 7.3), and particularly 1828 were good. In 1827 *Abram* was beset in the ice in late September, but was quickly liberated and able to return home in November. This contemporary report gives a striking description:

> The following melancholy accident befell this vessel *(Abram)* on 23rd September near Cape Sorrell. Having killed a fish, an extra boat's crew was sent off to assist in recovering the lines which were entangled among the ice, and a thick fog coming in, accompanied by a strong gale, the running ice beset the ship, and cut off all communication with the unfortunate boat's crew, consisting of fifteen men, the best hands in the ship, six natives of Orkney and nine Englishmen, who were unavoidably left behind.

Happily, the crew did not perish:

> A letter has been received at Hull, from Aberdeen, stating that the 15 men belonging to the Abram, of the former port, who had been left behind on the ice in Davis's Straits, had been picked up by the *Harmony* belonging to Hull.[15]

On this occasion *Abram* had been fortunate to escape being frozen in over the winter. During the 1830s this became an increasing danger.

Abram played a central role in the dramatic events of 1830. That year was the first of two disastrous whaling seasons which left the industry on its knees. Of the 91 British ships in Davis Strait during that season, 19 were lost and 21 returned clean. Practically all of the shipwrecked sailors were rescued by other whalers, but with 1,000 men camped on the ice at one time after nine ships were lost and four badly damaged in a single day (an event that became known as 'Baffin Fair'), the dangers of whaling in Davis Strait could not be clearer. *Abram* was involved in two of the rescues, and brought John Reed and Captain Edward Dannatt back to Hull. John Reed, who had lost the use of his feet from frost-bite, was found by the mate of *Abram* on shore on the point of starvation. Reed claimed that he had left the French whaler *Madamoiselle*, which had earlier rescued him, on account of bad treatment. The ill feeling appears to have caused the French captain to ignore the *Abram*'s request for the return of Reed's clothes.[16] Dannatt had been captain of *Progress* which had sunk on 2 July. Initially he took refuge on *James* of Peterhead, but on the morning of 6 July he walked across the ice to *Ariel* of Hull which he reached that evening. He remained on board *Ariel* until 17 August and then travelled overnight across the ice to *Swan* of Hull. He rested there and the following day crossed to *Harmony*. He left *Harmony* on the same day and continued to *Abram* which he reached on 20 August, 18 days after his ship was wrecked.

Nearly 20 per cent of the Hull fleet was wrecked that year, and those ships that returned had only caught 77 whales between them. The resulting shortage of whale oil caused the price to rise to £60 per ton which was to the advantage of the successful ships.[17] *Abram* was amongst the more successful whalers with three catches, and as the first Hull ship to return to the Humber she brought the bad news about the events in Davis Strait. Although casualties were surprisingly few, the whaling community at all the ports suffered severe financial distress largely because their crews' pay was stopped from the day the vessel was abandoned. In Hull a meeting presided over by the Mayor was held at the Guildhall and a subscription was opened for the seamen and their families.[18]

The value of the industry to the port of Hull was questioned by a contemporary writer who wrote that he believed that 'the Greenland fishery has been greatly overdone and is proving injurious to the general trade of this port, by withdrawing an undue proportion of capital from other branches of Commerce'.[19] The owners of *Abram* were clearly not convinced that there was a future for the industry, and she was put up for sale. The advertisement described *Abram* as being 'remarkably fast' and claimed that the ship was in good condition:

> She is well found and in excellent condition having been thoroughly repaired since her return from the Fishery: has Casks for carrying Blubber, to produce from 220 to 230 Tuns of Oil, and will require nothing but provisions to send her to sea.[20]

However, there does not seem to have been a buyer and she continued to sail for Messrs. Tidd, Mercer and Co.

Hull maintained an interest in whaling, but sent fewer ships to Davis Strait and Baffin Bay from 1832. For those vessels still whaling, 1832 was a successful year, but *Abram* was fortunate to have four good seasons between 1831 and 1834, taking 59 whales. Not all ships were so successful and accidents continued to happen. Another Hull whaler, *Shannon*, struck an iceberg during the 1832 season and sank. When *Abram* returned to port in November 1832 her crew subscribed £1 4s. 6d. for the relief of the widows and families, as well as the surviving crew of *Shannon*, some of whom were 'in a mutilated and debilitated condition'.[21]

In 1835–36 *Abram* was trapped in the ice (see Chapter 8) but after just two months back in Hull she set sail again for Davis Strait in April 1836. This turned out to be another disastrous season, not just for *Abram*, who returned 'clean', but for the whole whaling fleet. In the autumn six ships became frozen in, although on this occasion *Abram* was not one of them. The death toll was considerable as the whalers had become trapped at a higher latitude than in 1835, with the result that it took longer for them to drift south and be released from the ice. When *Advice* returned to Britain only seven crew out of 49 were left alive, and on *Dee* there were 15 survivors out of 60. It seemed as if nothing had been learned from previous unforeseen over-winterings and the ship owners were blamed for not equipping their ships with enough supplies and fresh food (such as lemon juice) to prevent scurvy.

Only the Peterhead ships had a good season with their sealing in 1837.[22] For the Hull whalers it was so poor that *Abram* returned as early as the 20 August. This enabled the ship to embark on a second voyage in the autumn. She left Hull for St Petersburg on 21 September, with a crew of 14. Only the master, John Hibbs, the carpenter and the three apprentices had been part of the crew that had been in Davis Strait earlier in the year. There is no record as to whether she was in ballast or took a cargo to Russia, but she returned on 2 December with a cargo of cranberries, hemp, linseed oil and wood.[23] This ensured that the ship's owners made some profit that year.

The initiative shown by William Penny, the Dundee whaler, in pursuing new opportunities in the Cumberland Sound area of Baffin Island, led to 1838 and 1839 being better years for the Hull whalers and *Abram* in particular.[24] Our knowledge of the 1839 voyage of *Abram* is so extensive that it forms the subject of Chapter 9.

The improved catches of 1838 and 1839 were not maintained during the 1840s. The size of the whaling fleet reduced nationally, and the decline in Hull was particularly marked. In 1840 only four ships departed from Hull for Davis Strait, 13 per cent of the UK total.[25] *Abram* was one of these ships, but she returned 'clean'. Tidd, Mercer and Co. ceased trading during the year as a result of a 'rupture' between the partners that caused great interest in the town.[26] During 1840 the mills, warehouses and even the homes of Tidd and Mercer were auctioned off. No doubt a fracas at Lerwick, which saw Captain Couldrey of *Abram* brought before the Sheriff's Court accused of slander and not paying his Shetland pilots, was not helpful, and *Abram* was put up for sale.[27]

Thomas Barkworth of Hull became the new owner when he purchased the ship outright in 1841.[28] The Barkworths were shipbuilders, merchants and ship owners – the company owned a number of ships including another whaler *Comet*, which had operated in both the Northern and Southern Whale Fisheries, and which was lost in 1843. *Abram* sailed in 1841, but success eluded the Hull fleet. *Abram* was described as being 'laid up from 26 October 1841 to 11 March 1844', presumably to prevent the company incurring losses during this lean period for whaling.[29]

When *Abram* sailed again in 1844 she was under the command of Captain R.W. Humphreys, one of Hull's most famous whaling masters. In 1833 he had been commander of *Isabella*, the whaling vessel which had rescued Captain John Ross and Commander James Clark Ross from Lancaster Sound after their epic voyage in search of the North West Passage during which they had spent four winters frozen in at various locations to the east of Boothia Peninsula. Two years later in 1835 Captain Humphreys' reputation ensured that he was at the centre of the mission to rescue the eleven ships trapped in the ice in Davis Strait. Unusually, in 1844 Humphreys sailed via Stromness in Orkney, where 22 Orcadians were taken on; it was an indifferent whaling season and he returned with the produce of just two whales on board *Abram*.

By 1845 the industry was improving again, but catches continued to vary from season to season. During the final years at Hull (1844–53) *Abram* averaged 51 tons of oil per year. In 1849 Captain Gravill had to decide between his instructions to search for Sir John Franklin (see Chapter 10) and the financial advantages to be gained from concentrating on the hunt for whales. In 1852 and 1853 the income derived from whale oil was supplemented by the oil from several thousand seals. 1854 was described as 'a coarse year' and three Hull ships were wrecked while sealing. The effect of the Crimean War on trade was a problem for Hull's industries. The local oil mills suffered particularly badly, with only three or four of the 27 working in 1855.[30] There was very little demand for linseed and rapeseed oil and virtually no demand for whale oil. It is, therefore, not surprising to discover that Thomas Barkworth sold *Abram* to new owners in Kirkcaldy in early 1855.[31]

References

1   Copies of the accounts of *Exmouth* and *Neptune* can be found in Hull History Centre.

2   *Hull Packet*, 5 April, 1819.

3   Lubbock, *Arctic Whalers*, p. 210.

4   Bellamy, *Trade and Shipping of Nineteenth Century Hull*, p. 63.

5   Hull Trinity House, MSF/2/43 p. 276.

6   The average catch for Hull whalers in the Greenland Sea that year was 6.5 whales, producing 2 tons 13 cwts of bone and 51 tons of oil per ship.

7   Jones, *Polar Portraits*, p. 187.

8   Lloyd's Registers and the registers of the Society of Merchants, Ship-owners and Underwriters list *Abram* as intending to sail to the Greenland Sea in every year up to 1831. However reality was not always the same as intention, and it is clear that from

1822 she sailed to Davis Strait. See A.G.E. Jones, *The Greenland and Davis Strait Trade, 1740–1865*, n.p., 1996.

9   Copies of these tracts can be seen at Hull Maritime Museum.

10   T. Sheppard and J. Suddaby, *Hull Whaling Relics and Arctic or Historical Records of 250 Years*, Hull, Hull Museums Publications, no. 31, 1906, p. 12.

11   For information on the character of whaling crews see: Jordan, 'Captains and crews', pp. 188–89. Hull History Centre, Accounts of the ship Exmouth, 1819.

12   *Abram* caught an above-average number of whales (average = 27.5 whales) and was responsible for 6.6% of the total Hull catch.

13   Quoted in Sheppard and Suddaby, *Hull Whaling Relics,* p. 13.

14   *Liverpool Mercury,* 5, 12 & 26 Dec. 1823.

15   *Liverpool Mercury,* 23 Nov. 1827. The ship *Harmony* was not the same *Harmony* as previously referred to, but another Hull ship of the same name.

16   Lubbock, *Arctic Whalers*, p. 281.

17   Lubbock, *Arctic Whalers*, pp. 281–83.

18   Lubbock, *Arctic Whalers*, p. 284; J. Leslie, R. Jameson & H. Murray, *Narrative of Discovery and Adventure in the Polar Regions and Seas*, (6th ed), Edinburgh, Oliver and Boyd, n.d. (*c*.1845).

19   J. Greenwood, *Picture of Hull*, (1835); quoted in Bellamy, *Trade and Shipping of Nineteenth-Century Hull*, p. 27.

20   *Hull Packet*, 25 Dec. 1832 and Jan. 1833, various editions. The same advertisement appeared in *Aberdeen Journal*, 16 Jan. 1833.

21   *Hull Packet*, 27 Nov. 1832.

22   In 1838 Peterhead ships killed 28,646 seals. A.G.E. Jones, 'Captain Robert Martin: a Peterhead whaling master in the nineteenth century', in Jones, *Polar Portraits*, pp. 190–91. Reprinted from *Scottish Geographical Magazine*, 1969.

23   Hull History Centre, Bills of Entry for the Port of Hull, 1837.

24   In 1839 the catch of nine whales produced 310 butts of blubber (100 tons of Train Oil) and 6.5 tons of whale bone. Hull History Centre, Bills of Entry for the Port of Hull, 1839.

25   Bellamy, *Trade and Shipping of Nineteenth-Century Hull*, p. 24.

26   Personal communication from Arthur Credland, Hull Maritime Museum (April 2009). Tidd, Mercer and Co. was dissolved on 22 March 1844, *London Gazette*, 29 March 1844.

27   Shetland Archives: SC12/6/1840/130 (7 April 1840) Lerwick Sheriff's Court Records; See Archibald, *Whalehunters*, p. 130.

28   Hull History Centre, DPC/1/10/19 (1841). Barkworth owned all 64 shares.

29   Trinity House, Hull, Muster Rolls, MSF/3/40/174.

30   Bellamy, *Trade and Shipping of Nineteenth-Century Hull,* p. 33.

31   An advertisement was inserted in the *Hull Packet*, 5 Jan. 1855 seeking a new master for the ship. However, by the time of the departure to Davis Strait, *Abram* had been acquired by owners in Kirkcaldy as on her return in October she is referred to as *Abram* of Kirkcaldy. *Aberdeen Journal*, 24 Oct. 1855.

CHAPTER 8

1835: Rescued from a 'dreadful death'

The 1835 season was one of the most notorious in the entire history of whaling, and *Abram* played a central part in the drama. We know of her role in the events of that year because of the journal kept by Alexander Dunn, an ordinary seaman on board the ship. Although his journal has not survived, much of what he wrote was published in a series of articles in 1875 in the Hull newspaper, *The Criterion*, to mark the fortieth anniversary.[1]

Abram, under the command of John Hibbs, departed from Hull on 24 March 1835 with a crew of 28. She was seen off by 'a dense multitude', 'a waving of hands' and 'three tremendous cheers'. On 1 April the ship arrived in Lerwick where a further 20 seamen were engaged (Figure 8.1).

The day before she departed on 5 April one of the three Hull apprentices, John Lee, absconded. She crossed the north Atlantic in a series of storms, and when ice was seen on 1 May the crew were ordered to get 'all our fishing gear in order'. She avoided being driven onto a reef off the west Greenland coast, and then sailed north to Disco Bay where 'we found nothing but large floes and floe pieces'. The ship continued northwards but was unable to penetrate the ice in Melville Bay, so she skirted round the ice to the south and west heading towards Baffin Island. There she was able to turn north again, and in the company of *Mary Frances, Hector, Lady Jane* and *Dordon* entered the pack. The ice then closed in, and Dunn describes the work involved in keeping the ship safe in the ever moving pack ice:

> As soon as the ice begun to open we kept warping and tracking at all opportunities. The ice was very heavy. For three weeks we hardly knew what it was to get an hour's rest; all our clothes were packed in a bag ready for a run. Scarcely a day passed but that some of the ships were nipped by the ice. We fully expected that some of the ships would be buried underneath the ice. We were always cutting docks; two or three times in a day. Sometimes before we had got finished the ice would sally upon us and break all in together. We were always in jeopardy, not a moment to call our own. It made the stoutest hearts tremble. We had some very narrow escapes with our ship; sometimes we were lifted above three feet out of the water; then it would ease in a moment.

8.1. *Abram* Muster Roll, 1835–36: Hull History Centre. C DSTR/53/113. (Reproduced by courtesy of Hull History Centre and Hull Trinity House.)

The only escape from this pack ice was to the north, and *Abram* and *Dordon* made their way as far as 72°N, but they found no whales. A northerly gale forced the ships south again where they came across *Lady Jane* who had rescued the crew of *Mary Frances*, which had sunk. As was customary *Abram* embarked some of the survivors, in this case ten of the rescued men, including the master, Captain Coldray. Alexander Dunn empathised with Coldray's situation: 'he was now destitute; had lost his all, a fine ship – the pride of the country. The owners had expended £2,000 in repairs, besides her provisions. He is now, as it were from home, obliged to some one or other for what little comfort, if comfort there is any on board a strange ship.' By now it was late September and *Abram* 'picked up two dead fish…and flinched them…little thinking they would prove of such service as they afterwards did'. During the first weeks of October, both *Abram* and *Dordon* desperately tried to escape from the ever thickening ice. On 20 October, *Dordon* sank, and *Abram* took on board half her crew along with as much of the provisions and equipment that could be saved. As was the custom, the wrecked ship was then set on fire. *Abram* now had 96 men on board, twice her complement, and as she had become frozen in, it seemed that she would have to over-winter. As was usual at that time her owners had not equipped her for this. There was neither the necessary clothing nor enough food to sustain the normal crew, let alone one augmented by the sailors from the wrecked vessels. Alexander Dunn described the conditions they endured as the winter advanced.

> Towards the latter end of October the frost was very severe. Our master further reduced our weight of provisions to 2lbs. of bread a week. It was very little in a cold climate, where your appetite is very keen. We were all getting very weak, having the ship to attend warping and tracking at all opportunities, when the ice opened… About the 15th November it was very severe, freezing fourteen or fifteen inches in a night. We always went every other day to fetch ice to make water for the ship's use, and it rarely happened but the most of us got frost-bitten before we came back, especially if there was any wind… We had prayers and a sermon three days in the week; but a few others met together every night to supplicate the throne of grace for pardon for our past sins. We found ourselves getting weaker and weaker every day. It would have melted the heart of a stone to see us sit down to get a meal, a sup of weak tea or coffee and one-third of a biscuit; it was very little…We had a warm dinner every day; it was soup (alias spoilt water); three pints of barley or peas to serve the whole ship's company…29th November: Our coals being very low, our master ordered the jaw bones and rump and tail [of the two captured whales] to be got out of the hold to burn…I am certain that there was not one fourth part of the rump and tail used for the fire;

the rest was stolen and eaten by us starving sinners…we never found any bad effects from eating the putrid and mortified rump and tail. On the evening of the 8th December, the swell was very heavy; every moment we were expecting the ice to come right through her…I am confident that not a man of us would have lived four hours upon the ice that night; it was a dismal night.

Conditions did not improve, even with the shooting of some foxes and two polar bears. Because of their hunger the men ate the poisonous liver of the bears and were subsequently very ill. However, as the winter advanced the ice was drifting south and slowly took the ship towards the ice edge. The master of another ship, *Grenville Bay*, calculated that the ships were drifting 'down the straits about eight miles a day'.[2]

News of the freezing in of eleven whaling ships was brought back to Hull by the Whitehaven-built *Alfred*. Before long the fate of the ships was being reported in newspapers across the country.[3] In Hull, the *Hull Packet* urged that as 'it was never contemplated that (the vessels) would have to winter in the Straits, their necessities will be great before the breaking up of the winter', so 'the earlier the relief is attempted the better, and we think the voice of the public is with us'. Colonel Thompson, MP for Hull, endorsed this view in a letter to the Admiralty, and urged action as the rescue of the whalers 'was a much juster measure of national energy than any race, however honourable, for planting the first standard upon the ices of the pole'.[4] The more radical *Hull Advertiser*, reacting to what some saw as the ship owners' greater concern at the potential loss of their property (the ships were valued at £59,000 and the oil and whalebone at about £13,500), than in the fate of more than 600 crew members trapped in the ice, took a more strident approach, referring to the 'lukewarmness' of the maritime community's response, and making it clear that it had little confidence that the Admiralty would support the private interests of the Hull ship owners.[5] The paper urged that the ship owners should marshal local expertise to find more effective means to 'relieve the seamen who…are doomed to endure hunger and hardship for several months amid the gloomy rigours of the extreme North'.[6]

The following week the more moderate *Hull Packet* responded to its rival's call for action:

We regret that an attempt has been made to give a party colouring to the exertions made in behalf of the crews of those vessels, by our radical contemporary the *Advertiser*, by insinuating that there has been a want of sympathy in certain classes, with the unfortunate men in question; nothing can be further from the truth.

In order to prove its point the paper went on to print the texts of the two 'Memorials' sent by the town to the Admiralty as evidence of the action being taken in the community.[7]

The first Memorial asked for assistance from the Admiralty to take the form of 'two vessels, with a supply of provisions, coals, and other necessaries, to enable the crews of the detained vessels to remain with their ships'.[8] As nothing was said about the rescue of the ships' companies, the *Hull Advertiser* saw this as another indication that the owners were more interested in the ships than the welfare of their crews. The Admiralty stalled. 'My Lords....do not think it is possible, from the advanced period of the season, to afford them the assistance required'. Consequently a second Memorial was sent on 11 December. Both Memorials were endorsed by one of Hull's most respected whaling masters, Captain Humphreys, who two years earlier had been commander of the whale ship that had rescued Captain John Ross and Commander James Clark Ross from the North West Passage, and who in 1844 was to become the master of *Abram*.

A few days later the Mayor of Hull, perhaps stung by the 'lukewarmness' criticism, called a public meeting at which the Mayor commented, to loud applause, on how pleased he was to see 'gentlemen of all classes... Christians of every denomination...men professing every grade of the political creed' meeting together and 'laying aside differences' to devise 'means whereby we may come to the rescue of our fellow creatures'. A subscription quickly raised over £5,000. Petitions from across the country reached the Admiralty, which was forced to reconsider its position. Sir John Barrow, Second Secretary at the Admiralty, sanctioned the creation of a relief expedition, although he required that much of its cost had to be met by the local community. It was to be the responsibility of the owners and underwriters to fit out a ship and provide a crew, while the Admiralty would restrict itself to paying the wages and providing the equipment and stores. By mid-January 1836, James Clark Ross, the celebrated polar explorer, had offered his services as commander of the expedition, and had selected *Cove* as the most suitable ship available in the port of Hull. Several hundred men, placed under the authority of Captain Humphreys, fitted her out with stores and provisions shipped from Deptford and Woolwich Dockyards. Within a fortnight the ship sailed with Humphreys as master, and a crew made up of Arctic veterans and whalers. *Cove* was to be followed by two other ships, *Erebus* and *Terror*.

By the time Ross left Hull he already knew that two of the trapped ships had returned, and a few days later he received news that two more had reached Britain. One of them, *Grenville Bay*, brought news of *Abram*. The master, Captain Taylor, said that she had last been seen in latitude 62°N and that he thought that at that time she had 150 men on board, three times her original crew, although he believed (correctly) that she had obtained a share of the provisions of *Dordon* which had been lost. He suggested that *Abram* could soon be freed from the ice although he could not say when.

The situation seemed to be becoming less serious by the time Ross reached Stromness in Orkney, and the equipping of *Erebus* and *Terror* was put on hold. *Cove* left Stromness on 11 January, but by 28 January had been so damaged in a series of storms that she had to return for repairs. On 30 January, *Abram*, which had drifted from Davis Strait into and out of Hudson Strait, was released from the ice at latitude 54°N and longitude 54°W (Figure 8.2). She had on board 98 hands which included some of the crews of *Mary Frances*, *Dordon* and *William Lee*.[9]

8.2. The approximate route of the drift of *Abram* in the ice, 1835–36.

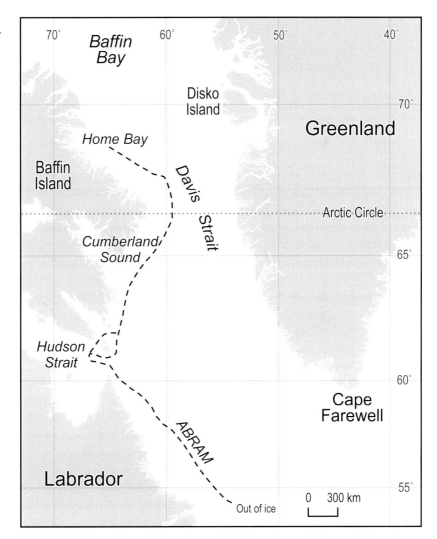

Using what strength they had left, the crew of *Abram* sailed the ship to Lerwick, which was reached on 9 February and where the Shetlanders disembarked, and then on to Hull (15 February) where Dunn recorded that 'thousands cheered us and welcomed us, as it were from the dead. May the Lord in heaven make us truly thankful for our great deliverance.'[10] The *Hull Advertiser* described the homecoming rather more vividly.

> Her arrival was greeted by thousands who lined the piers and quays;...
> – pleasure beamed on every countenance; the various vessels in the
> dock had hoisted their colours; the bells of the churches sent forth a
> merry peal; the sun shone brightly on all – the whole town seemed
> to rejoice that so many brave fellows were rescued from that dreadful
> death which it was feared had befallen them. Not the least pleasing
> and affecting part of the whole was the meeting between relatives
> and friends; many a rough hand was raised to wipe away the tear
> from the weather beaten cheek. Cordial greetings were everywhere
> passing around, and dozens of little knots were formed where the
> sailors – objects of great interest for the time – were rapidly telling
> the adventures in which they had participated. It is a matter of
> thankfulness that, under all the privations to which the crews have
> been exposed, only two that we are aware of – a Shetlander in the
> Dordon and the cook of the Abram – have perished, and both, it
> would appear, from constitutional consumptiveness.[11]

The fact that despite all the difficulties faced by the ship's company only one man died, reflects well on the leadership of the master John Hibbs, and on the skills of the surgeon W.J. Johnson. It is ironic that the cook, George Ward, having survived the worst of the winter, died two days after the vessel had become free of ice and started on her return journey.[12]

Abram's return was newsworthy enough for local newspapers with no significant whaling interests amongst their readers, such as the *Westmorland Gazette*, to run the story.[13] After all the difficulties, *Abram* returned with what little remained of the produce of the two whales – eight tons of train oil and one ton of whale fins.[14] The 1835 whaling season was a financial disaster for the ship owners of Hull.

Ross learnt of the return of *Abram* while still in Stromness. Two more of the ice-bound ships arrived at Stromness in a pitiable state, leaving only two ships unaccounted for. One of these returned in May, leaving only *William Torr* to be located by Ross. No evidence of her fate had been found at the time of Ross's return to Britain in August 1836. During that summer some flotsam from the ship was found by whalers, but an explanation of what had happened was not forthcoming until 1840 when Captain Harrison of *Norfolk* discovered from local Inuit that she had been crushed by the ice off Cape Fry in December 1835. Twenty two sick crew members had been left to be looked after by the Inuit but all had died despite their efforts. A second party of fitter men, led by her master, Captain Smith, had set off across the ice in search of rescue, but was never heard of again.

Table 8.1: Muster Roll for *Abram*, 1835–1836.[15]

Note: the document is damaged and some entries cannot be read.

Names	In what capacity engaged	Place of birth

Hull crew: date of entry 24 March 1835; discharged at Hull 15 Feb. 1836.

Names	In what capacity engaged	Place of birth
John Hibbs	Master	Hull
Robert Nicholson	Mate	Hull
W.J. Johnson	Surgeon	Peterborough
Leonard Conyers	Harpooner	Hull
William Cawcutt	Harpooner	Hull
Emanuel Wells	Harpooner	Hull
John Burgess	Harpooner	Hull
Charles Thomlinson	Harpooner	Hull
George Simpson	Carpenter	Whitby
William Haggitt	Cooper	Hull
John Todd	Sailmaker	Hull
William Lankester	Seaman	Hull
John Brown	Cooper's mate	Hull
Alexander Dunn	Seaman	Hull
John Anderson	Seaman	Stockton upon Tyne
William Marshall	Seaman	Gainsborough
……. Bowmaker	Seaman	North Shields
George Stephenson	Seaman	Cullercoats
Edward Frost	Seaman	Hull
William Ellison	Seaman	Hull
John Brookes	Seaman	Hull
Matthew Bryan	Seaman	Hull
Robert Meggett	Ordinary Seaman	Hull
William Lusby	Carpenter's mate	Hull
George Ward[1]	Seaman	York
William Weatheral	Seaman	Boston
George Simpson	Apprentice	Hull
Robert Dickson	Apprentice	Hull
John Lee[2]	Apprentice	Hull

Shetland crew: date of entry 1 April 1835; discharged at Lerwick 9 Feb. 1836.

Names	In what capacity engaged	Place of birth
……. Christie		
……. …….		
……. Halcrow	*On the Hull muster roll the*	
……. Akister	*Shetland crew were listed by*	
……. Christie	*name with no further details.*	
……. Sinclair		
……. Anderson		
……. Cowper		

Names	In what capacity engaged	Place of birth
……. Sinclair		
……. …….		
……. Anderson		
……. Leask		
Andrew Scollay		
Andrew Smith		
Oliver Clarke		
Malcolm Anderson		
Simon Smith		
Thomas Tullock		
James Ollerson		

[1] 'Died at sea – natural causes' 2 Feb.1836.
[2] 'Run at Shetland' 4 April 1835.

References

[1]   *The Criterion*, 10, 17 and 24 April 1875.

[2]   Quoted in Barrow, *The Whaling Trade of North-East England*, p. 98.

[3]   For example, *Westmorland Gazette,* 19 Dec. 1835.

[4]   *Hull Packet*, 4 Dec. 1835.

[5]   See for example the reports in *Caledonian Mercury* 4 Dec. 1835, *Liverpool Mercury* 4 Dec. 1835 and *Hull Advertiser* 4 Dec. 1835 which quoted the previous papers.

[6]   *Hull Advertiser*, 4 Dec. 1835.

[7]   *Hull Packet*, 11 Dec. 1835.

[8]   *Hull Advertiser*, 4 Dec. 1835.

[9]   *Nautical Magazine*, vol. 5 March 1836; *The Times*, 17 Feb. 1836.

[10]   Alexander Dunn's account of the 1835–36 voyage is supplemented by A. Cooke and W. Gillies Ross, 'The drift of the whaler *Viewforth* in Davis Strait, 1835–36, from William Elder's Journal', *Polar Record*, 92, 1969, pp. 581–91.

[11]   *Hull Advertiser*, 19 Feb. 1836.

[12]   Hull History Centre, C DSTR/53/113.

[13]   *Westmorland Gazette*, 20 Feb. 1836. *Lancaster Gazette* also ran two short reports on 20 and 27 Feb. 1836. In the former *Abram* was described as returning to the Humber via an Irish port where some crew were disembarked.

[14]   *Hull Packet*, 26 Feb. 1836.

[15]   Hull History Centre, C DSTR/53/113.

CHAPTER 9

Life on board *Abram*: the journal of Thomas Phillips, surgeon, in 1839

'A journal kept during a voyage to Baffin Bay in the ship *Abram* of Hull in search of whales: commencing on the 11th day of March' provides a vivid account of the 1839 whaling season.[1] After the poor season (and over-wintering) in 1835 the Hull fleet, including *Abram*, continued to struggle financially during the seasons of 1836 and 1837, and during the 1840s business was so bad that whaling was almost abandoned at the port, and *Abram* herself was laid up for a number of years. The successes of 1838 and 1839 stand out in marked contrast, so it is particularly fortunate that the journal gives us an account of the last good season *Abram* enjoyed while on the Hull register.

The journal was kept by Thomas Phillips, whose signature appears at the end. Phillips was the 23-year-old surgeon on board *Abram*, but, unlike many surgeons who signed on for a single season, he made a number of voyages. He had previously sailed to the Arctic on *Swan*, and in 1840 he was once again surgeon on *Abram*. Phillips was well educated and may have taken books of poetry on the voyage, and his learning is obvious from the style and contents of his journal.[2]

From 1733 the British Parliament had required whaleships to carry a surgeon as a condition of claiming the bounty. Beyond their medical role they had no real work to do. For much of the time the on-board life of a surgeon in the Northern Whale Fishery was probably little different from that described by Dr John Wilson while whaling in the South Seas between 1839 and 1843, 'No one can conceive the dreary monotony & utter solitude of a South Seaman's life & particularly that of the Doctor, who has no routine of duty, no fixed or regular employment to divert his mind'.[3] For a ship's master, the surgeon was an extra mouth to feed. Consequently they were often found other roles, and given that they were often the most educated member of the ship's company, this was sometimes the job of ship's clerk and purser. In 1880 Arthur Conan Doyle, surgeon on *Hope* of Peterhead, found himself the confidante of the master, as he was the only other person on board who had the education to converse and debate with

Date	Winds	Remarks &c on board May.
Sunday 19th May.	N E ... ... E	animals skin & his unfavourable position the harpoon would not enter higher than the withers. The Captain & myself fired two balls at him at a distance of a few feet one into his body and the other at his head but they seemed not to make the least impression on him & during the time the Mate was thrusting at his breast with the harpoon the monster erected his head as high as the mates and keeping his front constantly exposed to the enemy he gradually receded & dropped off the ice as slow and as apparently unconcerned as possible we never saw anything more of him but believe that he had not power remaining to regain the surface & consequently "duck down" a circumstance often noticed when mortally wounded & entangled by an harpoon
Monday 19th	E N E	Light breezes & tolerably clear weather Ship reaching towards the Land 3 P M saw a great number of gulls hovering near the surface of the water which was very greasy put the helm hard a weather and run towards the spot when we found the cause of it to be a great wounded walrus not far of kicking the bucket but possessing sufficient life so as to enable him to avoid the harpoon of the Eliza Swan's boat which tried for some time to hook him to no purpose. no doubt it is the same Walrus

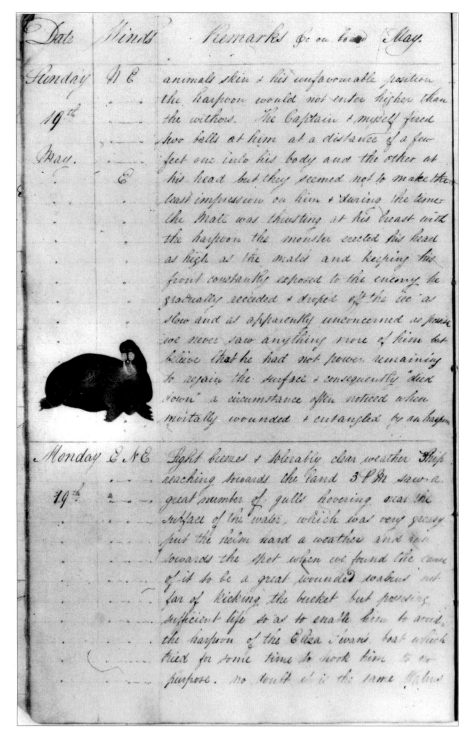

Fig 9.1. Two pages from the Journal of Thomas Phillips, surgeon on *Abram*, 1839: Archives of Manitoba, MG11 A7 MB. (Reproduced by courtesy of Archives of Manitoba.)

Date.	Wind	Remarks. on board August 1839
Sunday 4th	S.W.	Strong breezes & thick hazy weather, running northward with all possible sail set. 8 P.M. saw 2 whales & sent 2 boats away in pursuit hauled ship to & in studding sails 8.15 James Denton fastened to one of the fish 9 got 4 harpoons in 1 got her dead alongside and commenced flinching. 6 A.M. got done cleared away the decks and set the watch length of whalebone 11f.3in. supposed weight of Blubber 17 ton. Thick weather & nearly calm during the remainder of the day. the Truelove (Bark) of Hull in company.
Monday 5th	North	Light winds and calms throughout the 24 hours. 4 P.M. saw a whale and sent away 2 boats. The Truelove of Hull dodging the same fish 5 called all hands & manned the remaining boats in ¼ of an hour after 2nd Wells chief mate struck socket up into the said whale 8 P.M. killed her with four harpoons & got her alongside and began to flinch. 11 P.M. got done. decks cleared and watch set. Length of Bone as p. Margin. Supposed weight of Blubber 15 ton Fine clear and warm weather during the remainder of the day ship reaching in shore the watch employed in making preparations for 'making off'
Tuesday 6th	N.E. Calm	Light winds with thick hazy weather 6 H.M. called all hands & commenced making off the Truelove. Advice & 1 Other Ship in sight

the master as an equal.[4] Many surgeons turned to writing a journal as a way of passing the time, and as a means of recording all they witnessed. Their interests ranged widely, from wildlife to whale hunting, and from the people they encountered to marine and atmospheric phenomena. Only rarely did they record their medical duties.

When writing the journal Phillips would not only have his own previous experience to draw upon, but also what he had learnt from sailors with much more experience than him. He would no doubt have been aware of the many artefacts and models made by these sailors or acquired from the Greenlanders and the Inuit of Baffin Island, some of which were on display in Hull from time to time (Figure 9.2).

9.2. Nineteenth-century model of a whale boat showing the arrangement of whale lines coiled by the line-manager. (Reproduced by courtesy of Hull Maritime Museum: Hull Museums.)

We know he had read Leslie, Jameson and Murray's *Narrative of Discovery and Adventure in the Polar Seas and Regions*,[5] with its chapter on the history of whaling and its lengthy descriptions of the whale ships and the process of catching and flensing whales. He may also have read the accounts of whaling written by the best-known early nineteenth-century whaler, William Scoresby junior.[6] Scoresby's interest in so many aspects of the Arctic environment and people, in part inspired by the development of scientific observation and classification during the eighteenth century, may have influenced Phillips. His subject matter, like that of Scoresby, ranged across meteorology, the natural world, the environment, mapping, people and archaeology. In addition there had been much publicity surrounding the voyages of explorers who had been seeking a North-West Passage since 1818, and versions of some of their journals had appeared in book form, often accompanied by vivid illustrations created by, or based on, the works of the amateur artists amongst the officers. Phillips may also have had the opportunity to visit the Arctic panoramas displayed in Hull in 1836. One depicted 'the voyages of Sir John Ross painted on 2330 square feet of Canvas, displaying where he passed four successive winters', and the other a scene of the Hull whalers of 1835–36 icebound in the Arctic, an event which had involved the ship on which Phillips was travelling.[7] He probably saw the kayak brought back from Greenland by Captain Andrew Barker in 1613, and displayed at Trinity House in Hull. Phillips would have absorbed all this information through a range of filters resulting from his own experiences and personality. His journal is, therefore, a nuanced account of one man's experiences and observations on a single voyage. It is a valuable record, and it is the only original account surviving of one of *Abram*'s voyages.

From Hull to the Arctic

William Couldrey, aged 40, was appointed master, and the ship's company of 27 men was engaged on Monday 11 March 1839, and spent the morning of the following day 'employed in getting their chests etc. on board'. The pilot was taken on that afternoon, and no doubt with the usual throng of families and well-wishers on the quayside, the ship left the quay on the River Hull and entered the Humber on 13 March. Navigating the river was a slow process and it was not until Friday 15 March that *Abram* 'proceeded out of the Humber…discharged the pilot' and passed 'Flambro Head light' and headed north.

Seven days later, *Abram* sailed into Lerwick harbour. She was by no means the first of the season's whalers to anchor, as there were already five other ships in the port, and during the four days she was there a number of others arrived and some departed. She arrived in the middle of 'the Greenland time'. Thomas Phillips does not say much about the time spent at Lerwick, beyond reporting that the 'men [were] employed in sundry work under the boatswain', and that there were 'snow showers'. However other journals are more revealing of events that took place during 'the Greenland time'. Some time later another surgeon, Alexander Trotter, on *Enterprise* of Fraserburgh, wrote a vivid account of time spent in Lerwick in 1856. By chance he refers to *Abram*, by this time no longer sailing from Hull but registered at the port of Kirkcaldy.

Enterprise was anchored at Lerwick from 9 February to 4 March 1856. Trotter described the town with 'its beautifully commodious harbour'. He estimated the town as of 'perhaps 500 houses such as they are'. He was most taken with 'the curious character of the streets…simply lanes… about a yard and a half wide, with only one exception, namely what is called Commercial 'Street', in which are nearly all the shops and places of business. It is certainly a street although a very irregular one, at one place 10 yards wide, and at another only 2, but throughout its whole extent remarkably dirty… As for the houses they are all hereaway, thereaway: some have their broadsides to the street; some have their gables to the street; some unmannerly ones have fairly turned their back to the street…I could not have believed such an outlandish place was in existence.'

On the evening of Wednesday 20 February 1856 Trotter recorded in his journal that 'a bagpiper and second mate from the *Abram* barque of Kirkcaldy…..came on board our ship on their way to Lerwick in order to astonish the inhabitants'. Trotter agreed to join them and become their bodyguard. This trio clearly made quite an impact because 'we got three cheers from the hundreds of folk at our heels, for almost all Lerwick was out to see what was the matter'. Perhaps inevitably the evening ended with the piper in a bar, and Trotter making his own way back to his ship.

He also had a lot to say about a Saturday night in Lerwick. 'There was a great many people apparently respectable enough walking about. But for my part I would not give much for their respectability especially the female part of them. Indeed to tell the truth in Lerwick it is said to be impossible to tell what woman is decent and what one is respectable'. Later he had even less flattering thoughts about the men. 'I am told that [when] the Shetland men come home [from the whaling] they live on their money setting their wives and daughters to cultivate their little bit of land: their own lazy lordships standing giving orders with their hands in their pockets.' He noted that as the sailors came into Lerwick to sign on for the whaling season, 'you may see sailors and their wives coming into the town, the wives almost invariably carrying the husbands' trunks and boxes slung on their backs: his supreme highness walking alongside quietly smoking his pipe or it may be riding on a pony to keep him from the trouble of travelling and perhaps hurting his very delicate and valuable feet.'[8]

Rather surprisingly, Phillips's journal of 1839 makes no mention of the signing on of a Shetland crew, but we do know that the Hull company were supplemented by 20 men from Shetland (Table 9.2). The ship's company consisted of the following:

Table 9.1: The voyage of *Abram*, 11 March 1839 – 21 October 1839.

Master	1
Mate	1 (mate and harpooner)
2nd Mate	1 (2nd mate and harpooner)
Boatswain	1 (boatswain and harpooner)
Surgeon	1
Spectioneer	1 (spectioneer and harpooner)
Boatsteerer	5
Line Manager	*
Loose Harpooner (a harpooner on trial)	1
Carpenter	2
Cooper	2
Sailmaker	1
Steward	1

Skeeman	1 (skeeman and harpooner)
Cook	1
Seaman/Ordinary Seaman	26

* There would have been five line managers but unusually they have not been identified on the crew list.

Lerwick provided the last opportunity to collect and stow stores for the rest of the whaling season and to carry out repairs to the ship, so the crew were no doubt engaged in these activities.

On Monday 25 March 'work end[ed] at noon', providing the crew with 12 hours ashore before the commencement of 'nautical time' and the beginning of the voyage to Davis Strait. *Abram* departed from Lerwick on the following day, initially sailing south and 'rounded Sumbro Head and shaped our course across the Atlantic'. Crossing the North Atlantic was not straightforward. On 30 March there was 'a stiff gale' and on 6 April a 'strong gale with a very heavy sea'. However, 6 April ended with 'midnight calm, the *Hecla* (of Kirkcaldy) about 8 miles distant'. It was obvious that *Abram* was entering Arctic waters on 7 April when she 'passed several icebergs' off Cape Farewell, and on 10 April she reached the pack ice off the south-west coast of Greenland: 'a strong gale to the end of this day the ship plying along the Pack edge under double reefed topsails'.

The weather was variable, even within a 24 hour period. On Thursday 11 April the 'day commenced with strong gales and cloudy weather; the Ship reaching along the Pack edge. Middle part more moderate…the day ending with fine weather and nearly calm. The crew actively employed in preparations for the fishery'. This was known as 'spanning on', and the first tasks were to post a look-out at the top of the mast to keep an eye on the ice conditions, and to make the whale boats ready. On 12 April 'the crew employed in coiling the Quarter boats lines etc.'. This involved the careful coiling of up to one and a half kilometres of rope which would be attached to the harpoon, and had to be paid out smoothly as the injured whale would initially dive to a great depth, before resurfacing exhausted. At the same time the harpoons and lances would have been sharpened and stowed ready for the chase. When this work was completed 'the crew assembled on the afterdeck where a glass of grog was poured out and a toast loudly proclaimed to the success of the hunt'.[10]

Sailing conditions were not easy. On 18 April the ship was 'running among streams of loose ice', and on 23 April there were 'strong gales with showers of snow the whole of these 24 hours, the Ship plying along the Pack edge'. On 27 April a whale was sighted: '3pm saw a whale on the lee bow lowered away 2 boats immediately. 4pm the ice closing obliged us to take the boats up'. As the pack ice is always on the move, lowering and using the small boats was always hazardous. The journal makes it clear that most whale sightings did not lead to a successful kill.

Abram was now north of the Arctic Circle and ice conditions were becoming more difficult. On 28 April the crew had to act quickly to save the rudder: '2pm made the ship fast to a floe. 6pm the ice closing fast, unship'd our rudder to preserve it from receiving any damage'; and on the following day when within sight of the Whalefish Islands, the ice had become so solid that the men had to get out onto the ice floes and were 'actively employed in warping and heaving the ship through the ice'.

By 1 May the ship was lying to the south of Disco Island. May Day provided an excuse for an initiation ceremony involving those on board who were participating in their first season in the Arctic. Phillips was not a first-timer, and unfortunately his journal says little about the day's activities: 'Our garland was hoisted this morning with the usual ceremonies peculiar to ships in crossing the equator, 9 novices chins and faces having suffered under the delicate hand of Neptune's barber'.[11] Other sources tell us that the garland would have been 'fancifully decorated with ribbons, presents by sweethearts and friends before sailing' and was placed midway on the main mast and remained there until the voyage was over. Neptune's barber was no doubt equipped with 'a formidable razor, made out of a piece of iron hooping. The blade was eighteen inches long, with huge gaps in the edge. The poor innocent was then lathered with coal tar, and his hair powdered with crushed chalk and resin, well rubbed in.'[12]

From this point on the journal becomes more detailed. Fortunately, Phillips not only reported on the weather, sailing conditions and whale hunting, but also on other crew activities such as foraging to supplement their diet, meeting the local 'esquimaux', the comings and goings of other ships, and curiosities of general interest. On one occasion he reported that he 'saw the Graves of some Europeans ashore, poor seamen! Their bones bleached white by the climate. Many a cold blast has whistled over their Grave – a serious subject for reflection'. On another he reported on the Arctic postal service of the day: 'On returning from Lievely received a parcel from Hull which had arrived by the *Swan* Capt. Dring who sailed three weeks after us'. Unfortunately we are not told what was in the parcel!

Sailing in high Arctic waters

Abram, in company with the rest of the whaling fleet, was destined for waters even further north. As they sailed north the temperature became colder, and 1839 seems to have been a particularly cold year, in a cold decade. Even as early as 13 May, at 58° 30'N the thermometer read 'average 44°'.[13] Heavy ice meant that on many occasions it was necessary, as at 1.30pm on 2 June, to call 'all hands to track and warp ship along the land ice'; and on 10 June 'called all hands to tow ship'. On 14 June 'the men employed in sawing a passage for the ship through a large field of ice', and on 5 July '6.30pm seeing danger of loosing [sic] the ship the ice closing very fast called all hands and sawed a dock in the ice for her safety'.

While anchored at Upernavik on 18 June, the opportunity was taken to check out the sea conditions to the north: '9am went on top of the island about 300 feet high to get a good look to the northward which did not present a good appearance there being very little water'. Upernavik was the last Danish settlement where a stop could be made to collect mail, learn about ice conditions, meet up with the crews of other whalers, and 'fraternise' with the Greenlanders. By 26 June Phillips recorded that they had reached 73° 35'N, 'the highest latitude attained by the whalers in 1835 and the prospect this year of getting round the ice to the northward is equally or nearly as bad. Nothing but a continuance of Northerly winds, and that soon will be of any service to us in attempting the Northern Passage to the N West Coast of America where the great object of our voyage lies at present in undisturbed security'.[14]

On the 29 June, when at 74° N, the journal records: 'very cold for this season of the year the thermometer averaging only 32°…being the coldest summer that some of the older hands ever felt'. By 2 July the temperature had fallen still further, 'at noon this day being as low as 28°'. Such low temperatures were not good news for the whalers as 'exceedingly cold weather for this time of year evidently proving that the straits to be full of ice'. Virtually no progress had been made for many days and it now seemed as though there would be no opportunity for the fleet to reach the North Water and be able to access the fishing grounds around northern Baffin Island. In their joint predicament it seems that by 6 July much of the fleet was anchored within sight of each other '24 sail lying at anchor at different bergs with in a small distance of each other'.

The work was often very hard. A 24-hour period in late June is typical:

Saturday 22 June. Light winds and hazy weather. 3pm cast off from the berg. 4 called all hands and tried to heave ship through several barriers of ice. 7pm a large field of ice set down on a berg to leeward and closed the passage. Made the vessel fast to the floe and set the watch. 10pm the ice opening astern. Cast off and run back to the same berg from which we sailed and anchored ship at 12pm and went on a small island about a mile from the ship and got a lot of Eider ducks eggs. [Sunday] 8am cast off again from the berg and reached north, a boat and crew having been on the top of Berry's island. Saw three ships to the southward and suppose the nearest to be the *Bon Accord* of Aberdeen about 15 or 20 miles distant. 9.20am called all hands and warped ship among large floes during the remainder of the day.

The weather during July remained variable. On 14 July 'thermometer rising as high as 50° in the shade', but within 24 hours there were 'heavy gales with Hail and snow showers, the ship made fast to a floe unable to proceed …in any direction'. On 21 July the fleet abandoned its attempt to reach the North Water. Once this decision had been made the weather seemed to improve and the tension on board lessened. On the following day Phillips once again has time to remark on the beauty of the Arctic seascape. 'Light airy winds with beautiful weather with a great deal of refraction on the Icebergs at the verge of the Horizon assuming a thousand fantastic forms'. However, a beautiful scene could in a moment become one of considerable danger. At 3pm on the same day 'while in the act of passing to windward of a large ice berg the current swept the ship alongside, but fortunately she weathered it, but that close that the men were enable to bear off with their hands out of the boats. A foot farther to leeward would have entirely swept away the whole of the boats on that side'. On 23 July the temperature reached '58° in the shade, causing the ice bergs to crack with an awful noise like thunder'.

By 30 July *Abram* was once again far enough south to be 'reaching to the westward in search of a passage through the ice to the West land or American side of the Straits. 14 sail in company'. At 2pm on 1 August 'the N W coast of America hove in sight about 60 miles distant'. By the following day Cape Searle on Baffin Island was only 15 miles distant, but the ice was heavy and the ship 'received some tremendous blows fore and aft; damage sustained not known'. The remainder of the season was spent on the central Baffin Island coast. This region had only become a popular whaling ground after John Ross's voyage in 1818, and the maps available to the crew of *Abram* dated from that time. It was not difficult to find inaccuracies, such as those noted in the journal on 29 August. 'Went on shore on what is supposed to be the mainland, but after walking several miles into the interior found it to be an island and one of very many situated between Cape Searle and the Main, yet the Cape is set down on Parry and Ross's chart as a continent!'. The crews of the whalers, such as *Abram,* played an important part in improving the mapping of these waters and coasts.

Hunting whales, walruses and seals

Initially *Abram* had little success in her hunting. The first sighting was on 5 May: '7pm saw a whale and sent away 2 boats in pursuit. 10pm took the boats up'. On 8 May, while about eight miles west of Disco Island off the coast of Greenland: '9pm saw a whale in the pack headed towards the ship. Sent away two boats when shortly afterwards William Wells got fast and soon after got a second harpoon in. 3am unfortunately lost her by both the harpoons breaking after lancing her severely and being fast for 5 hours. 5am took the boats up and set the watch, the sun during the night being only 5 hours below the horizon'. On 12 May the crew 'at 9pm observed *Truelove* of Hull in the ice about 8 miles distant towing a dead whale alongside, and believe it to be the same fish we lost on the 8th. A very mortifying thing after having such trouble, for another ship to get the prize; a very heavy fish and would be worth £700'. Although the whalers were often in sight of each other, it was each ship to herself when it came to hunting. This could lead to disagreements. On 8 September 'James Denton (harpr) would have been fast to a whale but was prevented by the shameful conduct of the Pr of Orange's boats'. Phillips does not tell us exactly what had happened. However, whale hunting could also lead to comradeship. On 15 May *Abram* had come to the help of *Neptune*: '11am made the ship fast astern of the Neptune of Aberdeen, and let him have 2 whale lines, he having lost 17 lines attached by the Harpoon to a whale on Sunday last, a length of 12,240 feet or more than 2 miles and 1 quarter'.

It was not until the week of the 4 August, on the east coast of Baffin Island, that *Abram* was successful in her whale hunting (Figure 9.1). Suddenly whales were everywhere. One was caught on the 4th, another on the 5th, and yet another on the 7th. One was left to escape on the 8th because the crew were too busy flensing (or flinching) the earlier catches, but another was caught on the 10th and yet another on the 11th. The journal entries for Saturday 10th and Sunday 11th give a vivid impression of the activity in the fleet when times were good, despite the author appearing, perhaps unsurprisingly, to become rather muddled about the sequence of events.

Saturday 10th August
Light breezes and fine clear weather. Saw the *Advice* harpoon and kill a whale. Two boats in pursuit of a fish ahead. 2pm saw two more whales on the starboard bow, called all hands and sent away 6 boats. 6pm the boats returned having been unsuccessful owing to the whales running fast to the northwards. 10pm made the ship fast to a floe piece, 2 of our boats in pursuit of a whale. 7am Thomas Mills, Harpooner, struck a fish and got her killed in 2 hours. Thick hazy weather at the same time, could not see either boats or whale, but heard the crews cheering when she died. 11pm got her alongside and began to flense. Several whales on [illegible] and 2 boats on beam to the end of the day.

Sunday 11th August
Light winds and clear weather. All hands employed in flensing. 4pm several fish being on [illegible], knocked off flensing and sent away all the boats. A great number of whales in sight but very unsettled. 5pm after several starts, J Soughberry got fast. Cast the ship off from the floe and plyed towards the fast boat. 11pm got the fish dead alongside and commenced flinching. 4pm got done. The decks cleared and watch set. Length of Whalebone 10 ft, supposed weight of oil 12 ton.

Other sources of oil were seals and walruses, the latter having the additional benefit of providing ivory from their tusks. On 16 May 'at 11am saw two walruses asleep on a piece of ice', and one was harpooned. Two days later William Wells was out in a boat 'after seals'. However, hunting walruses was almost more difficult than hunting whales. The following day another walrus was spotted. Initially 'the harpoon would not enter higher than the withers. The captain and myself fired two balls at him at a distance of a few feet one into his body and the other at his head but they seemed not to make the least impression on him and during the time the Mate was thrusting at his breast with the harpoon the monster erected his head as high as the mates and keeping his front constantly exposed to the enemy he gradually receded and dropped off the ice as slow and as apparently unconcerned as possible. We never saw anything more of him but believe that he had not power remaining to repair the surface and consequently "died down"'.

There were weeks of frenetic activity, and others during which nothing happened. Obviously the crew were very busy during early August when they successfully caught so many whales. Earlier in the season they were at times equally busy, but with much less success. For example on the week beginning 12 May the whale boats were launched on 12 May and 14 May on sightings of whales, on 16 May to kill a walrus, and on 18 May to hunt seals. In contrast the boats do not seem to have been launched at all during the following week.

Re-supplying the ship

Opportunities needed to be found to replenish the barrels with fresh water. In winter this would be done by chipping ice from an iceberg, but in summer it was possible to collect water from streams on the land. On Friday 24 May the captain 'made the ship fast to a berg...the crew employed in fetching water from the land and filling the ship's casks'. The crew also welcomed the opportunity to acquire fresh food after their diet of salted and preserved food. On 2 May, which was the first opportunity to tread on dry land since leaving Lerwick, some members of the crew 'went ashore on the south end of Fortune Bay only saw two Ptarmigan and killed one'. On the same day, at low tide, they also 'gathered several buckets full of fine muscles [sic]'. On 24 May 'shot 13 Ptarmigan this day'. On 10 June 'shot 2 Ptarmigan, 1 Plover and 1 Snipe' but failed to shoot five reindeer despite 'using a great deal of stratagem'. On 22 June 'went on a small island...and got a lot of Eider duck eggs'. On 21 August the crew were less successful. Despite following 'tracks of Hares, Bears and Foxes in abundance', they saw no animals.

The polar bear could provide large quantities of fresh meat as long as the poisonous liver was avoided. Its fur also had a market, as did bear cubs, if caught alive, as they could be sold to zoological gardens back in Britain. However they were not easy to hunt. At 6.00am on 18 July 'a large bear' was seen 'making his way towards the ship. At 6.15am he altered his course and steered towards the *Comet* of Hull, and when within a few yards of his boat which was at the ice edge, after firing at him with 2 guns, not a ball touched him, and the report frightened him away. He was that close to the boat that they might have put the musket into his mouth. I wish he had come towards us as he would have met with a different reception. The weather being thick and light winds, he was soon out of sight.' On 13 August the crew of *Abram* were more fortunate and shot a bear.

Meetings with the 'Esquimaux'

When *Abram* was sailing along the west coast of Greenland, she passed a succession of Danish settlements. Both Danes and 'Esquimaux' were encountered at these places. On 25 May 'several Esquimaux (came) on board from the new settlement "Noosak" together with the governor, his Esquimaux wife and 5 children'. The most northerly of these communities was Upernavik at 73° 47'N. Phillips described the town in some detail, and in particular a whaler's grave, a reminder of the dangers of their trade.

> The Danish settlement of Upernavik consisting of the Governor with wife and family, the Clergyman, 8 Danes and 319 Esquimaux. At this place was buried one of the men belonging to the John of Greenock, which was lost in 1830 (for the particulars of which see Murray's *Polar Seas and Regions*). The following is the inscription cut out on a triangular piece of Deal and faced over his grave by his unfortunate companions. "To the memory of Wm Simpson of South Shields, late seaman on board the *John* of Greenock, who died at Upernavik on the 15th of October 1830, aged 21 years". Near the same spot but enclosed with rails lie the bodies of the Clergyman's wife and 3 children who all died of scurvy.

By the 1830s the native people, both Greenlanders and the Inuit of Baffin Island expected the annual arrival of the whaling fleet. They could often provide the whalers with information about the location of the whales, about ice conditions and sometimes information about the fate of ships in previous years, and would seek to barter 'souvenirs'. In return they were often given some help with their hunting, acquired materials to which they normally had no access, and were given parts of whales which were of no use to Europeans but, to the more resourceful native people, were extremely valuable. For example on Friday 3 May, near the start of the voyage, Abram was anchored off the community of Lievely: 'several of the native Esquimaux and Danes on board with seal skins etc. 1pm walked to the settlement and entered all the huts. 7pm returned on board'. The opportunity was taken on 21 August to enquire of an Esquimaux who was on board 'as well as could be done by actions and gestures whether any Europeans or Kablunas were on the land, in hopes of getting some intelligence of the unfortunate crew of the Wm. Torr,[15] but the poor fellow seemed astonished at our actions and could make nothing out of him'. On 1 June while a group of Greenlanders were visiting *Abram*, 'one of the Esquimaux harpooned a narwhale not far from the ship, when the Neptune of Aberdeen sent a boat to his assistance and soon killed it for him; after taking the skin and blubber off for themselves the carcass formed a good feast for the dogs of which there are between 50 and 60'. While off Baffin Island on Tuesday 20 August the journal reports '6pm saw 5 Esquimaux approaching towards the ship in their canoes and shouting loud – took the first on board and made him a present of a knife and saw that he made motions for a file which was soon found for him, but that would not do until the Carpenter had fixed it in a handle. At 7pm he left the ship'. A fortnight later on 5 September again at '6pm 2 canoes and an Umiak or skin boat full of Esquimaux women, children and dogs hove in sight… they seemed highly delighted with some pieces of iron hoop which was given them and some blubber and skin of the whale which forms their chief article of food'.

At times, when anchored near to native encampments, these acts of fraternisation affected the running of the ship. When *Abram* was in the area of Upernavik, two groups of Greenlanders came on board on 11 June, another group on 12 June; on 13 June 'the Esquimaux (were) constantly going and coming from the land the whole of the day' and many seemed to have remained on board, or nearby, until 15 June when nine sledges and over 60 dogs finally left. Further groups of Greenlanders were on board on 16 June (including one who had made a 15 miles sledge journey), 17 June when 13 sledges and 100 dogs arrived bringing amongst others three infants, and again on 20 June.

The crew found the behaviour of the 'Esquimaux' both interesting and at times amusing. Similarly the Greenlanders were often amazed by the actions of the English. When *Abram* reached the settlement of Upernavik again on 26 July they 'went ashore among the Esquimaux. Several Englishmen bathing were viewed by the natives with evident signs of astonishment and delight some kept paddling round them in their canoes or kayaks while the beach was lined with young and old laughing heartily at their splashing and diving'.

Not only did the crew meet with living Greenlanders, but they also found evidence of past 'Esquimaux' cultures. On 1 July the journal records the discovery of 'an Esquimaux grave or pile of stones under which lay the bones of a female Esquimaux and those of a child about 12 months old[,] the remains of an old hut also on the island'.

Recording the unfamiliar

Most of the official log books which have survived from the whaling era focus on the task in hand, namely seamanship and the capture of whales. It is in journals, such as this one from *Abram*, that one gets a sense of the work involved in the day to day grind of sailing a vessel in difficult waters, and also of the bouts of intense activity that accompany the sighting and capture of a whale. However, the Arctic environment was so unfamiliar that the authors often commented on the unusual. Meteorological conditions were of constant interest, not least the atmospheric conditions that enabled coastlines to be seen at extraordinary distances. On 30 July the author noticed 'the highland of the island of Disco lifted up with the refraction although 90 or 100 miles distant', and even more remarkably on 29 August from the top 'of a very high mountain…saw the refracted part of the E land or Greenland side of the straits although 180 miles dist.'. The discovery of wrecks and the flotsam and jetsam of earlier whaling voyages were always of interest: '14th September. On the beach we found a boat's mast and 2 oars, 1 of them marked Clarendon. A handspike marked '*Dordon*' [lost 1835]. A blubber spade's sheath, a mitten marked W, part of a harpoon stock and various other articles evidently belonging to a ship's boat'.

The journal gives an insight into the interests, thoughts and beliefs of the more educated and articulate crew members. This is well illustrated by quoting in full the entry for 26 August where Phillips refers to meteorological conditions, ornithology, earlier whaling history, Inuit skills and the differences in missionary activity between Greenland and Baffin Island, and quotes from the English poet William Cowper.

Monday 26th August
Strong breezes and clearer weather. Malamauk Head or Cape Searl heaving within sight although not more than a mile distant, yet the constant thick and hazy weather has obscured it until now. Myriads of Fulmars hovering over this Singular Headland, while the land adjoining is covered with Ravens, Burgomasters, Snipes, and the beach covered with remains of Skeletons of whales and wreck. Part of the wreck of the *Dauntless* whaler lost on the bar in 1829, with 12 whales lies on the beach. The low land exhibiting proof of the recent habitations of Esquimaux. Numbers of Traps for foxes made by the natives, simple yet effectual, and presenting to the eye on a first appearance as a heap of stones piled carelessly together, shows how everything is ordained by Nature for the comfort and support of the inhabitants of this dreary country. How the Eternal welfare of the inhabitants of this place has been overlooked and still unnoticed by the Missionary Societies of each denomination is a wonder to me. From Hudsons Bay to Lancaster Sound a distance of 840 miles

are numerous tribes of inhabitants in a wild and savage state. How different Denmark and Germany have acted on the E coast of the straits; their missionaries are found as high as the 73° 30'N and to use the language of Cowper:

> "Fired with a zeal peculiar they defy
> The rage and rigour of a Polar Sky
> And Plant successfully sweet Sharon's ease
> On icy plains and in eternal snows".

Two whales seen this day but took the boats up without success.[16]

The end of the season and the return to Hull

By early September it became clear that winter was once again approaching. After the involuntary over-wintering that had taken place earlier in the decade, the master was determined not to be caught out again. On the night of Thursday 5 September it was 'snowing hard'. As dawn broke Phillips commented that the snow cover had caused 'the land since Monday last' to have 'entirely changed its appearance'. By 15 September it was decided that it was time to prepare for the voyage home: 'seamen and mechanics actively employed in clearing the decks and making preparations for sea intending to take our departure tomorrow and bear up for Old England'. The voyage back to Lerwick took over three weeks. On 8 October *Abram* sailed into Lerwick harbour and the author concluded his journal.

> So ends this log having run 1790 miles without seeing land and arrived at Sumburgh Head within 1 hour of the expected time!!!!!!
> Albion thou jewel of the earth
> Whose fields first fed my childish fantasy
> Whose rocks and mountains were my boyhood's wild delight.[17]

Nothing is recorded about the arrival of the Shetlanders in Lerwick, but one wonders whether their return in any way fulfilled Walter Scott's observation of the scene in 1814: 'Lerwick will suffer severely if the Fort is not occupied by some force or other; for between whisky and frolic, the Greenland sailors will certainly burn the little town'.[18] A postscript records that a fortnight later, on 20 October, *Abram* once again sailed up the Humber estuary to a berth in the Greenland Yards on the River Hull. A successful voyage such as this meant that the crew would return with enough money to allow them to remain at home until the start of the next whaling season. The ship would be repaired, cleaned and re-equipped during the winter months, ready for the next voyage in 1840. Never again, during her time at Hull, was *Abram* as successful as she was in 1839 when she caught nine whales.[19]

Table 9.2: Crew List of *Abram* 1839.[20]

Name	Age	Place of birth	In what capacity engaged	Ship in which he last served
Hull crew: date of entry 11–12 March 1839.				
William Couldrey	40	Thirsk	Master	*Mary Frances*
Thomas Phillips	23	Chepstow	Surgeon	*Swan*
Emmanuel Wells	38	Hull	Mate + harpooner	*Rosetta*
Thomas Briggs	35	Hull	2nd Mate + harpooner	*Coatham*
Thomas Mills	36	Grimsby	Boatswain + harpooner	*Planter*
James Denton	42	Shields	Specktioner + harpooner	*Gem*
John Loughborough	25	Hull	Skeyman + harpooner	*Abram*
William Wells	24	York	Loose harpooner	*Volunteer*
Marshall Batty	34	Sunk Isle	Carpenter	*Comet*
William Halcrow	23	Hull	Cooper	*Swan*
Henry Bowen	25	Hull	Carpenter's mate	*Abram*
David Brown	29	Hull	Cooper's mate	*Abram*
Samuel Armitage	29	Hull	Boatsteerer	*Comet*
David Thompson	21	Dundee	Boatsteerer	*Tearne*
John Graham	28	Hull	Boatsteerer	*Consort*
William Elliotson	31	Hampton	Boatsteerer	*Andrew Marvel*
William Courtnay	27	Hull	Sailmaker	*Brunswick*
Thomas Bourne	24	Hull	Boatsteerer	*Zephyr*
Charles Lancaster	24	Grimsby	Seaman	*Chase*
Robert Park[1]	55	Hull	Cook	*Abram*
William Darrill	26	Louth	Ordy seaman	Landsman (first voyage)
John Homan	33	Hull	Seaman	*Sisters*
William Birch	19	Hull	Ordy seaman	*Shamrock*
Christopher Hicks	23	Hull	Seaman	*Latona*
William Denton	22	Hull	Seaman	*Duncombe*
John Smith	29	Hull	Seaman	*Bravo*
William Wetherill	29	Spalding	Steward	*Abram*
Thomas Roberts	18	Hull	Seaman	*Abram*
John Taylor	48	London	Cook	*Shamrock*
Shetland crew: date of entry (Lerwick) 22 March 1839.				
Lawrence Malcolmson	33	Sound, Shetland	Seaman	*Sisters*
John Georgeon	37	Sandness, Shetland	Seaman	*Hecla*
Andrew Johnson	37	Sandsting, Shetland	Seaman	*Hecla*
David Robertson	37	Nesting, Shetland	Seaman	*Abram*
William Sinclair	27	Unst, Shetland	Seaman	*Abram*
Senelais Thompson	27	Sandness, Shetland	Seaman	*Riby Grove*
Arthur Johnson	34	Sound, Shetland	Seaman	*Resolution*
Thomas Manson	22	Yell, Shetland	Seaman	*Alfred*
Simon Smith	30	Cunnings, Shetland	Seaman	*Ellison*
James Malcolm	29	Sound, Shetland	Seaman	*Resolution*

Name	Age	Place of birth	In what capacity engaged	Ship in which he last served
John Thomas Scolley	24	Delting, Shetland	Seaman	*Alfred*
William Williams	26	Gulberwall, Shetland	Seaman	*Fame*
William Hendry	25	Yell, Shetland		Landsman (first voyage)
John Lawson	39	Cunnings, Shetland	Seaman	*Abram*
James Gray	19	Unst, Shetland	Seaman	*Riby Grove*
William Hunter	34	Tingwall, Shetland	Seaman	*Hecla*
William Manson	24	Easting, Shetland	Seaman	*Abram*
Robert Williamson	33	Yell, Shetland		Landsman (first voyage)
Archibald Lesk	19	Trondra, Shetland	Seaman	*Christian and Jean*
Lawrence Williamson	22	Nesting, Shetland	Seaman	*Riby Grove*

[1] unshippd 11 March'.

References

[1]   Thomas Phillips's journal is in the Archives of Manitoba Government Records, MG 11 A7 M13.

[2]   Thomas Phillips uses the word 'Esquimaux' when referring to the native peoples of Greenland and Arctic Canada. This term has been retained when quoting from his journal. In the explanatory text modern words have been substituted: 'Greenlander' for the inhabitants of Greenland and 'Inuit' for the inhabitants of Arctic Canada.

[3]   J. Druett, *Rough Medicine: Surgeons at Sea in the Age of Sail*, New York, Routledge, 2001, p. 90. The journal of John Wilson is in the collection of the Royal Geographical Society, London.

[4]   A.C. Doyle, *'Dangerous Work': Diary of an Arctic Adventure*, ed. J. Lellenberg and D. Stashower, London, The British Library, 2012, pp. 5–6.

[5]   Leslie, Jameson, Murray, *Narrative of Discovery.* This was an extremely popular book and was already in a fifth edition by 1845.

[6]   Scoresby, *Account of the Arctic Regions.*

[7]   *Hull Advertiser*, 2 Sept. 1836.

[8]   I. Macleod (ed.), *To the Greenland Whaling: Alexander Trotter's Journal of the Voyage of the 'Enterprise' in 1856 from Fraserburgh and Lerwick*, Sandwick, 1979. Various entries from 9 Feb. to 4 March.

[9]   TNA, BT 98/297.

[10]   Francis, *Arctic Chase*, p. 8.

[11]   A similar ceremony was traditionally performed when ships crossed the equator.

[12]   Barron, *Old Whaling Days*, pp. 116–17.

[13]   All temperature recordings are given by Phillips in degrees Fahrenheit.

[14]   Phillips seems to have recorded some of these lines of latitude incorrectly. 73° 35'N lies to the south of Upernavik which he said that they had reached eight days previously.

[15] *William Torr* was the only ship to be lost with all hands during the over-wintering of 1835–6 in which *Abram* was also involved.

[16] This quotation is from William Cowper's satirical poem 'Hope' published in 1782. He was referring to the activities of the Moravian missionaries in Greenland.

[17] This quotation is from Joseph Ritchie 'A Farewell to England'. This poem was published in 1828 in *The Poetical Album and Register of Modern Fugitive Poetry* edited by Alaric Alexander Watts.

[18] Quoted on a display of Arctic whaling in Shetland Museum and Archives, Lerwick (February 2013).

[19] In 1839 the catch of nine whales produced 310 butts of blubber (100 tons of Train Oil) and 6.5 tons of whale bone. Hull History Centre, Bills of Entry for the Port of Hull, 1839.

[20] TNA, BT 98/297.

CHAPTER 10

Searching for Sir John Franklin

In 1849 *Abram* became involved in one of the most famous episodes in the history of Arctic exploration. At a time when the whaling industry and its troubles were of little interest beyond the east coast whaling ports, the nation's attention became focused on the fate of Sir John Franklin's expedition to search for the route of the North West Passage.

Since William Scoresby had reported the reduction in Arctic sea ice in 1817, the British Admiralty was as interested as the whaling fleet in the more favourable navigational opportunities. John Barrow, the Ulverston-born Second Secretary to the Admiralty, promoted a succession of expeditions to find the elusive North West Passage route to the Pacific Ocean. Incidental to their main purpose, these voyages helped to open up the new more northerly whaling grounds in Baffin Bay, and aided the whalers by charting, not always very accurately, the east coast of Baffin Island.[1] A symbiotic relationship developed between explorers and whalers and the government recognised the contribution that whalers could make to Arctic exploration when it announced that the whale ship owners were equally eligible for the awards which parliament was offering for the discovery of 'a northern passage between the Pacific and Atlantic Oceans, or for approaching within one degree of the Northern Pole'.[2] Whalers had already supported the Admiralty by reporting sightings of expedition ships, as well as by rescuing Sir John Ross and his crew in 1833 after they had spent four winters trapped in the pack ice.[3]

In 1845 Sir John Franklin, the veteran Arctic explorer, was re-engaged by the Admiralty to lead an expedition of two ships, HMS *Erebus* and HMS *Terror*, on a voyage which, it was hoped, would finally establish the existence of a northern route to the Pacific. By then few expected that the discovery of such a route would be of any commercial or strategic significance, but given Britain's earlier commitment to the project, its resolution was considered to be an issue of national honour.

The disaster that befell Sir John Franklin's expedition once again provided the whalers with an opportunity to contribute to a rescue attempt, by helping with the search alongside their whaling activities, carrying supplies, providing manpower and demonstrating ice techniques if circumstances in the search area demanded it. They could also help with communications, taking messages to the Admiralty ships in the spring and returning with messages in the autumn.

Abram and the search for Sir John Franklin

The last sighting of *Erebus* and *Terror*, moored to an iceberg and awaiting a favourable passage from Melville Bay into Lancaster Sound, was by two whalers, *Enterprise* of Peterhead (Captain Robert Martin) and *Prince of Wales* of Hull (Captain Edward Dannatt), in July 1845. As the expedition was equipped to survive a number of winters, there was no undue concern at the lack of information as to its progress during 1846 and 1847, although the veteran Arctic explorer Sir John Ross suggested to the Admiralty at the beginning of 1847 that, as nothing had been heard from Franklin, he thought that his ships must be imprisoned in the ice. In February the Admiralty asked the whaling fleet and the Hudson's Bay Company to keep a look out for Franklin, and offered rewards for information.[4] The Dundee whaling master William Penny, the most experienced and successful whaling captain of the time, initiated the first of many searches, spending a number of days during the 1847 season searching in Lancaster Sound and making enquiries amongst the Inuit of Pond Inlet on Baffin Island, but to no avail.[5]

In the autumn of 1847 the Admiralty began planning for a major search in 1848. It was intended that expeditions would be dispatched to approach Franklin's assumed position from the east via Lancaster Sound, from the west through the Bering Strait, and overland from the south by descending the Mackenzie and Coppermine rivers. These expeditions were to be led by the friends of Sir John Franklin who were amongst the most accomplished polar explorers of the time. At the same time the Admiralty offered a reward of £100 'to any whale ship which should give authentic information about the *Erebus* and *Terror* in Lancaster Sound'.[6]

Despite this Sir John Franklin's wife, Lady Jane, was not convinced that everything was being done to discover the fate of the ships, so she made independent contact with the whaling community. On 25 February 1848 she wrote to the veteran Arctic whaling master William Scoresby, saying that although she was 'deeply grateful for the interest' shown by the Admiralty, she was concerned that every effort must be put into that summer's search, and she indicated her willingness to fund her own search expeditions:

> It appears to me my private resources may be made available for this purpose – I venture to ask of you who have so much knowledge in these matters how I could best employ a couple of thousand pounds or more, if necessary, to the relief or rescue of the missing ships or any portions of their crews. Is there any scale of rewards that could be offered with advantage to the Captains, Crews or Owners of whaling vessels?[7]

It was obvious to Lady Jane that the whalers were in a good position to assist in a search, and if necessary a rescue, because of their experience in

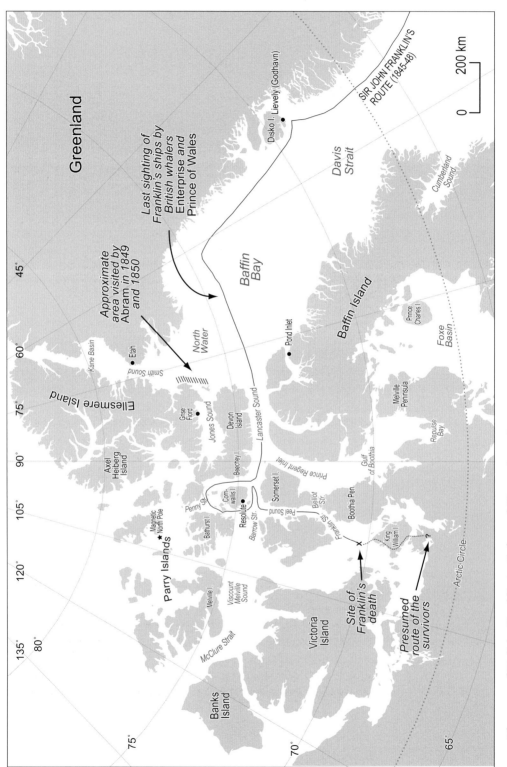

101. The route of Sir John Franklin in *Erebus* and *Terror*, 1845–48.

10.2. Portrait of Sir John Franklin by Thomas
Phillips, 1828. Bequeathed by Lady Franklin's niece,
Miss Sophia Cracroft, 1892. (© National Portrait
Gallery, London.)

10.3. Portrait of Lady Jane Franklin by Amélie
Romilly, 1816. (© National Portrait Gallery,
London.)

ice navigation, and their knowledge of the entrance to Lancaster Sound
which Franklin would have passed through in 1845. Scoresby reminded
Lady Jane that Sir John Ross had earlier survived four winters frozen in the
Arctic pack ice, and therefore urged her to remain optimistic as Franklin's
expedition had taken supplies for three years.

Later that spring Lady Franklin made an offer of a reward which was
printed by the Admiralty and distributed at the whaling ports:

Two Thousand Pounds offered by Lady Franklin to Whalers.
With the view of inducing any of the whaling ships which resort
to Davis Straits and Baffin Bay, to make efforts in search of the
expedition under the command of Sir John Franklin, in those parts
which are not within the scope of the expeditions about to be sent out
by the Government, I hereby offer £1,000 to be divided as follows: to
the owner, captain, officers and crew of any ship which shall depart so
far from the usual fishing ground as to explore Prince Regent's Inlet,
Admiralty Inlet, Jones' Sound or Smith's Sound, provided such ship,
finding the above expedition in distress, shall communicate with and
afford it effectual relief.

To the owner two-tenths or £200
To the captain, one-tenth or £100
To the chief mate one-twentieth or £50
To the next two officers one-fortieth or £25 each
The remaining six-tenths or £600 to be divided amongst the rest of
the ship's company.

And further I hereby offer an additional sum of £1,000 to be
distributed in the same proportions to the owners, officers, and
crew of any vessel which shall at an early period of the season make
extraordinary exertions for the above object; and if required bring Sir
John Franklin and his party to England.

The whole or part of this last thousand pounds will be granted
according to the decision of Sir John Franklin or the commanding
officer of the expedition relieved. In other respects the decision of
the following gentlemen who have kindly consented to act as referees
in awarding the above £2,000 is to be final, viz: Admiral Beaufort,
Captain Sir W.E. Parry, R.N., and Thomas Ward, Esq., of Hull.[8]

20 March 1848   Jane Franklin, 21 Bedford-place, London

Before the end of the year Captain Thomas Lee, the master of the whaler
Prince of Wales, returned to Hull claiming that he had seen a cairn
during his voyage. When Lady Jane Franklin heard the story, she joined
with William Scoresby and her niece and travelling companion, Sophia
Cracroft, and visited Lee in Hull. Sophia described the meeting:

> She saw & questioned the Captn the veteran Lee of Hull – but he…
> is very ignorant of navigation or charts, & in fact knows nothing but
> the best way of getting thro' ice, & of catching whales – so he had a
> very bungling story – being sure of only one thing, viz – that they had
> been in some place north of Lancaster Sound, & that (the weather
> being very foggy) they had run some 100 or 150 miles up it, to the
> westward, fr the entrance in Baffin's Bay.
>
> As to the cairn, he did not seem to have, anything to say abt it.
> Some of the men <u>thought</u> they had seen one was all he admitted. He
> probably & with reason, thought that to admit its existence wd. be to
> incur blame for not examining it.[9]

Lady Franklin and Scoresby went on to examine the log book of the
voyage but (according to Sophia) it was 'most confused & told nothing of
the kind'.[10] It would appear that Lee fabricated this story, enticed by the
possibility of the reward.[11]

During 1848 there was one Admiralty searching expedition in the area.
Sir James Clark Ross had sailed on HMS *Enterprise* in May with instructions
that the commander of the vessel accompanying him, Captain Edward
Joseph Bird of HMS *Investigator*, should, after wintering, 'go by ship or

steam launch…to the west coast of Baffin's Bay, to communicate with the whale ships' in the early summer of 1849. The so-called Arctic Council, made up of the most experienced polar explorers including William Scoresby, met in January 1849 and recommended that the Admiralty should 'send out by a certain number of whaling ships (selecting the most desirable), copies of new instructions to Captain Bird, and [should offer] some inducement to the masters of the whaling ships to deposit these communications at certain points [previously identified by Ross].' The Admiralty identified seven whaling ships, including *Abram*, and gave each twelve 'copies of the [new instructions] hermetically sealed up in metal cylinders, which they were requested to deposit' at the seven locations left by Ross 'should opportunities offer'. Of the twelve metal cylinders 'not less than four watertight casks of large size [were] to be fitted with a short pole carrying a small flag or tin vane, each cask to enclose one of the cylinders carefully packed to prevent it being damaged, and to drop these casks in different places four or five leagues apart as far to the westward as possible in Lancaster Sound'. In the event *Abram* did not sail until mid-June. It is not clear whether *Abram* did in fact carry the new instructions in the metal cylinders, but the Dundee whaler *Advice,* commanded by the veteran whaling master, Captain Penny, did do so. Robert Goodsir, the brother of the assistant surgeon, Dr Harry Goodsir, in Franklin's *Erebus*, whom Penny had taken on board *Advice*, wrote in a despatch to the Admiralty that on 3 August 'in the forenoon, whilst off Cape Hay [south of Lancaster Sound], an Admiralty cylinder was put overboard, enclosed in a cask, according to the Admiralty Instructions, marked with a pole and vane, and properly ballasted'. And again on the 9 August 'an Admiralty cylinder was here got ready, and enclosed in a small cask, along with some of the latest newspapers which we had on board, and two boats were despatched on shore to bury it in the most conspicuous place possible'.[12]

By the end of 1848 there was no more information available about the fate of Franklin than there had been at the beginning of the year. It was becoming clearer that the expedition was in some difficulty, so in 1849 the Admiralty raised the reward which it offered to any ship which brought help to Franklin and his crew to £20,000. This increase was announced too late for the whaling ships as they had already left for the whaling grounds. Lady Jane asked the Admiralty to widen the search to include everywhere that Franklin might have ventured if he had followed the orders given him to the letter, which she was certain he would have done. However the Admiralty refused to do more than they had already scheduled for that year – namely the sending of a store ship, HMS *North Star*, to support Sir James Clark Ross who was still searching Lancaster Sound. So in April Lady Jane also eloquently wrote to the President of the United States requesting that country's help, a request that was favourably received by the government of President Zachary Taylor.

Early in 1849 Lady Jane took the decision to become more involved in the search. In February she visited Hull with William Scoresby in order to confer with 'the captains and owners of vessels bound for the Davis Straits'.[13] In March she increased her reward to £3,000 and in the printed broadsheet announcing this change she encouraged the whalers to enter the maze of channels beyond Lancaster Sound and to search more widely. Although she was confident that her husband and the ships' companies could still be found alive, she was perhaps aware that her view was no longer shared by all so she indicated that for any whaler which could prove that they had searched diligently, but had no success, 'the case of such whaler, with a view to reward, will be taken into favourable consideration'.[14]

In May she wrote to Scoresby that she was thinking of purchasing a whaler – *Abram* of Hull:

> I have almost decided on purchasing the '*Abram*' of Hull (which) is I am told a sound & good ship & could be ready for sea in a fortnight. I have sent a person down to look at her and expect the result immediately. I wished we had looked at her when at Hull – it was an omission not to look at the Whalers, but we were so busy.[15]

Later that month Lady Jane noted 'the return of our friend Captn Gravill from Greenland when he lost his ship in a tremendous gale'.[16] She went on to comment to Scoresby:

> You know how highly I thought of this man and wished he had been going to Davis Straits & admired his spirit of discovery which was chiefly directed to the northern passages & rejoiced to hear him say that please God, he wd yet go to Davis Straits this year. Poor man! He did not foresee by what unfortunate circumstances, this wished for want was to be brought about. Having first written to Hull to ascertain that no blame attached to Gravill for the loss of his ship, I sent for him to town & told him my desire that he shd combine with his fishing the exploration of one or both of the sounds in Baffins Bay but especially Jones' Sound, for which I was ready to pay a proper consideration. He told me that three fourths of the shares [in *Abram*] were taken – that he thought I had better take the remaining 4th which wd enable the ship to start immediately & it was left to me to propose a sum for searching the sound. Mr Barkworth, the owner, who himself takes one fourth of the shares wd not name any price thinking I shd name a better, so I offered (£)500 for exploring one or other Sound which I suppose was more than was necessary as no difficulty at all was made on that cunning man's part, except that I must pay the addl insurance for putting the ship in more danger than usual – and thus the bargain is concluded & I am become a whale fisher! & shall get I trust part of the places searched about which I am

anxious, tho' not the principal which is still Wellington Channel – I trust Gravel will penetrate Jones Sound far enough to look into that inlet.[17]

Clearly Lady Jane was suspicious about the honesty of Thomas Barkworth, a suspicion which revealed just how canny a negotiator she was becoming. Despite the promise of rewards, humanitarian actions were secondary to the needs of commerce.

The public was made aware of events on 8 June. The *Hull Packet* reported:

> The well-known whale ship, *Abram*, is now fitting out at this port as quickly as possible, for a voyage to Davis Straits. We understand that Lady Franklin has purchased a considerable share in her, and although she is to be fully equipped as a whaler, instructions have been given, if circumstances are favourable, to search Smith's Sound and Jones's Sound, in quest of Sir John Franklin. She is to be commanded by Captain Graville, late of *William Ward* of this port.[18]

10.4. Portrait of Captain John Gravill. (Reproduced by courtesy of Hull Maritime Museum: Hull Museums.)

Later in the month the crew signed on for a voyage 'to Davis Straits, Cumberland Straits, Lancaster Sound and inlets and sounds of every description in the seas adjacent…for the purpose of striking, killing, taking and securing Seals, Whales and other creatures in the said seas', but a further clause made clear the additional responsibility of searching for Sir John Franklin's expedition (Figure 10.5):

> It is also agreed by the said parties hereto that in case any Bounty or reward is obtained from the Government or from Lady Franklin for any assistance rendered to or information obtained of the Expedition which sailed under the command of Sir John Franklin, one half of such bounty or reward, whatever may be the amount shall wholly belong to the parties who have taken shares in this adventure and that the other half shall be considered as produce to be divided amongst the shareholders, the Master, Officers and crew in the same proportions as are specified in this agreement every £500 of the said reward or bounty being considered equal to a Whale producing Thirteen Imperial Tuns of Oil.[19]

It is also agreed by the said parties hereto that in case any bounty or reward is obtained from the Government or from Lady Franklin for any assistance rendered to or information obtained of the Expedition which sailed under the command of Sir John Franklin, one half of such bounty or reward, whatever may be the amount shall wholly belong to the parties who have taken shares in this adventure and that the other half shall be considered as produce to be divided amongst the shareholders. The Master, Officers and Crew in the same proportions as are specified in this agreement every £500. of the said reward or bounty being considered equal to a Whale producing Thirteen Imperial Tuns of Oil —

When Gravill left Hull on 14 June 1849 it was already late in the season, but it was necessary for the vessel to visit Lerwick to engage the Shetland crew.[20] During July, Lady Jane and her companion Sophia Cracroft travelled to the Orkneys and Shetlands in order to talk with the crews of other whaling ships as they returned from the Arctic. Spirits were raised when in September a whaling ship returned with a bottle with a message from the expedition which was dated 1845. A few days later a sailor reported that the whaler *Truelove* had met some 'esquimaux' who had claimed to have seen *Erebus* and *Terror* and Sir John himself in Prince Regent's Inlet in March 1849. Although *Truelove* had failed to reach the area because of sea ice, she had left a depot of food and fuel for the beleaguered expedition.

From Orkney, Lady Franklin went to Kirkcaldy in October to 'avail herself of all the information which George Turnbull Esq. (long a proprietor and manager of the whalers here), and Captain Kinnear, who for a long period of his life had been familiar with that desolate country, could afford her'.[21] She stayed at a local hotel awaiting Captain Kerr's return with any information he could provide about her husband's whereabouts. Unfortunately he had nothing to report. Lady Jane then went to Dundee to talk with Captain Penny, whose ship *Advice* had returned from Davis Strait on the 24 October.[22] Captain Penny had again taken Robert Goodsir, the brother of the assistant surgeon on Franklin's ship with him. Although Goodsir discovered no information about his brother or about the expedition, he wrote to Lady Jane on his return, urging her to remain positive: 'I trust you are not allowing yourself to become over-anxious. I know that, although there is much cause to be so, there is still not the slightest reason that we should despair.'[23]

The return of Sir James Clark Ross and Sir John Richardson to London early in November, with the news that they had also found no trace of the expedition, increased despondency.[24] On 21 November *Abram* returned to

10.5. The agreement written on the Crew List for *Abram* in 1849 relating to a reward or bounty resulting from finding evidence of Sir John Franklin: TNA, BT 98/1905. (Reproduced by courtesy of The National Archives, London.)

MENS' NAMES.	Age.	PLACE OF BIRTH.	QUALITY.	Amount of Wages per Calendar Month, Share, or Voyage.	Hand Money in advance.	Striking.	Fish Money.	Oil Money, per Imperial Tun.	Bone Money.
Magnus Tait	42	Trigawell	Seaman	1 15/				1/3	
Lawrence Froatt	39	Walls	do	1 10/				1/6	
Archibald Jameson	29	Melly	do	1 15/				1/3	
Magnus Tait	21	Aithsting	do	1 2/				1/-	
Andrew Froatt	25	Sandness	do	1 10/				1/3	
Jeremiah Morrison	20	Lerwick	do	1 2/				1/-	
Thomas Gawder	39	do	do	1 10/				1/3	
Gilbert Lawrenceson	19	do	do	1 2/				1/-	
William Henderson	21	Gulberwick	do	1 2/				1/-	
Henry Nicolson	27	Lerwick	do	1 15/				1/3	
Alexander Goodlad	22	do	do	1 10/				1/6	
George Lawrenson	19	Bressay	Ordin'y do	" 16/				6°	
James Robertson	18	do	do	" 16/				6°	
John Thomson	25	Weisdale	Seaman	1 15/				1/3	
Magnus Thomson	33	do	do	1 15/				1/3	
Erasmus Hunter	20	do	Ordinary Seaman	" 16/				6°	
John Jameson	20	Walls	Seaman	" 18/				10°	
Robert Lawrenson	22	Whiteness	do	1 2/				1/-	
Andrew Manson	18	Bressay	do	1 4/				1/-	
John Manson	21	do	do	2 "				1/6	
William Gear	43	Nesting	do	1 15/				1/3	
1849.									
Abram.									
Agreement for the Davis Straits Voyage.									
James Georgeson	20	Sandness	Seaman	1 10/				1/-	
Robert Slatter	24	Walls	do	1 10/				1/3	

10.6. Crew list of the ship's company of *Abram* who signed on at Lerwick, Shetland Islands, 1849: TNA, BT 98/1905. (Reproduced by courtesy of The National Archives, London.)

Hull with three tons of whale bone and 49 tons of oil. Gravill had taken the ship as far north as any whaler had yet been, and he had become the first European to set foot on Ellesmere Island. However, he had concentrated on whaling and seemed not to have carried out a search of Jones Sound; he returned without any further information about Sir John. The year therefore ended badly for Lady Jane. Her offer to pay only £100 'for [Gravill's] attempt, or whatever it may be called' was rejected by Mr. Ward, Thomas Barkworth's manager, who threatened legal action.[25]

Gravill sailed again in *Abram* in 1850, and the crew signed up to search for Sir John Franklin, with the promise that the bounty would be divided as before. It is unclear whether Lady Jane took a share in the ship that year. Ten of the 1849 crew rejoined the ship in 1850, perhaps in part persuaded by the promise of the reward.[26] In October 1850 Lady Jane was waiting for the return of *Abram* in order to go to Hull, but not, it seems, to discover whether anything had been found of her husband's expedition. Rather, she sought to settle the dispute that had arisen over what had actually taken place in 1849. It seems that Lady Jane had learnt of a conversation between Captain Gravill and Captain Penny in which the former had said that 'at the entrance to Jones Sound [he] had called his men together and asked them whether they wd explore the Sound or go to their fishing; the latter being carried unanimously'. She hoped to meet with Captain Gravill on his return as she had little doubt that 'the poor man who is of a cautious & timid nature (as I am told) & whose bread depends on his not offending his rich owners, will be frightened into denying or contradicting himself'. Her opinion of Gravill had clearly changed since the previous year, and she hoped that if William Scoresby could come to Hull too, his 'knowledge and position' would instil some 'firm discipline with Mr Ward' and bring the dispute and the threat of legal action to an end.[27] Lady Jane's correspondence provides no information about the outcome of this dispute.

Lady Jane's role in the promotion of the search for her husband and his ship's company was acknowledged by the author of the first account of Franklin's voyage and the searches written in 1852:

> All those who read these pages will, I am sure, feel the deepest sympathy and admiration of the zeal, perseverance, and conjugal affection displayed in the noble and untiring efforts of Lady Franklin to relieve or discover the fate of her distinguished husband and the gallant party under his command, despite the difficulties, disappointments, and heart-sickening "hope deferred" with which these efforts have been attended…The name of the present Lady Franklin is as "familiar as a household word" in every bosom in England; she is alike the object of our admiration, our sympathy, our hopes, and our prayers.[28]

Although *Abram* had played a rather inglorious part in the search for Sir John Franklin, it was anticipated that the whaling ships and their crews would continue to be involved. Sir James Clark Ross's expedition of 1848–49 had left a large depot in a hut built by the expedition, along with one of his steam launches. It was hoped that if this was found by Franklin it would enable the surviving members of his crew to reach the entrance to Lancaster Sound and meet the whale ships.[29] While the whaling industry was in the doldrums in the early 1850s, masters and crews were easily persuaded to search for Franklin. For example, Peterhead whale men made up the crew of *Felix*, a schooner commanded, and largely financed, by the veteran Arctic explorer Sir John Ross, on an expedition in 1850–51. At the same time Captain William Penny once again became involved in the search as commander of HMS *Lady Franklin*. The skills and knowledge of the whalers were acknowledged by Rear-Admiral Sir Francis Beaufort in his memorandum to the Admiralty in which he endorsed this voyage because of Penny's 'local knowledge, his thorough acquaintance with all the mysteries of the ice navigation, and his well known skill and resources'.[30] However, we now know that by this time Franklin and the entire ships' companies were dead, and neither whalers nor naval ships had been able to save them.

Table 10.1: Crew List of *Abram*, 1849.[31]

Name	Age	Place of birth	In what capacity engaged	Ship in which he last served
Hull crew: date of entry 11 June 1849.				
John Gravill	47	Gainsborough	Master	--------------
John Hilton	23	Duckinfield	Surgeon	First voyage
William Dannatt	52	Kirton in Linsley	Mate and harpooner	*William Ward*
Joseph Henderson	54	Gateshead	2nd Mate and harpooner	*Cleveland*
Paul Whiteman	57	Stamland	Spectioneer and harpooner	*Lord Gambier*
Richard Tether	24	Hull	Boatswain	*William Ward*
Henry Trott	43	Hull	Skeeman and harpooner	*Pledge*
Thomas Hall	49	Hull	Loose harpooner	*Nevan*
John Watt	42	Hull	Carpenter	*Abram* (prior to 1848)
William Harrison	33	Hull	Cooper	*Abram*
Henry Harrison	25	Patrington	Carpenter's mate	First voyage
John Brown	45	Hull	Extra cooper and boatsteerer	*William Ward*
William Nicholson	36	Hull	Sailmaker and boatsteerer	*William Ward*
Thomas Ward	20	Gainsborough (on crew list) Whitby (on muster roll)	Steward and boatsteerer (on crew list) Cook (on muster roll)	*Marchioness of Queensbury*
Thomas Pinder	26	Hull	Boatsteerer	*Duke*
John Goodhutt	23	Hull	Boatsteerer	*Charles Saunders*
John Harrison	23	Hull	Boatsteerer	*Pledge*
William Grant	22	Hull	Boatsteerer	*Ann*
Richard Byers	18	Hull	Apprentice (1845)	--------------
Thomas Lee	15	Hull	Apprentice (1848)	--------------
James Smith	15	Hull	Apprentice (1849)	--------------
Robert Nicholson	62	Whitby	Cook (on crew list)	*James Gibson*
Shetland crew: date of entry (Lerwick) 19 June 1849.				
Magnus Tait	42	Tingwall, Shetland	Seaman	*Plum*
Lawrence Twatt	39	Walls, Shetland	Seaman	*Swallow*
Archibald Jameson	29	Melly, Shetland	Seaman	*Victor*
Magnus Tait	21	Aisting, Shetland	Seaman	*Victor*

Name	Age	Place of birth	In what capacity engaged	Ship in which he last served
Andrew Twatt	25	Sandness, Shetland	Seaman	*Flamingo*
Jeremiah Morrison	20	Lerwick, Shetland	Seaman	*Victor*
Thomas Gaudie	39	Lerwick, Shetland	Seaman	*Scotia*
Gilbert Lawrenson	19	Lerwick, Shetland	Seaman	*Victor*
William Henderson	21	Gulberwick, Shetland	Seaman	*Hamilton Ross*
Henry Nicolson	27	Lerwick, Shetland	Seaman	*Victor*
Alexander Goodlad	22	Lerwick, Shetland	Seaman	*Victor*
George Lawrenson	19	Bressay, Shetland	Ord. Seaman	First voyage
James Robertson	18	Bressay, Shetland	Ord. Seaman	First voyage
John Thomson	25	Weisdale, Shetland	Seaman	*Victor*
Magnus Thomson	33	Weisdale, Shetland	Seaman	*Bon Accord*
Erasmus Hunter	20	Weisdale, Shetland	Ord. Seaman	First voyage
John Jameson	20	Walls, Shetland	Seaman	*Hebe*
Robert Lawrenson	22	Whiteness, Shetland	Seaman	*Lark*
Andrew Manson	18	Bressay, Shetland	Seaman	*Victor*
John Manson	21	Bressay, Shetland	Seaman	*Victor*
William Gear	43	Nesting, Shetland	Seaman	*Superior*
James Georgeson	20	Sandness, Shetland	Seaman	*Flamingo*
Robert Slatter	24	Walls, Shetland	Seaman	*Flamingo*

References

[1] A. Savours, *The Search for the North West Passage*, London, Chatham, 1999, pp. 39–55.

[2] Dundee City Archives, KRS/CE70.2.12, 24 March 1818; quoted in Archibald, *Whalehunters*, p. 44.

[3] For an overview of the whalers contributions to the Franklin search see: W. Gillies Ross, 'Whalemen, Whaleships and the Search for Franklin', in P.D. Sutherland (ed.), *The Franklin Era in Canadian Arctic History 1845–1859*, Ottawa, National Museums of Canada, 1985, pp. 54–68.

[4] F.J. Woodward, *Portrait of Jane: A Life of Lady Franklin*, London, Hodder and Stoughton. 1951, p. 256

[5] C.A. Holland, 'William Penny', p. 34.

[6] Lubbock, *Arctic Whalers*, p. 347.

[7] Quoted in T. & C. Stamp, *William Scoresby: Arctic Scientist*, Whitby, Caedmon, 1975, pp. 209–10.

[8] House of Commons Papers, 1847–48, XLI/211: quoted in E.B. Elce (ed.), *As affecting the fate of my absent husband: Selected Letters of Lady Franklin Concerning the Search for the Lost Franklin Expedition, 1848–1860*, Montreal and Kingston, McGill-Queen's University Press, 2009, pp. 63–64. See also Lubbock, *Arctic Whalers*, pp. 347–48.

[9] S. Cracroft, Letter to mother and sisters, 9 June 1851. Cambridge, SPRI, Ms248/247/24; D. Quoted in W. Gillies Ross, 'False Leads in the Franklin Search', *Polar Record*, 209, 2003, p. 136.

[10] Cracroft 1851; quoted in Ross, 'False Leads', p. 136.

11   Over the next few years the story of the cairn persisted and became emboldened with telling. In *The Weekly Times* 14 Oct. 1849, Lee had expressed his conviction that the cairn had been built by Franklin. In May 1851, one of Lee's crew, William Millar, revived interest in the story when he came forward with further details of the location and a reason why the cairn had not been examined (in fact he suggested that the crew were in the middle of opening it, when weather conditions changed and they were recalled to the ship). This new twist appeared in *The Weekly Times* 15 June 1851, and Lady Jane got Millar to put his signature to his statement in *John O'Groats Journal*, 20 June 1851, and then amended the orders she had given to her *Prince Albert* expedition, to include investigations in Jones Sound where this cairn was supposed to be. See Ross, 'False Leads', pp. 131–60.

12   House of Commons papers, 1849, *Arctic expeditions: extracts of any proceedings or correspondence of the Admiralty, in reference to Arctic expeditions*, pp. 1–7, 22–24.

13   *Hull Packet*, 16 Feb. 1849.

14   Elce, *As affecting the fate of my absent husband*, pp. 66–7.

15   Whitby Literary and Philosophical Society, Jane Franklin letter to William Scoresby, 12 May 1849. Copy at SPRI: MS1100/3/5. Referred to in Ross, 'False Leads', p. 136.

16   This was the whaler *William Ward*. Fortunately there was no loss of life.

17   Whitby Literary and Philosophical Society, Jane Franklin letter to William Scoresby, 12 May 1849. Copy at SPRI: MS1100/3/5. Referred to in Ross, 'False Leads', p. 136. John Gravill (1802–66) was a whaling master with over 30 years' experience in the industry. In 1866 he was master of *Diana* when she was beset in the ice in Baffin Bay and only returned to Shetland the following spring. Gravill and 12 other men died over the winter. See Credland, *Whales and Whaling*, p. 26.

18   *Hull Packet*, 8 June 1849.

19   TNA, BT 98/1905.

20   *Hull Packet*, 6 July 1849.

21   *Fifeshire Advertiser*, 20 Oct. 1849, p. 3.

22   *Fifeshire Advertiser*, 3 Nov. 1849, p. 4.

23   P.L. Simmonds, *Sir John Franklin and the Arctic Regions*, 1852; republished Stroud, Nonsuch, 2005, p. 212.

24   Woodward, *Portrait of Lady Jane*, pp. 267–70.

25   Whitby Literary and Philosophical Society, Jane Franklin letter to William Scoresby, 24 Oct. 1850. Copy at SPRI Ms 1100/3/16; D. Referred to in Ross, 'False Leads', p. 136.

26   Hull Trinity House, MSF/3/60/97. TNA, BT 98/2188; BT 98/2529.

27   Whitby Literary and Philosophical Society, Jane Franklin letter to William Scoresby, 24 Oct. 1850. Copy in SPRI Ms 1100/3/16; D. Referred to in Ross, 'False Leads ' p. 136.

28   Simmonds, *Sir John Franklin*, pp. 155–56.

29   Savours, *Search for the North West Passage*, p. 190.

30   Simmonds, *Sir John Franklin*, pp. 198–99.

31   TNA, BT 98/1905; Hull History Centre, Muster Rolls, C DSTR MSF/3/60/97.

CHAPTER 11

Abram at Kirkcaldy 1855–1862

When *Abram* arrived in Kirkcaldy in 1855 she had already seen 49 years of service, and this meant that she was older than Kirkcaldy's other two whaling ships, *Chieftain* and *Lord Gambier* (Figure 11.1). On 16 March George Turnbull transferred the ship to the Kirkcaldy Whale Fishing Company. The principal shareholders were all Kirkcaldy businessmen. Patrick Don Swan, founder of Swan Brothers was a flax spinner, bleacher and yarn merchant; Andrew Currie of A. Currie and Sons was a wholesale tea, wine and spirit merchant; George Beveridge and John Russell were both linen manufacturers.[1] A year later on 27 March 1856 she was re-registered when ownership passed to a larger group of merchants and manufacturers, thereby spreading the risk, a pattern common at a time when ships faced so many dangers at sea.[2] At that time Alexander Hay was named as master.

11.1. Photograph of *Lord Gambier* at Kirkcaldy, prior to 1862. (Reproduced by courtesy of Fife Council Museums: Kirkcaldy Museum and Art Gallery.)

1855 was the first year when the new Kirkcaldy fleet of three ships sailed to Davis Strait. *Lord Gambier* left first on 24 February because she was destined initially for sealing off the Labrador coast. *Chieftain* and *Abram* left Kirkcaldy in mid-March for the whaling in Davis Strait 'to prosecute their adventurous calling in the icy north. The owners dined together, as usual, before the sailing of their vessels, on board the *Abram*, on Thursday last'.[3] However, the season turned out to be a failure, not just for the Kirkcaldy ships, but for the entire United Kingdom fleet. *Abram* caught two whales, *Chieftain* three, and *Lord Gambier* returned with 55 tons of seal oil. The newspaper considered that 'the cause of the failure this year is much the same as the cause of previous ones – the impossibility of forcing the vessels through the ice to the *real* fishing-ground by means of sail only. The cry should therefore be "steam, steam, steam!". We hope the owners of our whaleships will now see the propriety of fitting up their vessels with the screw propeller.'[4]

The early departure of *Abram* in February 1856 indicates that she was bound initially for the sealing areas. A report in May stated that she had caught 4,800 seals before proceeding to the Davis Strait whale fishery on 29 April. *Abram*'s seal catch was claimed to be the best in the United Kingdom fleet, which in that year numbered 33 ships. 1856 was a successful year for everyone, including the Kirkcaldy fleet. The resultant prosperity caused the *Fifeshire Advertiser* to comment: 'We cannot refrain from expressing the wish that the crews may be able to carry their cup of prosperity somewhat steadily'.[5] The call for steam power was quietly dropped.

Table 11.1: Tonnage of oil brought back to Kirkcaldy by the whalers, 1856–1860.[6]

	Chieftain	*Abram*	*Lord Gambier*
October 1856	145	140	140
November 1857	16	45	clean +3 live bears
October 1858	clean	60	25
October 1859	14	40	38
October 1860	70	54	75

The success of the 1856 season encouraged the Scottish ports to send 50 ships to Davis Strait the following year. The departure of the whalers from their home ports was always a colourful occasion which was written up at length in the local press. The departure of *Abram* and *Lord Gambier* was described in vivid detail:

> The weather being fine, a great crowd had assembled on the quay to bid the hardy venturers God-speed, and the hearty cheers of the crews from the rigging of their respective ships were enthusiastically responded to from the shore…Both vessels, apart from the holiday display proper to the occasion, presented a most seaworthy appearance

– the result of the unstinted liberality of the Company in making repairs…We have said that considerable hilarity was observable as they left the shore, and certainly the crews and the spectators generally seemed borne away with the excitement of the moment; but here and there, especially among the females, was to be seen a dim eye and a husky voice which spoke plainly enough of the severance of tender ties for a season, and the undistinguishable throng of hopes and fears at work in the heart within.[7]

However, the 1857 season was not so productive for the Kirkcaldy Whale Fishing Company, and in the same year all three ships came to the attention of the Kirkcaldy Harbour Commissioners for infringing harbour rules. In January *Chieftain* damaged the capstones of the Quay Wall on Sailors Walk while repairs were being carried out. The company was ordered to pay the repair bill, but the following month it was reported that it had not responded.[8] In March *Abram* was in collision in the harbour with *Jeannie* of Glasgow, and the company was charged with the damage. Later the same year it was reported that *Lord Gambier* had not paid the pilotage dues to James Walker, Pilot.[9]

The uneasy relationship between the Company and the Commissioners resurfaced during the winter of 1861 when it was reported that 'on account of the state of the Dock Gates the Owners of the Whale Vessels had refused to pay the extra charge made for the use of the Docks.' It seems that they had a case because the Commissioners resolved to establish what the repair costs would be and appointed an engineer to report back. In the event the Commissioners did not make any decision until 1863, by which time the whale company had lost its three ships and its operations were being rapidly scaled down.[10]

With continuing poor catches it was becoming obvious that the days of Kirkcaldy whaling were numbered. The evidence from Dundee increasingly suggested that steam power was more efficient than the sails of the three old ships at Kirkcaldy. In 1861 the weather and ice conditions were terrible. *Abram*, commanded for the first time by the relatively inexperienced Dundee-born David Soutar, and *Lord Gambier* were whaling in the difficult waters of Melville Bay off the north-west coast of Greenland.[11] William Barron, who was master of *Truelove* that year, described what happened:

A few miles to the westward there was a deep bight, and we (the masters of all the ships whaling in that area) held a consultation, on board one of the ships, which would be the most prudent course to take, so we concluded to remain by the fast ice.

In a short time the whole Bay broke up into floes, and no fast ice remained. A calm, prevailing for a few hours, made an opening, so we towed and tracked until the ice closed again, and we then made fast.

A dark sky was shewing to the southward, and the barometer began to fall, which denoted a strong wind from that quarter. No time was lost preparing for the safety of the ships, and we began to saw docks. The *Abram* and *Lord Gambier* were in one, and the *Hudson*, of Hanover, in another. Our ship was placed in a third, and the *Anne* brig of Hull, remained sheltered by a point, whilst the *Commerce* of Peterhead, was about two miles in the offing, jammed between two floes. A furious gale with heavy rain and sleet came upon us.

When the weather cleared we saw the *Commerce* a total wreck, and the *Anne* was badly stove. When the gale abated, every precaution was taken for the safety of the vessels, such as sawing, etc., getting the [whale] boats further from the ships and provisioning them, as there were signs of more bad weather coming. The storm came on again and raged with greater fury, and in a short time the *Anne* also became a total wreck. Momentarily we all expected to share the same fate. Providentially we stood the test, although we had heavy pressures put on us. The *Hudson* had her stern post started, but the others did not suffer materially.[12]

On this occasion *Abram* and *Lord Gambier* survived the storm. However, the following year neither they, nor *Chieftain*, were so fortunate. 1862 was another year of appalling weather. William Barron, who was on *Polynia*, commented that for the sealers off the east coast of Newfoundland it was 'a disastrous year. About fifty sail (of the Newfoundland fleet) were lost on the ice along the coast during our stay, and it was the most severe time experienced by the oldest sealer in St. John's since 1831'.[13] Conditions were as bad for the whalers later in the year. The mate on board the barque *Emma* commented that 'the weather – during the whole voyage – has been exceedingly stormy; in fact it has been such an unfavourable year in this respect, as is not remembered by the oldest mariners'.[14] In October *The Times* reported that Captain Wells of *Emma*, who had lately returned to Hull, stated 'that from the time he left Hull on the 15th of March last, up to his arrival at the Orkneys on his return voyage, there has been a succession of violent storms'. He had gone on to say that 'nearly all the sailing vessels have returned clean, and many have been lost, the ice having closed in upon them almost without warning'.[15] Amongst those lost were all three ships in Kirkcaldy's whaling fleet.

The first of the town's three ships to be wrecked was *Lord Gambier*. A report, provided by Captain Robertson of *Alibi*, appeared in the *Fifeshire Advertiser* on 20 September. In response to an enquiry from the paper, Robertson wrote:

On the 4th July, in company of *Lady Franklin* and *Polar Star*, saw the wreck [of *Lord Gambier*] a little north of Hingston Bay, but saw or heard nothing of the crew until I got amongst the rest of the ships, which was the same night, when I was told the *Gambier* was wrecked on the 25th June, weather very thick, ship fast to a floe which set up against a berg, and left her a complete wreck before they had time to get her clear, likewise destroying three of their boats, they seeking their way south for the Danish settlements.[16] The *Gambier* had no fish.[17]

The same report stated that *Abram*, once again commanded by Captain Soutar, had caught two whales. However, it was not long before news came that she too had been wrecked. Just over a fortnight later the *Caledonian Mercury* reported 'On Saturday evening Kirkcaldy was again thrown into considerable excitement by a rumour that a telegram had been received by a share holder of the Whale Fish Company, stating that the *Abram*, Captain Soutar, was lost. This, on investigation has turned out quite correct...the crew was reported all saved...we understand the vessel is fully covered by insurance, as also the "oil money" of the crew'.[18] A few days later the *Fifeshire Advertiser* repeated this report, but there were still few details. The report, which was supplied by *Polar Star*, from Peterhead, confirmed earlier reports that the steamers had got through Melville Bay in good time for the Pond's Bay fishing off Baffin Island, but the sailing vessels had become trapped in the Melville Bay ice.[19] Information about the events that took place in Melville Bay can be found in the log books of the ships that witnessed the destruction of *Abram*. David Gray, master of *Active* of Peterhead wrote in his log:

> July 1. Off the Duck Islands (74° 05'N, 56°W). Visited the wreck of *Lord Gambier*. Beset in Melville Bay.
> July 26. Still beset (75° 35'N, 63°W); strong gale from the West South West. Ice tight and squeezing; the *Abram* and the *Alexander* were both lost this morning.[20]

Captain Wells of *Emma* recorded these same events rather more vividly. 'The vessels were overtaken by a hurricane of a most dreadful character... During the latter part of the gale, the *Abram* was crushed to atoms so that not a vestige of her was seen again. It was truly distressing to see the shipwrecked dragging the few clothes they had saved towards the surviving ships'.[21] The *Fifeshire Advertiser* later reported that:

> ... the crews of both ships escaped, and made of [sic] the nearest vessels, which happened to be the *Polar Star* and the *Augustine* of Peterhead, both of which have arrived. They left the ice nearly at the same time. They proceeded down the Middle Water under great difficulties, and finally left the ice at 62 degrees on the 12th September. Both vessels had run short of provisions, and could not have stayed longer; indeed the captain of the *Polar Star* on this account intended to have put a portion of the *Alexander*'s crew on shore at Discoe

Island, to have come home in a Danish vessel, but the coarseness of the weather prevented this.[22]

Further information was provided by *The Times* quoting Captain Wells of *Emma*. He reported that 'The *Abram* was crushed with such suddenness, that although provisions, boats, clothes, etc., were on deck in readiness for an emergency, everything went down with the vessel, and the crew was with difficulty saved'.[23]

The people of Kirkcaldy were awaiting every scrap of news. On 16 October the *Caledonian Mercury* quoted the text of a telegram from Copenhagen under an ominous headline 'Loss of *Chieftain*, the last of the Kirkcaldy whalers'. The telegram was from Captain Couldrey of *Lord Gambier* who wrote 'I am glad to state my arrival here with 10 of my crew, 23 of *Chieftain*'s, and some of the *Resolution*'s; *Abram* and *Alexander* also lost. Crews saved.'[24] The report was picked up by the *Fifeshire Advertiser* which commented that 'from the above telegram, it is inferred that the last of these three old vessels which sailed from this port in the spring of the present year for the Straits fisheries has either been lost, or abandoned, by its crew'.[25] *The Times* pulled no punches in its report of 18 October: 'Thus in one season, the Kirkcaldy fleet of three vessels has been totally destroyed'.[26] The paper went on 'From the above it is concluded that the *Chieftain* has also been lost…so all the vessels belonging to the [Kirkcaldy Whaling] company have been lost this season'. Information from Captain Souter of *Abram* followed four days later. He had not heard of the fate of *Chieftain* and reported that the ship had been in Melville Bay, 'firmly beset with ice, but clean', and that with nearly 100 men on board [the consequence of picking up crew from other wrecked ships] she could not have 'wintered out' as 'death from starvation would have been the consequence'. He went on to confirm the previous reports that 'not withstanding all his precautions to keep the *Abram* free of bergs, yet she was so severely crushed that she sank almost instantaneously, leaving the crew time to save nothing.'[27]

As the Scottish newspapers, and in particular the *Fifeshire Advertiser*, reported on one disaster after another, gloom must have settled on the town of Kirkcaldy. No whaler registered there had sunk in the Arctic since *Egginton* in 1830. It became increasingly uncertain whether Kirkcaldy could survive as a whaling port. By this time it was obvious that the industry's future lay with steam ships and Kirkcaldy lacked both the experience of working with steam, and investors with the cash to purchase a steam vessel. The *Fifeshire Advertiser* acknowledged that though the ships had been insured, their insured value had unfortunately been reduced for 1862, perhaps to reduce costs, so that the shareholders could not expect to recoup very much, and the purchase of a steam vessel would cost about £10,000. The paper went on to report that 'the Company is about to be 'wound up', but urged the town not to abandon its interest in whaling. 'The question arises shall we abandon the fishing, or try it again in steam vessels – sailing ones being quite out of the question – as is being done so successfully in Dundee. We must hope that there is sufficient energy still left among us to get up another Company, and in order to popularise it £10 shares have been spoken of. It will be rather hard to see Dundee bringing home fortunes yearly from the fishing, while we are doing nothing'.[28]

The edition of 1 November contained a lengthy letter from 'an old shipmaster' endorsing the paper's recommendation that those involved with the whaling trade in the town should purchase a steam vessel to 'continue a branch of trade which has been successfully pursued by many of their forefathers for the general prosperity of the place and its inhabitants'.[29] By 8 November there had been talks amongst local businessmen about purchasing 'two screw steamers for the fishing next year, the shares to be from £10 to £20 each'. The paper hoped that 'nothing would come in the way to thwart their object, as it ill afforded employment for those next season who otherwise would probably be thrown out of work'.[30] However, it seems that despite the paper's encouragement, the townspeople were dispirited by the disaster of the 1862 season and perhaps sceptical about the profit that could be made. By 22 November it reported that only one third of the shares had been taken up.[31] On 20 December thoughts had apparently turned to buying an old sailing vessel – *Sir C. Campbell*.[32] This did not happen, and an advertisement in January 1863 suggests that the Kirkcaldy Whale Fishing Company was beginning to sell off its whaling equipment including casks 'mostly newly coopered' and a variety of machines and implements including 'seal clubs'.[33] A vessel is recorded by Lubbock as being registered at Kirkcaldy from 1863–65, and Lockhart refers to two ships. Firstly, a whaler called *Brilliant*, which was acquired from a Peterhead company in 1865 and made a single voyage to Davis Strait in that year under the command of Captain Hay. On returning empty, she was resold back to Peterhead. Secondly, he cites an oral tradition of a steamer *Ravenscraig* which brought 55 tons of oil and four tons of whalebone to Kirkcaldy in 1868. If true, this was Kirkcaldy's last link with the whale trade.[34]

The events of 1862 removed an employment opportunity for the mariners of Kirkcaldy and district. However, David Soutar continued whaling from Dundee. His run of bad luck continued in 1863 when he was mate on board *Lady Seale* which was also shipwrecked in Melville Bay. Despite this, he continued his career as mate or master on Dundee whalers for at least another ten years.[35] The destruction of the whaling fleet also reduced income at the port, and meant that local industries that still used whale oil, such as linoleum manufacture, had to look elsewhere. They looked especially to Kirkcaldy's neighbour Dundee. However, that city itself needed about 1,200 tuns of whale oil annually for the manufacture of jute. In a good year this could be supplied by its own fleet and there was enough in excess to be sold to other consumers, such as Kirkcaldy's linoleum factories. When conditions were difficult, as in 1862, it meant that there was considerable shortfall in Dundee and little or no surplus for the manufacturers of Kirkcaldy.[36]

The boom years of whaling were already over. The United Kingdom whaling fleet numbered 46 ships in 1861, but within a decade it had been reduced to 21 ships, and although numbers remained steady during the 1870s, the industry never recovered. In 1861, 1,947 tons of whale oil and 1,768 cwts. of whale bone were brought back to Britain in British whalers, figures which were never again reached. Although sealing continued to bring some prosperity, Britain's declining need for whale oil was, by the end of the nineteenth century, increasingly supplied from Norwegian whalers operating in the South Atlantic, using new techniques and equipment that did not make Britain dependent upon the declining whale stocks of Davis Strait or east Greenland.[37]

Had *Abram* not been wrecked in 1862, it is arguable that, as a sailing ship, her days as a whaler were numbered anyway. She might have been retired, broken up or relegated to coastal trading. As it was she finished her days doing what she had been created to do over forty years previously, in an environment for which she had been specifically, and very successfully, rebuilt.

Table 11.2: Crew List of *Abram* 1862.[38]

Name	Age	Place of birth	In what capacity engaged	Ship in which he last served
Kirkcaldy crew: date of entry 3-13 March 1862. (The master's employment 'continued'.)				
David Soutar	29	Dundee	Master	*Abram*
William Brown	31	Dundee	Mate	*Abram*
Charles Myers	42	Heligoland	1st Harpooner	*Abram*
Samuel Burd	28	Dalkeith	Surgeon	First ship
Hepburn Neilson	53	Kirkcaldy	Spectioneer	*Chieftain*
Thomas Yorker	37	Kirkcaldy	Harpooner	*Abram*
William Dickson	47	Dundee	Harpooner	*Abram*
Alexander Booth	28	Dundee	Harpooner	*Abram*
David Vallance	31	Kirkcaldy	Loose harpooner	*Chieftain*
George Smith	33	Dysart	Boatsteerer and skeeman	*Abram*
John Baxter	34	Kirkcaldy	Boatsteerer	*Alexander*, Dundee
John Beveridge	35	Kirkcaldy	Boatsteerer	*Abram*
David Esplin	30	Dundee	Boatsteerer and boatswain	*Camperdown*, Dundee
George Wallace	25	Pathhead	Line manager	*Lord Gambier*

Name	Age	Place of birth	In what capacity engaged	Ship in which he last served
Thomas Pearson	52	Kirkcaldy	Line manager	*Chieftain*
James Dickson	44	Kirkcaldy	Line manager	*Abram*
James Wilson	27	Kirkcaldy	Boatsteerer and sailmaker	*Sir Colin Campbell*, London
James Kerr	36	Pathhead	Carpenter	*Lord Gambier*
Alexander Wood	21	Leith	Carpenter's mate	First ship
James McKenzie	24	Kirkcaldy	Cooper	*Abram*
Adam Mackintosh	26	Kirkcaldy	Cooper's mate	(Underwriter, New York)
Alexander Williamson	42	Dysart	Cook	*Abram*
John Henderson	22	Kinghorn	Steward	First ship
August Spangle	22	Hamburg	Seaman	*Abram*
James Ross	30	Pathhead	Ordinary Seaman	*Abram*
David Smith	16	Pathhead	Ordinary Seaman	*Gardener*, South Shields
George Eaves	21	Leven	Seaman	*Isabella*, Leith

Shetland crew: date of entry (Lerwick) 29 March 1862.

Name	Age	Place of birth	In what capacity engaged	Ship in which he last served
Adam Wishart	57	Aithsting, Shetland	Line manager	*Abram*
James Hunter	23	Bressa, Shetland	Line manager	*Scotia*, Lerwick
Peter Johnson	23	Sandsting, Shetland	Line manager	*Abram*
Andrew Johnson	27	Quarff, Shetland	Line manager	*Abram*
James Thomson	22	Sandness, Shetland	Seaman	*Abram*
John Jamieson	28	Sandness, Shetland	Seaman	*Eliza*, Peterhead
George Leask	34	Aithsting, Shetland	Seaman	*Veracious*, Lerwick
Robert Williamson	29	Sandness, Shetland	Seaman	*Mary and Jane*, Macduff
Samuel McCourtney	58	Glasgow	Seaman	*Northerner*, Lerwick
Daniel Thomson	23	Yell, Shetland	Ordinary Seaman	*Abram*
Robert Arthur	32	Lerwick, Shetland	Seaman	*Alert*, Peterhead
Peter Dowall	22	Tingwall, Shetland	Ordinary Seaman	*Agostina*, Peterhead
James Andrew	17	Bressa, Shetland	Seaman	*Scotia*, Lerwick
John Hunter	21	Bressa, Shetland	Seaman	*Aeolus*, Hull
William Jameson	24	Walls, Shetland	Seaman	*Lord Gambier*
Thomas Jameson	21	Walls, Shetland	Ordinary Seaman	*Truelove*, Hull
Arthur Yell	21	Walls, Shetland	Ordinary Seaman	*Queen*, Peterhead
Robert Nelson	21	Bressa, Shetland	Seaman	*Aeolus*, Hull
William Tulloch	16	Yell, Shetland	Ordinary Seaman	*Kate*, Peterhead
William Gifford	31	Bressa, Shetland	Line manager	*Camperdown*, Dundee
Robert Jamieson	21	Lerwick, Shetland	Lad	First ship

References

[1] Kirkcaldy Register of Shipping 2:102, 17 March 1855. Information about the subscribers can be found in A.J. Campbell, 'Fife Shopkeepers and Traders 1820–1870', vol. 3, unpublished manuscript, n.d., Kirkcaldy Central Library.

[2] Kirkcaldy Register of Shipping, 27 March 1856; Lloyds Register 1859.

[3] *Fifeshire Advertiser*, 24 Feb. 1855, p. 3.

[4] *Fifeshire Advertiser*, 20 Oct. 1855, 17 Nov. 1855.

[5] *Fifeshire Advertiser*, 25 Oct. 1856.

[6] Lockhart, 'Kirkcaldy Harbour History', Kirkcaldy, 1940 (manuscript volume in Kirkcaldy Central Library).

[7] *Fifeshire Advertiser*, 14 Feb. 1857.

[8] Fife County Archive Centre, B/KDY/4/3, Kirkcaldy Harbour Commissioners' Minute Book 1856–71: Minutes of 13 Jan. & 10 Feb. 1857.

[9] Fife County Archive Centre, B/KDY/4/3, Kirkcaldy Harbour Commissioners' Minute Book 1856–71: Minutes of 10 March & 10 Nov. 1857.

[10] Fife County Archive Centre, B/KDY/4/3, Kirkcaldy Harbour Commissioners' Minute Book 1856–71: Minutes of 10 Dec. 1861 and subsequent entries during 1862 and 1863.

[11] London Metropolitan Archives, Ms18567/13, Captains' Registers of Lloyds of London. Soutar's previous officer experience was limited to Mate on *Tay*, 1859–60.

[12] Barron, *Old Whaling Days*, p. 135.

[13] Barron, *Old Whaling Days*, p. 149.

[14] *Hull Packet*, 17 Oct. 1862.

[15] *The Times*, 18 Oct. 1862.

[16] The Danish settlements contained both Danes and Inuit, who lived a more Europeanised lifestyle than many of their countrymen. The crew was probably billeted on both populations, possibly for as long as four months; Archibald, *Whalehunters*, p. 112.

[17] *Fifeshire Advertiser*, 20 Sept. 1862.

[18] *Caledonian Mercury*, 6 Oct. 1862.

[19] *Fifeshire Advertiser*, 11 Oct. 1862.

[20] D. Dobson, *Scots in the Arctic: Tales of the Whalers*, St Andrews, 1976. Also Lubbock, *Arctic Whalers*, pp. 458–59.

[21] Quoted in P. Hepton, *Captain William Wells and the Last Years of the Hull Whaling Fleet 1844–1869*, Hull, Malet Lambert Local History Originals vol. 17, nd., pp. 38–39.

[22] *Fifeshire Advertiser*, 11 Oct. 1862.

[23] *The Times*, 18 Oct. 1862.

[24] *Caledonian Mercury*, 16 Oct. 1862.

[25] *Fifeshire Advertiser*, 18 Oct. 1862.

[26] *The Times*, 18 Oct. 1862. A note attached to the ship's log reads 'The ship was lost at the Davis Straits on 26th July last. The crew were all saved and taken aboard other ships in company'; National Maritime Museum, *Abram* Crew List 18034, 1862.

[27] *Caledonian Mercury*, 20 Oct. 1862.

[28] *Fifeshire Advertiser*, 18 Oct. 1862.

[29] *Fifeshire Advertiser*, 1 Nov. 1862.

[30] *Fifeshire Advertiser*, 8 Nov. 1862.

[31]   *Fifeshire Advertiser*, 22 Nov. 1862.

[32]   *Fifeshire Advertiser*, 20 Dec. 1862.

[33]   *Fifeshire Advertiser*, 10 Jan. 1863.

[34]   Lockhart, 'Kirkcaldy Harbour History'; Lubbock, *Arctic Whalers*, p. 460.

[35]   London Metropolitan Archives, Ms18567/13, Captains' Registers of Lloyds of London.

[36]   *Fifeshire Advertiser*, 11 Oct. 1862.

[37]   Lubbock, *Arctic Whalers*, pp. 460–61; Jackson, *British Whaling Trade*, pp. 157–63.

[38]   National Maritime Museum, *Abram* 18034, 1862.

Reflections: more than
the story of a ship

Abram's story is, of course, unique to her,[1] but her voyages and the activities of the people associated with her in various capacities represent issues of global significance.

When she sailed to the Caribbean and the Arctic, season after season, she was contributing to a process which transformed the world commercially, culturally and environmentally, and also revolutionised the lives of people in those regions she visited. Ships such as *Abram* were essential to the foreign trade which fuelled the growth of British manufacturing, consumption and commerce from the late eighteenth century onwards. Indeed, it is impossible to explain Britain's industrial growth during this period, often portrayed as powered by coal and steam, without reference to the wind and sails which propelled both ocean-going vessels and the humble domestic coastal traders. The world's oceans were criss-crossed in the maritime equivalent of the world-wide web, linking Britain to its sources of supply and markets, and transmitting people and values around the globe. The sea, rather than railways, turnpikes and canals, holds the key to appreciating Britain's world supremacy in the nineteenth century and shaped the world we know today.

The Caribbean was an important contributor to British economic development during the eighteenth and early nineteenth century. Produce from the West Indies spawned large-scale industries such as sugar refining and cotton manufacturing which converted raw materials into valuable consumer products. Trade also contributed to the expansion of financial services such as banking and insurance, stimulated the manufacture of goods for the export trades and created the basis for an emerging domestic consumer society. Logwood and other dyes transformed printing on both textiles and paper. Imported hardwoods enabled high-quality cabinet and furniture making. Ivory, tortoiseshell and gold were used in ornaments and jewellery. As the activities of *Abram's* owners demonstrate, the profits of West Indian trade could also directly fund the construction of some of these early enterprises.[2] West Indian trade also sustained local shipbuilding and refitting and provided markets for British manufacturers and farmers who supplied the wide range of commodities and foodstuffs necessary to sustain life in the plantation economies.

Whale oil was also a vital raw material for British industry. Once refined, it was used for street and domestic lighting, and also the manufacture of soap, varnish and paint. Whale bone was used in ornaments, articles of clothing such as corsetry, household objects as diverse as sieves, riddles, trellises, umbrella spokes, brush bristles and watch springs as well as blinds and guards for shop windows, while other parts of the whale were used in glue and for chair stuffing. The shore facilities at major ports such as Hull provided employment for numerous trades associated with ship building and chandlery and seasonal work in whale oil processing plants. The Dundee jute industry and Kirkcaldy's manufacture of oilcloth and linoleum were dependent on whale oil. Whaling also supported the precarious, marginal Shetland economy by recruiting its crews during the 'Greenland time' at Lerwick.

Abram's career also reflects the fluctuations in fortune experienced by both the trades in which she was involved and the British economy as a whole. Some of the problems were created by the vicissitudes of the climate, notably hurricanes and pack ice, which affected plantations and whaling albeit in very different ways. The military conflicts of the late eighteenth and early nineteenth centuries increased the value of the Caribbean produce on the one hand but also posed additional dangers to shipping and the industries which were dependent on it. Indeed, what is remarkable about *Abram* is that she escaped largely undamaged in such dangerous waters for over half a century. Unfortunately for her backers, she was employed in the twilight of these trades. Although the British economy continued to grow, neither the West Indies nor the Northern Whale Fishery shared in its later prosperity. In both cases they were undermined by a combination of the availability of new sources of supplies and over-exploitation of natural resources.

Demand for sugar, cotton, hardwoods and other exotic produce remained high throughout the nineteenth century, but Britain's West Indian colonies did not share in the riches which this generated. This is evident in the declining fortunes of *Abram*'s owners in the years after 1815. In part the Caribbean's problems stemmed from soil exhaustion brought about by intensive plantation cultivation, but there were other factors at play. By the early 1800s the southern states of the United States eclipsed the West Indies as a source of raw cotton. Sugar producers also suffered as new post-emancipation plantations worked by indentured labour were established in other colonies such as Mauritius and Demerara, and the tariffs on foreign sugar imports into Britain were reduced. Hardwoods were also increasingly imported directly from the American continent.

Arctic whaling was undermined partly by declining demand but primarily by problems of supply. Unfortunately for the whaling industry, few industrial processes existed for which whale oil was the essential and irreplaceable ingredient. As more reliably available substitutes like linseed and rape seed oil were produced and coal gas supplanted whale oil as a source of street lighting, some key markets began to decline.

Nevertheless, other processes still depended on whale oil and the main reason for the industry's decline was in essence a failure of supply. The decline in the availability of whales is evident in *Abram*'s career. Initially she sailed successfully to the East Greenland Sea for three years, but after that she was forced to join the rest of the fleet in Davis Strait and Baffin Bay, tapping into new areas where whales, at least initially, were plentiful. However, as the season became longer and the climate deteriorated during the 1830s, whaling became more dangerous and catches again declined. With the rise of other whaling nations and the emerging significance of the Southern Whale Fishery, the Northern Whale Fishery increasingly became a backwater and, without investment, British whaling companies could not compete on a world stage. Ultimately the activities of the whalers were unsustainable, as over time they decimated the whale populations of both the Arctic and the Southern Ocean. Consequently they sowed the seed of the demise of the industry itself, and the parlous state in which they left the whale population did much to promote the iconic status of whales for contemporary environmentalists.

The West Indian trade and whaling also contributed to the transformation of elite and popular culture in Britain, although their influence was not entirely positive.[3] On the one hand sugar rapidly became integral to the new social customs such as tea drinking and coffee house culture. Thereafter, as Sydney Mintz noted, the assimilation of sugar into the British diet over the subsequent century led to increased consumption and the proliferation of 'New foods and beverages [which] were incorporated into daily life with unusual rapidity'.[4] Furniture production and styles in the Georgian era were also transformed by the adoption of imported hardwoods, such as mahogany and satinwood. But a slave society in which indigenous peoples, cultures, flora and fauna had been all but annihilated by Western plantation expansion did not generate a widespread influence on literature, art or architecture in nineteenth-century British mainstream culture in the way in which the Orient fascinated and enthralled.[5]

The whalers increased knowledge about the Arctic and in particular enabled people who lived at the whaling ports to engage, at arm's length, with inhabitants of the Arctic.[6] For example, a 14-year-old Inuit boy was brought to Kirkcaldy in 1846 on board the whaler *Caledonia*, and given an education before being returned to his homeland.[7] The arrival of such 'strange strangers...excited considerable interest' as it provided an 'opportunity of seeing a specimen of the tribes of the far North, and of their handicraft and way of life'.[8] More often whalers returned with Inuit domestic and hunting artefacts and models of igloos and kayaks, as well as preserved specimens and skeletons of Arctic mammals. Some were retained by the whaler's family, others were sold to merchants and shopkeepers and provided a useful source of additional income for members of the ship's company,[9] and yet others were gifted to museums. When they brought back captured polar bears, these by necessity were exhibited in zoological gardens. Authors such as Arthur Conan Doyle and W. Gordon Stables spent seasons on board whaling ships in the Arctic and used their experiences when writing their novels and children's stories.

Whereas artistic depictions of West Indian vessels were relatively rare, those of whale ships in the Arctic became the subject of panoramas, vast canvases displaying exotic and topical scenes, which were exhibited around the country. The over-wintering of whale ships, including *Abram*, in Davis Strait in 1835 became the subject of a panorama in Hull in 1836. Whaling ships were also depicted by professional artists. For example J.M.W. Turner was inspired by whaling stories to paint two canvases in 1846 which portrayed, although not very accurately, Arctic whaling. 'Hurrah! For the whaler Erebus! Another fish!' and 'Whalers (boiling blubber), entangled in flow ice, endeavouring to extricate themselves' were both exhibited at the Royal Academy.[10] John Ward, the most accomplished of the marine artists who made their living painting ship's portraits in whaling ports such as Hull, also exhibited in London. The paintings of lesser artists such as James Wheldon, who painted *Abram* (Figure 7.1), adorned the walls of company offices.

The impact of the West Indian trade and whaling was not restricted to Britain; they also significantly affected the lives and values of people in the regions they visited. Although *Abram* and her owners were not involved in the triangular African slave trade which was abolished in 1807, they were heavily dependent on slave plantations which supplied the produce which sustained their trade. Burrow and Nottage's extension of credit to planters like Abram Chalwill Hill ultimately resulted in them, rather than the nominal owners of the estates, receiving government compensation after slavery had been abolished in the British colonies in 1833. It is difficult to overstate the manifold consequences of the large-scale transportation of these tens of thousands of Africans to work in sugar and cotton plantations in the Caribbean and on the American mainland, consequences which have shaped the composition of these societies and the world more generally today. Although the colonies were essentially racially segregated societies, as the experiences of Abram Chalwill Hill and Edward Burrow demonstrate, sexual liaisons and even marital relationships between white merchants and planters on the one hand and black or mixed-race, coloured women on the other were not unknown and these further affected the ethnic composition of the islands. Nor was Abram Chalwill Hill unusual in promoting the efforts of Christian missionaries among the black population.

Although very different from the Caribbean experience, whale ships' penetration of the Arctic also had profound implications for indigenous peoples. Far more than the well-documented explorers, it was whalers who came into contact with the inhabitants of Greenland and Baffin Island. Trade and exchange provided northern peoples with access to sophisticated hunting weapons and equipment which altered their relationship with the natural world. As in the West Indies, sexual liaisons changed the ethnicity of the population while contact with Christianity and its different morals and behaviours, although not always well exemplified by whalers, shook the indigenous people's beliefs in their traditional cultural order.

The whalers also had particular value to those responsible for the parallel world of Arctic exploration. Their expertise in ice navigation was much sought after by the Admiralty and other explorers. In 1773 an expedition in search of a sea route to the North Pole led by Captain Constantine Phipps relied on four whalers who were employed as ice-pilots.[11] When explorers were in difficulties, experienced whalers were called upon for advice and whale ships assisted in search and rescue. It was the whaler *Isabella* who rescued John Ross and his crew in 1833 after his four polar winters trapped in the ice of the North West Passage, and when Sir John Franklin's expedition was missing in the late 1840s, both his wife, Lady Jane Franklin, and the Admiralty turned to the most experienced whalers – William Scoresby Jnr. and William Penny – for advice and help, and engaged whaling ships, including *Abram*, in the search. *Abram* operated in unfrequented seas and along what were often uncharted coastlines, and the master and his officers were at times, no doubt, able to contribute to the nineteenth-century mapping of the globe, although not on the scale of the Scoresbys, father and son, whalers from Whitby who had made outstanding contributions to the geography and science of the Arctic. In an age of empire, the whalers' naming of topographical features, and their presence in areas of 'undiscovered' lands, allowed new regions to be claimed for king or queen and country. William Scoresby Jnr. was particularly adept at this. For example, during his 1822 voyage to east Greenland he named Young's Bay after the Secretary to the Board of Longitude, Scott's Inlet in honour of Sir Walter Scott and Arundel Island after the Rev. John Arundel, his brother-in-law![12] Many of these names appeared in the atlases and board games of the Victorian era.

Ships like *Abram* were consequently responsible for much more than the transportation of raw materials and goods, important though this was. They were transmitters of culture, values, people and wealth, and the medium through which much of the world we know today was created.

References

[1]   Other ships from north-west England were involved in both trades but none had as long or as varied career as *Abram*. In the eighteenth century the Whitehaven-built ships *Thompson* and *Precedent* had both crossed the Atlantic to the West Indies and America for a few years, before being converted into whaling ships, and sailing from that port until the early 1790s when both were wrecked. R.G. David, 'Whitehaven and the Northern Whale Fishery', *Northern History*, 47, 2010, pp. 117–34. *Harmony* was constructed by Brockbank's in Lancaster in 1798 for a Glasgow company, where

she was 'intended for the West India trade'. She was sold to Hull in 1819 where she was registered as a whaler. However, she was lost in 1821 on her only voyage to the Northern Whale Fishery: *Cumberland Pacquet*, 13 Nov. 1798. The Whitehaven ship *Alfred* was also constructed in 1798 and sailed from Liverpool, and later Lancaster, to the West Indies. After being sold to Hull (1809) and later Bo'ness (1836), she served in the Northern Whale Fishery before being wrecked in 1847. *Jumna*, also of Whitehaven, sailed from Liverpool to India and China from 1833, before being sold to Dundee as a whale ship and being wrecked in the Arctic in 1863. R.G. David, '"A Perilous Situation": Whitehaven-built ships in the Northern Whale Fishery', *Transactions of the Cumberland and Westmorland Antiquarian and Archaeological Society*, 3rd Series, 10, 2010, pp. 197–216. This pattern of long distance traders being converted to whaling vessels is evident elsewhere. The Stockton-on-Tees-built ship *Grenville Bay* had also been employed in the West Indies trade between 1783 and 1816 before being converted to a whaler sailing out of the Tyne. T. Barrow, *The Whaling Trade of North-East England*, Sunderland, University of Sunderland Press, 2001, p. 59.

[2]   See chapter 4. The potential importance of investment is still debated nearly 70 years after Eric E. Williams, *Capitalism and Slavery*, North Caroline U.P., 1944, first argued that profits from the West Indian trade supplied the capital for investment in other British industries.

[3]   Mimi Sheller, *Consuming the Caribbean: from Arawaks to Zombies,* London, Routledge, 2003.

[4]   Sidney W. Mintz, *Sweetness and Power: the place of sugar in modern history,* London, Penguin, 1985, p. 120; James Walvin, 'A Taste of Empire, 1600–1800: how tea, sugar and tobacco hooked Britons into a fondness for the fruits of imperial expansion', *History Today,* 47.1, 1997, pp. 11–16.

[5]   Edward W. Said, *Orientalism*, New York, Pantheon, 1978; John M. Mackenzie, *Orientalism: History, Theory and the Arts,* Manchester, Manchester University Press, 1998; J.E. Crowley, 'Picturing the Caribbean in the Global British landscape', *Studies in Eighteenth-Century Culture*, 32, 2003, pp. 323–46; Kay Dian Krix, *Slavery, Sugar and the Culture of Refinement: picturing the British West Indies 1700–1840,* London, Yale University Press, 2008.

[6]   For further information about the arctic in popular culture see: R.G. David, *The Arctic in the British Imagination 1818–1914*, Manchester, Manchester University Press, 2000.

[7]   Kirkcaldy District Museums, *Whaling: The Maritime History of Kirkcaldy District*, Kirkcaldy, 1994. His name was Aukotook Zininnuck.

[8]   *Hull Advertiser*, 10 Dec. 1847. The quotations refer to an Eskimo 'couple' aged 17 and 15 brought by Captain Parker of *Truelove* to Hull where they were exhibited at the Mechanics Institute in the town and visited by 4,000–5,000 people.

[9]   For example William Brown, a Lerwick merchant, advertised a 'Fine Collection of Arctic Skins, Eskimo Goods and Shetland Curios'.

[10]   B. Venning, 'Turner's whaling subjects', *Burlington Magazine*, 983, Feb. 1985, pp. 75–82.

[11]   A. Savours, '"A very interesting point in geography" revisited: the Phipps Expedition towards the North Pole 1773' in S. Forgan, (ed.), *Northward Ho! A Voyage towards the North Pole 1773*, Whitby, Captain Cook Memorial Museum, 2010, p. 5.

[12]   W. Scoresby, *A Voyage to the Whale Fishery, 1822*, Edinburgh, Constable, 1823 (Caedmon Reprint, 1980), p. 104.

Appendix 1: Voyages of *Abram* to the Virgin Islands, 1806–18.

Crew Engaged	From	Captain	Ports of Call[1]	Crew Discharged	Return	Mths-days
Jan./Feb. 1806	Lancaster	W. Trasure	Tortola	4 Oct. 1806	Lancaster	8–21[2]
26 Oct. 1806	Lancaster	W. Trasure/T. Watson	Tortola	10 April 1807	Lancaster	5–15[2,3]
10 May 1807	Lancaster	T. Watson	Tortola	25 Sept. 1807	Lancaster	4–15
21 Oct. 1807	Lancaster	T. Watson	Tortola/St Domingo	11 April 1808	Lancaster	5–20
13 May 1808	Lancaster	T. Watson	Tortola/St Croix	18 Sept. 1808	Lancaster	4–5
2 Nov. 1808	Lancaster	T. Watson	Tortola/St Croix/St Thomas	25 March 1809	Liverpool	4–21
7 May 1809	Liverpool	T. Watson	Tortola/St Croix	9 Sept. 1809	Lancaster	4–1
9 Nov. 1809	Lancaster	T. Watson	Tortola/St Croix	10 May 1810	Lancaster	6–1[4]
3 June 1810	Lancaster	T. Watson	Tortola/St Croix	2 Sept. 1810	Lancaster	3–0
29 Oct. 1810	Lancaster	T. Watson	Tortola/St Croix	14 April 1811	Lancaster	5–16
15 May 1811	Lancaster	T. Watson	Tortola	20 Sept. 1811	Lancaster	4–5
9 Nov. 1811	Lancaster	T. Watson	Tortola/St Croix	10 May 1812	Liverpool	6–1
15 June 1812	Liverpool	T. Watson	Tortola/St John/St Thomas	9 Oct. 1812	Lancaster	3–24
Dec. 1812	Lancaster	T. Watson	Tortola/St Thomas	Aug. 1813	Lancaster	no data[5]

Crew Engaged	From	Captain	Ports of Call[1]	Crew Discharged	Return	Mths–days
24 Dec. 1813	Lancaster	T. Watson	Tortola/St Thomas/St Croix	late June 1814 / 12 Aug. 1814	Liverpool/Lancaster	7–19[6]
23 Aug. 1814	Liverpool	T. Watson	St Thomas/St Croix	9 April 1815	Lancaster/ordered to Liverpool	7–17
9 May 1815	Liverpool	T. Watson	Tortola/St Croix	11 Sept. 1815		3–10[7]
8 Jan. 1816	Lancaster	T. Rogerson	Tortola	6 Sept. 1816	Lancaster	6–28[8]
4 Nov. 1816	Lancaster	T. Rogerson	Tortola	11 June 1817	Lancaster	7–7
28 Oct. 1817	Lancaster	T. Rogerson	Tortola	17 May 1818	Lancaster	6–19
8 June 1818	Lancaster	T. Rogerson	Tortola/St Thomas	11 Oct. 1818	Lancaster then Liverpool for sale	4–3[9]

Sources: TNA, BT98/30 Muster Rolls supplemented from shipping reports in *Lancaster Gazette* and *Liverpool Mercury*.

Notes: Dates refer to crew's period of engagement shown in muster roll rather than date of sailing unless otherwise stated.

1. Additional ports of call taken from newspapers. It is likely that *Abram* called at St Thomas on more of her voyages but that this was not always specified.
2. Crew were hired up to several weeks before sailing on first two voyages. *Lancaster Gazette* gives dates of sailing as 18 Feb. 1806 and 8 Nov.1806.
3. William Trasure dies on return voyage.
4. Muster roll incomplete and not on official form – ports derived from newspapers.
5. Muster roll not identified; details from newspapers.
6. *Lancaster Gazette* reports that she initially sailed from Lancaster 10 Oct. 1813 but experienced a gale off Cork so may have turned back. Muster roll gives dates of crew's engagement as 24 Dec. from and back to Lancaster.
7. Muster roll not on official form.
8. Muster roll from Tortola dated 22 July 1816; English ports not given. Crew's length of engagements does not tally with dates given – return port taken from *Lancaster Gazette*.
9. Muster roll from Tortola; sailed 15 Aug. 1818 for Liverpool but *Lancaster Gazette* reports it initially returned to Lancaster.

Appendix 2: Voyages of the whaler *Abram* to the Arctic, 1819–62.

Hull, 1819–1854

Year	Master	Whales caught	Tons of oil	Tons of whalebone	Other products	Hull – total number of whalers	Hull – total number of whales	Hull – total tons of oil (tons of whalebone)
1819	W. Harrison	9	55			65	424	5183 (254)
1820	W. Harrison	13	118		147 seals	62	688	8086 (402) 1073 seals
1821	W. Harrison	3	54	2 tons and 13 cwts		61	498	5888 (322)
1822	S. Couzens	4	65			40	228	3112 (154)
1823	S. Couzens	31	205			41	636	5490 (297)
1824	W. Jackson	10	161			36	273	3459
1825	W. Jackson	2	30			36	223	2838
1826	W. Jackson	5	86			32	172	2495 (139) 1700 seals
1827	W. Jackson	10	98			30	373	4581 (260)
1828	W. Jackson	21	208			30	438	5297 (316)
1829	W. Jackson	4	53			33	336	3976 (235)
1830	W. Jackson	3	44			33	85	1271 (68)
1831	W. Jackson	15	88		2 seals, 8 'unicorns' (narwhal)	32	169	1829
1832	W. Jackson	6	56			30	539	4503 (251)
1833	J. Hibbs	22	191			27	589	(284)
1834	J. Hibbs	16	181			27	276	2696 (146)
1835	J. Hibbs	2	10			23	32	436 (26)[1]
1836	J. Hibbs	clean				15	14	145
1837	J. Hibbs	2	36		1500 seals	12		230
1838	J. Hibbs	11	79			6		594 (37)
1839	W.S. Couldrey	9	101			6	31	371 (24)
1840	W.S. Couldrey	clean				4	3	43 (2)
1841	I. Ward	1	24			2	5	52 (3)
1842	*No voyage*					2	1	46 2481 seals
1843	*No voyage*					4		
1844	R.W. Humphreys	2	25	1.5		10	2	

Year	Master	Whales caught	Tons of oil	Tons of whalebone	Other products	Hull – total number of whalers	Hull – total number of whales	Hull – total tons of oil (tons of whalebone)
1845	W.S. Couldrey		160	8		12		
1846	W.S. Couldrey		65	4		15		
1847	W.S. Couldrey	4	30	2		12		
1848	J. Good		30[2]	2		13		
1849	J. Gravill		49	3		13		
1850	J. Gravill		28	1.5		10		
1851	J. Gravill			6		12		
1852	J. Gravill		118	2.5		13		8400 seals
1853	J. Gravill					13	1	3800 seals
1854	*No record*							

[1.] *Abram* wintered in Davis Strait and returned to Hull on 25 February 1836.

[2.] According to the *Hull Packet*, *Abram* returned with three fish and 40 tons of oil.

Sources, 1819–1842: William Coltish, 'Whaling Statistics 1772-1842', unpublished manuscript, Hull History Centre, c.1843; 1843–1853: Philip Hepton, *Sailings of the Hull Whaling Fleet from the Port of Hull 1843 to 1869*, Malet Lambert Local History Originals, vol. 24, 1985 (compiled from local newspapers, Hull Customs Registers and Bills of Entry). See also www.hullwebs.co.uk/content/k-victorian/industry/whaling/masters.

Kirkcaldy, 1855–1862*

Year	Master	Whales caught	Tons of oil	Tons of whalebone	Other products	Kirkcaldy – total number of whalers	Kirkcaldy – total number of whales	Kirkcaldy – total tons of oil (tons of whalebone)
1855	A. Hay	2	25			3		
1856	A. Hay		140		4800 seals	3		425
1857	A. Hay		45			3		61
1858			60			3		85
1859	Capt. Stuart		40			3		92
1860	Capt. Stuart		54			3		199
1861	D. Soutar					3		
1862	D. Soutar	*Wrecked in Melville Bay*				3		

* There have been no compilations of whaling information for Kirkcaldy, unlike at Hull. Consequently it has not been possible to provide such complete data as at Hull.

Sources, 1855–1862: J.Y. Lockhart, 'Kirkcaldy Harbour History', Kirkcaldy, 1940 (unpublished manuscript); *Fifeshire Advertiser* (various editions); Shetland Archives, records of Hay and Co., D31/6; London Metropolitan Archives, Captains' Registers of Lloyds of London, Ms18567/13; TNA, BT 98/4183, BT 98/4508, BT 98/4966; National Maritime Museum, *Abram* crew list 18034, 1862.

Glossary

Bale (cotton)	size and weight vary depending on type of cotton and origin. West Indian cotton bales in 1856 averaged 212 lbs., but a marketable bag of West India cotton in 1805 was reported as around 300 lbs.
Baleen	also known as 'whalebone' or 'whalefins'. Baleen is the two rows of economically valuable whalebone plates in the head of the bowhead whale.
Barque	a sailing ship with at least three masts but with no square sails on the aftermost mast.
Barrel (sugar)	c. 250 lb.
Bight	a bay.
Boatsteerer	the person responsible for steering the <u>whaleboat</u> while pursuing a whale.
Bounty	a payment initiated by the government in 1732 which had been designed to encourage the conversion of merchant ships into whalers. The rate varied depending upon the supply of whale oil. The payment finally ended in 1824.
Bowhead whale (Balaena mysticetus)	The whale hunted throughout the Northern Whale Fishery. The name 'bowhead' was first given to *Balaena mysticetus* in England in the late nineteenth century. At the time of the whaling voyages described in this volume *Balaena mysticetus* was called the right whale or Greenland right whale.
Brig	a vessel with two fully rigged masts, as opposed to a ship which had at least three.
Clean	a whaling vessel that has returned without any whales.
Dock	in inclement weather the crew were detailed to construct a dock in <u>fast ice</u> or an <u>ice floe</u>. This involved crew members standing on the ice with large ice saws and sawing a rectangular 'dock' into which the ship could be pulled in order to prevent her being <u>squeezed</u> by other floating ice.
Drogher	a small West Indian vessel which transported produce to and from ships or between islands.

Fast	the word whalers used to describe the successful attachment of a harpoon to a whale.
Fast ice	solid ice connected to the adjacent land. In contrast <u>ice floes</u> and <u>pack ice</u> are loose ice that moves according to wind and tide.
Fishing	the activity of catching whales was known as fishing.
Flensing/flinching	the activity of stripping blubber from the carcass of a whale while it was tied up alongside the ship. The task was supervised by the <u>Spectioneer</u>, and usually performed by the harpooners. The rest of the ship's company then packed the blubber into barrels which were packed in the hold. The <u>Skeeman</u> was in charge of this operation.
Fustic	a yellow dye, originally from the mulberry tree. Widely grown in the West Indies.
Hogshead	a large cask containing 52-63 imperial gallons depending on the liquid. Also used for other commodities. A hogshead of sugar has been variously estimated at between 16 cwt. (812 kg.) and 12 cwt. because of weight loss in transit. Sometimes approximated to the produce of about one acre.
Hundredweight	usually 112 lbs. or 8 stones; it was made illegal in 1826 for merchants to apply it to 100 lbs.
Ice floe	a sheet of floating ice.
Indigo	a blue dye obtained from a shrub cultivated in West Indies.
Lignum vitae	a very hard wood used in furniture, carpentry and instrument making.
Logwood	a quick growing tree that is found in Mexico and northern Central America from which a dark purple-red dye is extracted. An inferior variety also grew on Jamaica.
Kablunas	an Inuit (Greenlandic) word for 'white people'.
Lead	a passage of open water through <u>pack ice</u>.
Line manager	a skilled seaman responsible for coiling and arranging the lines that are attached to harpoons in the <u>whaleboats</u>.
Nicaragua wood	or Brazil wood; a hard wood used in furniture making and which also yields a deep red dye. Some of this was grown on Jamaica.
Northern Whale Fishery	the name given to the Arctic whaling industry.
Pack ice	large areas of loose ice consisting of <u>ice floes</u> floating together. During the summer enormous quantities of pack ice floats south down the east coast of Greenland.

Pipe	cask of liquid of various sizes, usually containing about two hogsheads.
Puncheon	usually about 84 gallons of liquid.
Refraction	this refers to the peculiar property of light in the Arctic when ice and icebergs can seem to be upsidedown above the horizon.
Rocknosing	a term to describe whale ships working near land, often in uncharted waters where reefs were ever present dangers.
Sea Horse	a walrus.
Seron	a kind of skin or hide package, used for importing spices or other commodities such as indigo.
Ship	a fully-rigged vessel with three or more masts all carrying square sails.
Skeeman	the person responsible for packing the blubber into barrels on board the whaling vessel. A skeeman is not always listed as a separate occupation in crew lists.
Snow	similar to a brig but with a small trysail behind the main mast.
Southern Whale Fishery	the name given to whaling in the south Atlantic. (Originally it referred to any whaling south of the Northern Whale Fishery.)
Spectioneer	the principal harpooner and man responsible for organising the <u>flensing</u> of a whale.
Squeezed	the term used when a ship is caught between two or more <u>ice floes</u> which drift together. This is an extremely dangerous event as the power and size of the floes can break the timbers of the ship and/or force the ship out of the water and on to the ice.
Succades	fruits preserved in sugar.
Tamarind	a tree with hard yellow wood used for furniture making and for dyeing textiles, but more usually applied now to its pods and edible pulp which are used in cooking.
Tierce	approximately 60% of a hogshead or 42 gallons.
Tortoise Shell	sea turtle shell, widely used in decorative items.
Train oil	another term for whale oil.
Tun	a large cask of undefined measure but usually given as 252 gallons; according to Scoresby a tun of whale oil weighed 17 cwts.
Unicorn	a narwhal.
Warping	the process of pulling a ship with ropes through a <u>lead</u> in the ice.
Whaleboat	an open boat about 25 feet long which was used to

pursue a whale. Normally she had a crew of six, and a whale ship carried six whaleboats. Each whaleboat was equipped with harpoons, lances and five lengths of whale lines consisting of 120 fathoms (720 feet) of 2½ inch hemp coiled in the bottom of the boat. These whaleboats could also be used to seek rescue if the mother ship was wrecked.

Sources and Bibliography

Lancaster and the West Indies

Primary Sources

Manuscript Sources

Durham County Record Office, D/HH 3/1/5/12, Hanby Holmes, solicitors, collection.

Lancashire Archives (Lancs. Archives)

    DDX 70 Messrs. Swainson and Satterthwaite of Lancaster, solicitors, Tortola package.

    FRL/2/1/15/189; FRL/2/1/33/44, Lancaster Society of Friends.

    SS5/1 Lancaster Shipping Register.

    Lancaster Library Collection DDX 2743:

        MS 160 Lancaster Apprentice Rolls.

        MS 239 Voyage Book no 3, A. and J. Rawlinson.

        MS 241 John Brockbank's daybook 1795–1805.

        MS 242 John Brockbank's daybook 1806–13.

        MS 3726 Abraham Seward account book, 1805–13.

        MS 4689 Release of two plantations in Island of St Croix, West Indies.

        MS 5084 *William Ashton* log, 1810–11.

        MS 5179 Apprenticeship of James Greenwood, 1806

        MS 8127 John Brockbank's instructions for building ships.

        MS 8171 Letter Book etc., ships and goods, salvage insurance, 1783–93.

National Archives (TNA)

    BT 98/30–31 Muster Rolls for Lancaster ships.

    CO 142/20 Jamaica, return of shipping, 1787–88.

    CO 157/1 St Kitts, return of shipping.

    CO 259/2 (1808–1810) and CO 259/3 (1811–14) Naval Officers' returns for St Thomas.

    CO 317/1 Tortola return of shipping, 1784–86.

    CO 700 Plan of Tortola from actual survey by George King, London. Published 1 June 1798, by Robt. Wilkinson, London. Re-published with additions and corrections by William Darton, 3 June 1826.

    CO 152/104–105 Colonial Office and predecessors: Leeward Islands, original correspondence.

    CUST 34/814 Board of Customs: papers relating to plantations (A.C. Hill).

    PROB 11 Prerogative Court of Canterbury: wills.

T 71/370 (1818) and T 71/375 (1834) Office of Registry of Colonial Slaves
and Slave Compensation Commission: registers (Virgin Islands).
T 71/883 Register of Claims (Virgin Islands).
T 71/1040 Claims and Certificates (Virgin Islands).
T 71/1238–40 Counter Claims (Virgin Islands).

Published Primary Sources

Belisario, Arthur M., *A Report of the Trial of Arthur Hodge ... on the Island
of Tortola, 25th April 1811* (Middleton, 1812).
Craig R. & Jarvis, R.C., *Liverpool Registry of Merchant Ships, 1786–1788*
(Chetham Society 3rd series, vol. 15, 1967).
Danson, J.T.,'Some particulars of the commercial progress of the colonial
dependencies of the United Kingdom during the twenty years 1827–46',
Journal of the Statistical Society of London, 12.4, November 1849.
Lancaster City Library
Scrapbook 2 (2) printed extracts from *Lancaster Guardian*.
W. Hewitson, *Memoranda relating to Lancaster and District, c.* 1906,
2 volumes of cuttings from *Manchester Mercury*, Lancaster Central
Library microfilm, vol. 2.
Lancaster Gazette.
Liverpool Mercury.
London Gazette.
The Times.
Thornton in Lonsdale Parish Registers, 1576–1812 (Yorkshire Archaeological
Society vol. 89).
Williamson's Liverpool Advertiser.

House of Commons Papers

1808, *Select Committee on Distilleries.*
1812–13, *Account of Quantity of Sugar imported into Great Britain, 1812.*
1825, *Reports by Commissioners of Inquiry into State of Africans apprenticed
in W. Indies.*
1826–27, *Third report of the Commissioner of Inquiry into the Administration
of Civil and Criminal Justice in the West Indies.*
1828, *Reports by Commissioners of Inquiry into State of Slaves in H.M.
Colonies under Acts abolishing Slave Trade: (Tortola).*
1829, *Commission of Enquiry into the Charities of England and Wales.*
1837–38, *Return of Sums awarded by Commissioners of Slave Compensation*
(Virgin Islands).
1847–48, *The reports made for the year 1847 to the Secretary of State* (Virgin
Islands by E. Drummond Hay).
1847–48, *An Account of the Imports into the United Kingdom for the years
1831 to 1847.*

1847–48, *Third Report from the Select Committee on Sugar and Coffee Planting.*

1847–48, *Third Report from the Select Committee on the Slave Trade.*

1866, *Reports showing the present state of Her Majesty's colonial possessions for the year 1864, Part I.*

Web Resources

British West Indies (BWI) Study Circle Newsletter, vol. 80, 1974, pp. 16–17, http://www.bwisc.org/50_bulletins/b080_197403/b080_197403.pdf.

Census returns for St Croix, 1841 and 1846. http://stx.visharoots.org/db.html.

David W. Knight, *A Documentary History of the Cinnamon Bay Plantation 1718 – 1917,* Virgin Islands Historical & Genealogical Resource Center, 1999, originally accessed 12 November 2006 at http://www.friendsvinp.org/archive/cinnamon_history.pdf. Now (2013) archived on Internet Archive Wayback Machine in four parts: http://web.archive.org/web/20040423011420/http://www.friendsvinp.org/archive/Cinnamon/cinmer34.htm.

Sugar Refiners and Sugarbakers created by Brian Mawer, http://www.mawer.clara.net/loc-lanc.html.

Gent Family Papers, http://fjgent.zxq.net/henrygent/index.htm (Henry Gent letters re Tortola).

University College, London, *Legacies of Slave Ownership*, online database, http://www.ucl.ac.uk/lbs/.

Secondary Sources

Books

Craig, R. and Jarvis, R.C., *Liverpool Registry of Merchant Ships, 1786–1789* (Chetham Society 3rd series, vol. 15, 1967).

Crowhurst, P., *The Defence of British Trade, 1689–1815* (Folkestone, Dawson, 1977).

Dookhan, I., *A History of the British Virgin Islands, 1672–1970* (Caribbean Universities Press, 1975).

Dookhan, I., *A History of the Virgin Islands of the United States* (Kingston, Jamaica, 1974, 6th impression, 2006).

Edwards, M.M., *The Growth of the British Cotton Trade, 1780–1815* (Manchester University Press, 1967).

Elder, M., *The Slave Trade and the Economic Development of 18th century Lancaster* (Halifax, Ryburn Academic, 1992).

Howson, G., *The Making of Lancaster: People, Places & War, 1789–1815* (Lancaster, Carnegie Press, 2008).

Jenkins, C.J., *Tortola: A Quaker Experiment of Long Ago in the Tropics* (London, Friends Bookshop, 1923).

Krix, K.D., *Slavery, Sugar and the Culture of Refinement: picturing the British West Indies 1700–1840* (London, Yale University Press, 2008).

MacGregor, D.R., *Square Rigged Sailing Ships* (Watford, Argus Books, 1977)

Marshall, J.M. (ed). *The Autobiography of William Stout of Lancaster, 1665–1752* (Manchester University Press, 1967).

Mintz, S.W., *Sweetness and Power: the place of sugar in modern history* (London, Penguin, 1985).

Penson, L.M., *The Colonial Agents of the British West Indies* (London, 1924).

Pitman, F.W., *The Development of the British West Indies, 1700–1763* (Yale University Press, 1917, rpt. London, Frank Cass, 1967).

Ragatz, L.J., *The Fall of the Planter Class in the British Caribbean 1763–1833* (London, 1929, rpt. Octagon, New York, 1977).

Ross, D. and White, A., *The Lancaster Custom House* (Lancaster City Museums, Local Study, no. 9, 1988).

Schofield, M.M., *Outlines of an Economic History of Lancaster from 1680 to 1860: Part I Lancaster from 1680 to 1800* (Lancaster Branch of the Historical Association, 1946).

Sheller, M., *Consuming the Caribbean: from Arawaks to Zombies* (London, Routledge, 2003).

Sheridan, R.B., 'The Formation of Caribbean Plantation Society, 1689–1748', in P. J. Marshall (ed.), *The Oxford History of the British Empire, vol. 2 The Eighteenth Century* (Oxford University Press, 1998).

Stuart, S.E., *Gillows of Lancaster and London 1730–1840* (Woodbridge, Antique Collectors' Club, 2008).

Ward, J.R., 'The British West Indies in the Age of Abolition', in Marshall (ed.), *The Oxford History of the British Empire, vol. 2 The Eighteenth Century* (Oxford University Press, 1998).

White, A. (ed.), *A History of Lancaster* (2nd. edition, Edinburgh University Press, 2001).

White, A., *The Buildings of Georgian Lancaster* (Lancaster, Centre for North West Regional Studies, Lancaster University, 1992).

Williams, E.E., *Capitalism and Slavery* (North Caroline U.P, 1944).

Winstanley, M. (ed.), *Rural Industries of the Lune Valley* (Lancaster, Centre for North-West Regional Studies, Lancaster University, 2000).

Articles

Brown, G., 'The cotton mill at Westhouse', *North Craven Heritage Trust Journal*, 2006.

Crowley, J.E., 'Picturing the Caribbean in the global British landscape', *Studies in Eighteenth-Century Culture*, 32, 2003, pp. 323–46.

Ingram, K.E., 'The West Indian trade of an English furniture firm in the eighteenth century', *Jamaican Historical Review*, 3.3, 1962, pp. 23–37.

Morgan, K., 'Bristol and the Atlantic trade in the eighteenth century', English Historical Review, 107 1992, pp. 626–50.

Skidmore, P., 'New light on seamen, ships and trade of the port of Lancaster in the late eighteenth and early nineteenth century', *Transactions of the Historic Society of Lancashire and Cheshire,* 159, 2010, pp.63–81.

Walvin, J., 'A Taste of Empire, 1600–1800: how tea, sugar and tobacco hooked Britons into a fondness for the fruits of imperial expansion', *History Today,* 47.1, 1997, pp. 11–16.

Whaling

Primary Sources

Manuscript sources

Archives of Manitoba Government Records, MG 11 A7 M13 (Journal of Thomas Phillips, surgeon, *Abram* 1839).

Coltish, W., 'Manuscript of Whaling Statistics 1772–1842', unpublished manuscript, Hull, n.d., [transcribed by Credland, A.G., 1978].

Fife County Archive Centre, B/KDY/4/3 (Kirkcaldy Harbour Commissioner's Minute Book 1856–71.

Hull History Centre
  Accounts of *Exmouth* and *Neptune.*
  Bills of Entry for the Port of Hull.
  DPC/1 (Hull Register of Shipping).
  Trinity House muster roll DSTR/53/113.

Hull Maritime Museum, 'Five letters to the Officers and Crews of the fishing ships *Mercury*, William Jackson, Master, and *Abram*, Samuel Cousins, Master of the Port of Hull'.

Hull, Trinity House, MSF (Muster Rolls).

Kirkcaldy Central Library
  Campbell, A.J., 'Fife Shopkeepers and Traders 1820–1870' (vol. 3), unpublished manuscript, nd.
  Kirkcaldy Harbour Record.
  Kirkcaldy Register of Shipping.
  Lockhart, J.Y., 'Kirkcaldy Harbour History' unpublished manuscript, Kirkcaldy, 1940.
  Log of *Chieftain.*

London Metropolitan Archives, Ms18567/13 Captains' Registers of Lloyds of London.

National Archives (TNA), BT 98 Muster Rolls and Crew Lists.

National Maritime Museum, Crew List 18034, 1862.

Shetland Archives
    D25 Tom Henderson papers.
    D31 Hay and Co. Records.
    SC12 Lerwick Sheriff's Court records.
Whitby Literary and Philosophical Society, correspondence of Sophie
    Cracroft and Jane Franklin.

Published Primary Sources

Aberdeen Journal.
Barron, W., *Old Whaling Days* (London, Conway Maritime Press, 1996
    [first published 1895]).
Caledonian Mercury.
Fifeshire Advertiser.
Hull Advertiser.
Hull Packet.
Leslie, J., Jameson, R., Murray H., *Narrative of Discovery and Adventure in
    the Polar Seas and Regions: with illustrations of their Climate, Geology and
    Natural History, and an account of the Whale Fishery* (Edinburgh, Oliver
    and Boyd, 1830).
Liverpool Mercury.
Lloyds Register.
Nautical Magazine.
Scoresby. W., *An Account of the Arctic Regions, with a History and
    Description of the Northern Whale Fishery*, (Edinburgh, 1820) reprinted
    Newton Abbot, David and Charles, 1969.
Scoresby, W., *A Voyage to the Whale Fishery, 1822* (Edinburgh, Constable,
    1823) reprinted Whitby, Caedmon, 1980.
Simmonds, P.L., *Sir John Franklin and the Arctic Regions* (1852. Republished
    Stroud, Nonsuch, 2005).
The Criterion.
The Times.

House of Commons Papers

1849, *Arctic expeditions. Extracts of any proceedings or correspondence of the
    Admiralty, in reference to the Arctic expeditions.*
1850, *Arctic expeditions. Return to an order of the Honourable the House of
    Commons, copies of reports, plans, correspondence and instructions to and
    from the Admiralty.*

Web Resources

British Arctic Whaling (BAW), www.hull.ac.uk/baw.
Hull whaling, www.hullwebs.co.uk/content/k-victorian/industry/whaling.

Secondary Sources

Books

Adamson, P., *The Great Whale to Snare: The Whaling Trade of Hull* (Hull, Kingston upon Hull Museums and Art Galleries, nd).
Archibald, M., *Whalehunters: Dundee and the Arctic Whalers* (Edinburgh, Mercat Press, 2004).
Barrow, T., *The Whaling Trade of North-East England* (Sunderland, University of Sunderland Press, 2001).
Bellamy, J.M., *The Trade and Shipping of Nineteenth Century Hull*, Hull, East Yorkshire Local History Series, no. 27, p.37.
Credland, A.G., *Whales and Whaling* (Princes Risborough, Shire Publications, 1982).
Credland, A.G., *The Hull Whaling Trade: An Arctic Enterprise* (Beverley, Hutton Press, 1995).
Credland, A.G. (ed), *Baffin Fair: Experiences of George Laing, a Scottish Surgeon in the Arctic Whaling Fleet 1830 and 1831* (Beverley, Hutton Press, 2003).
David, R.G., *The Arctic in the British Imagination 1818–1914* (Manchester, Manchester University Press, 2000).
Dobson, D., *Scots in the Arctic: Tales of the Whalers* (St Andrews, 1976).
Doyle, A.C., *'Dangerous Work': Diary of an Arctic Adventure*, ed. J. Lellenberg and D. Stashower (London, The British Library, 2012).
Druett, J., *Rough Medicine: Surgeons at Sea in the Age of Sail* (New York, Routledge, 2001).
Dykes, J., *Yorkshire's Whaling Days* (Clapham, Dalesman, 1980).
Elce, E.B. (ed.), *As Affecting the Fate of my Absent Husband: Selected Letters of Lady Franklin Concerning the Search for the Lost Franklin Expedition, 1848–1860* (Montreal and Kingston, McGill-Queen's University Press, 2009).
Fenton, A., *The Northern Isles: Orkney and Shetland* (Edinburgh, John Donald, 1978).
Francis, D., *Arctic Chase: a History of Whaling in Canada's North* (St John's, Breakwater Books, 1984).
Hepton, P., *Captain William Wells and the Last Years of the Hull Whaling Fleet 1844–1869* (Hull, Malet Lambert Local History Originals vol. 17, 1984).
Hepton, P., *Sailings of the Hull Whaling Fleet from the Port of Hull 1843 to 1869* (Hull, Malet Lambert Local History Originals, vol. 24, 1985).

Holland, C., *Arctic Exploration and Development, c.500BC to 1915: an Encyclopedia* (New York and London, Garland, 1994).

Jackson, G., *The British Whaling Trade* (London, A. & C. Black, 1978).

Jamie, K., *Sightlines* (London, Sort Of Books, 2012).

Jones, A.G.E., *Polar Portraits: Collected Papers* (Whitby, Caedmon, 1992).

Jones, A.G.E., *The Greenland and Davis Strait Trade, 1740–1865* (n.p., 1996).

Lubbock, B., *The Arctic Whalers* (Glasgow, Brown, Son and Ferguson, 1978) first published 1937.

Macleod, I. (ed.), *To the Greenland Whaling: Alexander Trotter's Journal of the Voyage of the 'Enterprise' in 1856 from Fraserburgh and Lerwick* (Sandwick, 1979).

Ross, M.J., *Polar Pioneers: John Ross and James Clark Ross* (McGill, Queen's University Press, 1994).

Ross, W.G., *Arctic Whalers, Icy Seas: Narratives of the Davis Strait Whale Fishery* (Toronto, Irwin Publishing, 1985).

Rowley, J.C., *The Hull Whale Fishery* (Lockington, 1982.)

Savours, A., *The Search for the North West Passage* (London, Chatham, 1999).

Sheppard, T. and Suddaby, J., *Hull Whaling Relics and Arctic or Historical Records of 250 Years* (Hull, Hull Museums Publications, no. 31, 1906).

Spence, W., *Harpooned: the Story of Whaling* (Greenwich, Conway Maritime Press, 1980).

Stamp, T. and Stamp, C., *William Scoresby: Arctic Scientist* (Whitby, Caedmon, 1975).

Sutherland, P.D. (ed.), *The Franklin Era in Canadian Arctic History 1845–1859* (Ottawa, National Museum of Man, 1985).

Torrie, E.P.D., and Coleman, R., *Historic Kirkcaldy* (Edinburgh, Historic Scotland, 1995).

Vaughan, R., *The Arctic: a History* (Stroud, Alan Sutton, 1994).

Woodward, F.J., *Portrait of Jane: a Life of Lady Franklin* (London, Hodder and Stoughton. 1951).

Articles

Cooke, A., and Ross, W.G., 'The drift of the whaler *Viewforth* in Davis Strait, 1835–36, from William Elder's Journal', *Polar Record*, 92, 1969, pp. 581–91.

David, R.G., 'Whitehaven and the Northern Whale Fishery', *Northern History*, 47.1, 2010, pp. 117–34.

David, R.G., '"A Perilous Situation": Whitehaven-built ships in the Northern Whale Fishery', *Transactions of the Cumberland and Westmorland Antiquarian and Archaeological Society*, 3rd Series, 10, 2010, pp. 197–216.

Holland, C.A., 'William Penny, 1809–92: Arctic whaling master', *Polar Record*, 94, 1970, pp. 25–43.

Jackson, G., 'The British whaling trade', *Research in Maritime History,* 29 (International Maritime Economic History Association, 2005).

Jordan, K., 'The captains and crews of Liverpool's Northern whaling trade', *International Journal of Maritime History*, 22.1, June 2010, pp. 185–204.

Ross, W.G., 'False leads in the Franklin Search', *Polar Record*, 209, 2003, pp. 131–60.

Venning, B., 'Turner's whaling subjects', *Burlington Magazine*, 983, February 1985, pp. 75–82.

Index